... for Criminologists

# A Practical Guide

# Law for Criminologists

## A Practical Guide

Ursula Smartt

Los Angeles • London • New Delhi • Singapore • Washington DC

SAGE Publications Ltd
1 Oliver's Yard
55 City Road
London EC1Y 1SP

SAGE Publications Inc.
2455 Teller Road
Thousand Oaks, California 91320

SAGE Publications India Pvt Ltd
B 1/I 1 Mohan Cooperative Industrial Area
Mathura Road,
New Delhi 110 044

SAGE Publications Asia-Pacific Pte Ltd
33 Pekin Street #02-01
Far East Square
Singapore 048763


**Library of Congress Control Number Available**

**British Library Cataloguing in Publication data**

A catalogue record for this book is available from the British Library

ISBN 978-1-4129-4569-1
ISBN 978-1-4129-4570 7 (pbk)



Typeset by C&M Digitals (P) Ltd., Chennai, India
Printed in Great Britain by TJ International, Padstow, Cornwall
Printed on paper from sustainable resources

# CONTENTS

# ACKNOWLEDGEMENTS

My grateful thanks go to the following individuals who have helped to bring this book about. Specifically to:

**My husband Mike Smartt OBE** – once again for his patience for putting up with my nocturnal writing of the book; he took particular interest in the Northern Ireland chapters.

**Baroness (Lady) Kennedy of the Shaws** – Helena Kennedy QC for writing such a wonderful preface.

**Lord (Eric) Avebury** for constantly advising on new legislation and being such a really good friend.

**Caroline Porter** – my amazing editor at Sage Publications, who had the original idea for the book. She continues being strict but fair and had to restrain me regarding the word limit.

**Jennifer Crisp** for her cover design; another super inspirational idea other than the cover to my *Media Law for Journalists*.

**Stephen Pound MP, Member of the Northern Ireland Affairs Committee (2006–7)** for advising on the Northern Ireland criminal justice system and the future of the prison system in the province.

**Dr Jon Vagg** for alerting me to new forms of crime and the far-reaching globalisation of today's organised criminal activities.

**Gary Duffy**, former Ireland Correspondent of the BBC, for assisting with the Northern Ireland chapters.

**David Graham**, former chairman of the Independent Monitoring Board (IMB) for prisons (2003–6) and IMB member of HMP the Mount. He has helpfully advised on the role and function of IMBs.

**To the legal advisors at the Ealing Magistrates' Court,** West London, especially chief legal advisor, Christopher Jordan, for his continued advice on the complexities of ever-changing criminal justice legislation.

**To the anonymous reviewers of my book**. Whoever they were, they put in a lot of initial hard work, stating at one point that they really wanted this book to work.

**To Chris**, a friend and community volunteer with the Surrey Youth Justice Service.

# PREFACE

The law is entangled with our everyday existence: regulating our social relations and business dealings, controlling conduct which could threaten our safety and security and establishing the rules by which we live in community with each other. It is the baseline. Yet, too often law is covered in mystique and rendered remote by impenetrable language and the flummery of ritual. It is set apart from the everyday landscape in which it actually plays a seminal role. To parody the famous quote from L.P. Hartley – the law is a foreign country; they do things differently there. However, the lawyer and scholar, Ursula Smartt, comes to our rescue; her great gift is that she unmasks the mysteries and lays bare the complexities of law like few other writers on the subject.

It is increasingly vital that criminologists understand crime and the criminal justice system in some depth. The world is going through a period of dynamic change, presenting new and ever more complex problems to nations and to the international community. Societies are more complicated and mixed than they were in the twentieth century; people are better educated, more demanding and more conscious of their rights. The position of women has changed radically. Attitudes to homosexuality, marriage and legitimacy have all altered. The rigid divisions between classes have broken down but poverty is still a social ill. Crime is taking new and more sophisticated forms. While the police and security agencies have an incredible array of technology at their disposal, so too have those who commit crime.

The law has had to respond to this changed landscape. Increasingly, the answer to offending behaviour is sought in incarceration and prison numbers have almost doubled in the last 15 years. We create anti-social behaviour orders and other orders of social control, which often have the consequence of accelerating the trajectory to prison. New law is introduced at a furious pace by governments, anxious to show they are taking action in response to public fear. Then, a careful analysis of the crime figures shows that no increase in crime has in fact taken place and in some areas it has been greatly reduced.

Public fear is often the product of factors other than crime: fear of the 'other' in a nation which increasingly depends on immigration to support a stable economy and in a world where increasing numbers of people flee inhumane treatment by their own governments; fear of the young who seem less deferential and controllable, rejecting old social norms; fear of anyone who is different, like those who have mental illness, have a different race or religion.

Underpinning the public sense of insecurity is also a fear of the invisible powers which influence our lives, from international companies to intra-national governing bodies like the World Trade Organization or the European Union. Globalisation makes people fearful that their jobs and personal finances, such as pensions, are being affected by forces well beyond their control. Fear ignites the desire for strong government but it also fuels a lack of confidence in our own institutions, like parliament, the courts or the police, to handle the enormity of new problems. All the advances which have allowed the global market to flourish, such as ease of travel, opening of borders, electronic transfer of money, the internet and telecommunications, have also stimulated international crime. Drugs importation, the black market in arms, people trafficking and terrorism have all burgeoned in our new world and old systems of investigation often seem ill-equipped. Into this mix, we must add our reluctance as a society to accept the vicissitudes of life. We have become risk averse. We readily perceive ourselves as victims and we look to see who is responsible for everything that befalls us. This makes us more litigious and willing to engage in courtroom processes ourselves.

As our world has shrunk and crime has crossed borders, there has been a greater urgency to find synergies between our very different systems of law. This has led to changes in our own common law rules of evidence, the creation of new processes for extradition and better methods of receiving evidence from abroad. It has also forced us to restate the principles which should underpin all law, so that we do not receive evidence that has been obtained by unacceptable methods or surrender prisoners to systems which may punish in inhumane ways.

Finding common denominators between systems of law is never easy but that is what human rights law seeks to do, which is why I was so glad to see that Ursula Smartt had placed such emphasis on this comparatively new development in our own system. It sets out the values which should inform all legal systems – the right to liberty, to a fair trial, to freedom of speech, to family life. It reaches beyond the rights vested in us because of our citizenship and creates rights which everyone of us should have by virtue of our shared humanity. Human rights establishes a common language about law but it should also create a grammar for our everyday existence as lovers, spouses, parents and neighbours.

The criminal law changes more than many other parts of the law because it is so tied up with social development – that is what makes it so interesting and challenging and why I still feel so engaged after a lifetime in the criminal justice system. For example, when I first started in practice women had little voice within the system, either as practitioners, offenders or victims. Much has happened, though not enough has changed. There are many more women lawyers and judges but women involved in the processes still face stereotyping and a welter of mythology based on expectations about good womanhood. As victims of crimes such as rape they still have difficulty securing justice. However, it is within the criminal courts that social shifts are most tangible; it is also where the failure to make social change is most powerfully felt, as we see the poor and the dysfunctional as well as the maliciously aberrant.

When I read Ursula Smartt's writings on the law, I always wish she had been around when I was a student. She brings clarity to complex subjects and always manages to get to the heart of any matter. This book is a triumph in its clarity, scholarship and sheer scope. I am happy for the students of criminology for whom it was created but I would like to see it reach a far wider audience. This is *the* book on criminal law that should be on the shelf of everyone connected to the criminal law: students, judges, lawyers, criminologists, prison governors and officers, police and probation officers, social workers, magistrates, inmates and offenders and even the interested public. It is too good to keep to ourselves.

*Baroness Helena Kennedy* QC
*House of Lords, London*
*March 2008*

# INTRODUCTION: WHY STUDY THE LAW AS A CRIMINOLOGIST?

It is my firm belief that all students of criminology need to study some law as part of their course. The question is: how much law? And which areas of law are appropriate for study? *Law for Criminologists* goes further than basic criminal law, police and prosecution procedures and sentencing structures. It was my intention to provide the reader with both broader issues in criminology as well as an introduction to socio-legal studies to show how law is made in the form of statutes and explain the meaning of common law.

*Law for Criminologists* is based on my own teaching and lecturing on both criminology and law courses in higher education. Having studied and researched in both disciplines this book then offers a 'cross over' approach and seeks to provide students with a practical compendium of legal resources as well as criminological theories. Matters that up to a decade or so ago would have been considered obscure specialist legal issues, of little concern to the central themes of criminology, have increasingly become essential parts of our understanding of the causes of crime and the criminal justice system today.

Why is it important for a criminologist to study law? Reasons are manifold. Not only because your university course includes some law, but also because we will look at how the law connects with traditional criminological theories, where as a critical criminologist you will be asked to reflect on the causes of crime and criminality. Over the past 20 years or so, Britain has seen a plethora of new penal policies in the form of criminal justice legislation, such as the *Crime and Disorder Act 1998* or the *Criminal Justice Act 2003*.

To understand the workings of all three legal systems – England and Wales, Scotland and Northern Ireland – this book will provide a broad outline of all three jurisdictions with ample legislation and case law examples, coupled with current themes in criminology. For example, how does the government deal with persistent young offenders? How do control orders come about and how are they executed against those suspected of terrorism offences? What legislation allows the police to stop, search and question someone in the street?

Crime has spread across European borders and widespread organised criminal activity is a global law enforcement issue. *Law for Criminologists* draws the reader's attention to European legislation, the European Arrest Warrant, human rights legislation and the relevant courts, such as the European Court of Justice in Luxembourg, the European Court of Human Rights in Strasbourg and the workings of the International Criminal Court in The Hague.

Why does this book not simply feature criminal law? Based on my own teaching, I have long felt that criminology students need to learn about basic principles of law and how all the courts work, civil as well as criminal. Increasingly, private individuals are using civil courts to bring private prosecutions, where the criminal courts have failed to find a person guilty.

Each chapter is equipped with the following features:

- An overview of the topic
- Short case notes and summaries with full case citations in the appendix
- One full and detailed case study at the end of each chapter
- Sample examination and assessment questions
- Further resources comprising suggested additional reading

The case study at the end of each chapter serves as a legal research training exercise and is linked to a particular theme in the chapter. Students are encouraged to read each case cited in its original or electronic form (full law report) – as provided by either Westlaw or LexisNexis. Here follows a brief summary of what you can expect in the book.

**Chapter 1** introduces you to criminological theories and themes that discuss the distinction between crime and deviance. Questions will be addressed, such as: Why does a young person become deviant during his development? How does the environment, such as the family or the school, influence an individual? Why do some people turn to crime and others not? What are the causes of a person's criminal behaviour? What makes up a criminal offence? And how does the law address crime and why does criminal law change over time?

**Chapter 2** focuses on the English legal system and how it works in practice. You will learn about the main sources of English law, focusing on civil and criminal courts in England and Wales and their key personnel. Since English law is case law based – known as the 'common law' tradition – the learning of at least some of the leading cases and their precedents is advisable.

**Chapter 3** looks at the Scottish and Northern Irish legal systems and alerts you to the key differences in court and criminal procedures compared with the English and Welsh system. Scots criminal law is quite different from English law. It has a long history, dating back to medieval times and manifesting itself in Scottish independence with the *Acts of Union 1707* which abolished the Scottish Parliament and created a 'new' parliament at Westminster. Devolved government will be explained with the Scottish Parliament in Edinburgh and the Northern Ireland Assembly in Belfast.

A brief history of the Troubles in Northern Ireland will be provided so that you can understand some of the different court structures such as the juryless Diplock courts which were necessary in 'scheduled' offences in the Northern Irish province. With the Belfast Agreement of 1998 introducing normalisation in Northern Ireland, the book will then focus on changes in the criminal justice system including paramilitary prisoner releases from the Northern Irish prisons.

**Chapter 4** introduces you to European Union (EU) law and the European institutions confusingly spread between Brussels and Luxembourg, as well as giving you a brief history of the EU. You will learn about the supremacy of EU law over its 27 member states' legislations and the legislative function of the European Court of Justice. Though students tend to find the subject of EU law difficult, it has been my intention to make this area of law user-friendly by providing you with some interesting case law and trying to reduce the complexities and wordiness of EU directives and regulations.

Following the London and Madrid bombings it will be shown how the European Arrest Warrant has been used by EU law enforcement agencies in order to strengthen the third pillar of the EU, involving justice, home affairs, border control and the respective criminal courts.

**Chapter 5** provides you with the basic building blocks to what makes up a criminal offence in English criminal law: the *actus reus* and the *mens rea*. Though this chapter is volumous, I have tried to provide you with a user-friendly guide to some of the more difficult topics in criminal law, such as intention and causation, recklessness and the most common defences available, particularly in homicide offences.

The chapter includes important changes in sexual offences legislation as provided by the *Sexual Offences Act 2003*, with specific examples relating to rape and sexually transmitted diseases. The lengthy case of *Dica* [2004] will be highlighted, where a Somali defendant stood accused of knowingly infecting two women with HIV. It will also be argued that the law in the area of 'non-fatal offences against the person' is urgently in need of reform.

**Chapter 6** continues where Chapter 3 left off and focuses on the criminal justice systems of Scotland and Northern Ireland. It will be explained how the Royal Ulster Constabulary (RUC) was replaced by the Northern Ireland Police Force in 2001. The chapter then looks at new styles of policing and how a suspect is 'processed' through the criminal justice systems in England and Wales, Scotland and Northern Ireland and how policing in the community works in all three jurisdictions.

**Chapter 7** examines popular punishment theories and how they are linked to current sentencing practices, with specific focus on plenty of realistic sentencing examples used by the courts today, such as discharges, fines, community sentences and finally imprisonment.

At the time of writing this book, Britain's prisons were bursting at the seams and the prison population being the highest in Western Europe with 145 out of every 100,000 per population in custody, compared with France's 88 – though only a fraction of the United States' 738. You will learn to understand why the prison population of England and Wales in particular has been steadily rising.

The chapter will focus on continuing and high reoffending rates in that about 58 per cent of adult males will reoffend within two years of release from prison. Though the government has sought a quick fix by commissioning the building of more privately run and Titan prisons thereby providing about 8,000 more prison places, this may not necessarily address the causes of crime.

**Chapter 8** concentrates on human rights law in the UK and abroad and applied international case law, relevant to the study of criminology. One of the biggest changes to the law has taken place comparatively recently with the incorporation of *European Convention on Human Rights and Fundamental Freedoms of 1950* ('The Convention') by way of the *Human Rights Act 1998* into UK legislation. We will look at the way the *Human Rights Act 1998* has affected all general principles of law in the UK, especially in criminal proceedings and imprisonment.

The chapter then examines the arguments for and against capital punishment and alerts the reader to countries that have abolished the death penalty and those that have not. It will be argued that human rights law in conjunction with the rule of law and good governance should be among the strongest tools in the fight against terrorism of all EU governments today.

**Chapter 9** looks at legislation and criminal procedure regarding young people in England, Scotland and Northern Ireland. For a start, the age of criminal responsibility is different across the UK: a child aged 10 can be accountable for his crime in England, Wales and Northern Ireland, but an 8 year-old child can be charged with a criminal offence in Scotland.

This final chapter picks up where Chapter 1 left off trying to address the question of why children and young people commit crime and how the criminal justice systems treats young delinquents. You will learn about different youth and community support schemes in all three jurisdictions and how restorative justice is addressing the needs of victims.

It has been my prime objective that *Law for Criminologists* should motivate students of criminology to gain greater confidence when studying law as part of their curriculum. I have made every effort to keep this book up to date, since I am only too aware that legislation and common law change so rapidly. For this reason, I have added some useful websites in the appendices, together with statutes and case law across all three and EU jurisdictions, so that you can undertake updated research yourself. By the end of this book, you should be able to translate some criminological themes – such as what are the causes of youth crime – into the legal and procedural agenda, by thinking about social control, crime and deviance.

If there is one aim that I would like to achieve with this book it is that you become enthusiastic about the law and that *Law for Criminologists* broadens your general criminological knowledge horizon, joining up the two disciplines of law and criminology. Hopefully, this book will serve you well in your academic studies and help you to become an excellent criminologist.

*Ursula Smartt*
*London 2008*

# 1

## WHAT DETERMINES A CRIMINAL TODAY?

---

**Overview**

Chapter 1 examines:

- The distinctions between crime and deviance
- The rationale behind why the law changes over time
- The changing nature of criminal offences
- The way criminal statistics are presented and interpreted
- The role of the victim in criminal procedure

---

The study of criminology today includes the understanding of the concept of globalisation of crime which examines the role that crime plays as an agent of social change. Linked to criminalisation and social development, you can begin to understand the political economy of crime and crime in transitional cultures, such as the war on terror, the globalisation of economies, and the increasing social diversity and division in our societies.

The boundaries between public and private life have become increasingly blurred with high levels of private surveillance, from CCTV in shopping malls to credit checks in mobile phone shops. Some see the increasing surveillance as a net result of 'joined-up government' and as an interference with civil liberties. Governments might see it as dealing effectively with a range of social problems and crime control. The result is a mass of new criminal justice legislation which is both civil and criminal in nature. This book seeks to make the link between civil and criminal law and the relevant court structures in all three jurisdictions, England and Wales, Scotland and Northern Ireland.

Not only can the police increasingly patrol public and private spaces in the name of 'terrorism' now, but local authorities have also been given increased policing powers to impose Anti-social Behaviour Orders (ASBOs), to prosecute for fly-tipping and to evict noisy neighbours. Lord Anthony Giddens links today's criminal activities to consumerism and economic deprivation but also to terrorism and the notion of a new world order. He argues controversially that we live in a period of 'high modernity' (rather than in post-modernity) in which prior trends are radicalised rather than undermined. He links modernity to the post-industrialised world of the 1930s as that of a highly materialistic society and social control (Giddens, 1991a).

Giddens then comments on our 'surveillance society' with its 'visible super-vision' models, such as the police, private security services and CCTV and links these to Michel Foucault who argued that the state will always monopolise the control of crime and violence (Foucault, 1977). Giddens also refers us back to what Jeremy Bentham called the 'all seeing state' (Giddens, 1991b: 13ff).

Taking Giddens' model of 'risk society' we can link this concept to our post 9/11 era, namely the terrorism atrocities in New York, Washington DC and Pennsylvania on 9 September 2001 and the London bomb attacks of 5 and 21 July 2005, and see how governments are now dealing with terrorism threats and public fear of crime in a global agenda. The main facts surround-ing these attacks are too well known to recall here; it is enough to record that they were atrocities on an unprecedented scale, causing many deaths and destroying property of immense value.

Ulrich Beck, one of Europe's leading social theorists, has also analysed the impact of our global 'risk society'. Beck re-examined the essentially negative concepts of 'post-industrial' and 'post-Enlightenment' theories and how 'risk' has impacted on current social developments of personal and public life. He argues that increasing legislation has changed the whole social strata. By recog-nising that diversity, individualism, scepticism and fear are now part of our Western culture, Beck calls our society a 'new cosmopolitanism' and encour-ages a form of global morality, shared risk and a communal responsibility to crime (1992, 1999).

Putting these theories into context, whilst the UK has faced a variety of terrorist threats in the not so distant past, by the IRA or Al Qaida, a unique combination of factors has emerged, namely a globally united front by all members of society and within the European Union, or as the Labour Home Secretary, Jacqui Smith, put it in July 2007, that people in the UK will not be 'intimidated by those [terrorists] who wish to destroy our way of life and our freedoms' (Jacqui Smith's response to the terrorism threats to UK airports after the attempted bombing of Glasgow Airport on 30 June 2007).

## 1.1 ___ Making distinctions between crime and deviance _____

As part of your criminological legal studies, you may well be asked to note down some typical criminal offences. You might then mention burglary, rob-bery, assault or possibly rape. But, would you have made a note of identity theft, river pollution or the killing of passengers on a crowded commuter train?

The *Oxford English Dictionary* defines crime as:

An act punishable by law, as being forbidden by statute or injurious to the public welfare ... An evil or injurious act; an offence, a sin; esp. of a grave character.

Crime then has multiple meanings and definitions and comes down to a social construct, that is, every society defines 'crime' in different ways. And what would you call a 'priority crime' – a favourite term now used by law enforcement agencies? Would it be mobile phone theft by children from children at school? Or having your front teeth kicked in by your husband? Or graffiti on bus shelters? Or an attack on a gay bar?

First, you need to distinguish between the strictly legal definition of a crime, that is in statute (Act of Parliament) and the contravention of certain codes, conventions, or morals, known as normative definitions (see Chapter 2.1). The latter ones would not be 'law' but would reflect moral or religious codes which usually define socially acceptable behaviour. What may be against the law in one country might well be acceptable behaviour in another state, such as bigamy.

It is generally believed that those who act involuntarily do not deserve punishment nor would their punishment serve any useful purpose. An individual who lacks control over his criminal actions is generally not regarded as being responsible for the consequences of those actions and incurs no criminal liability (see Chapter 5.3). To summarise, a crime could be defined as:

- An activity that is classified within the criminal law of a country
- A strictly defined legal definition in form common law or statute in England and Wales
- Legally defined criminal acts
- An illegal act which deserves punishment by the state
- Criminal activity defined by the British Crime Survey (BCS)
- Some legally defined crimes in the UK may be legitimate acts in other countries (e.g. bigamy)
- An evolving social process in the criminal law, shaped by social forces and socio-political decisions made by individuals.

## Deviance

What then is the difference between a crime and what criminologists call 'deviant behaviour'? Deviance is a classical theme, which explains the causes of crime. The study of deviance is concerned primarily with the construction, application and impact of stigma labels. For example, there are strongly perceived links between juvenile offending and the home (familial) environment (see Chapter 9.1). Other theorists discovered that deviance and delinquent behaviour are learnt through observing, imitating and 'modelling' others (refer to McLaughlin and Muncie, 2006).

Critical criminologists like Professors David Downes and Paul Rock established that penal policies and resulting changes in criminal legislation are usually consequences of wider social changes. These, in turn, have influenced law enforcement priorities and legislation such as policing (see Chapters 6.2–6.4) Downes and Rock (2003) explained deviance as the difference between what is morally wrong and what is against the law – that is criminally wrong – within a given society:

> The sociology of crime and deviance is not one coherent discipline at all but a collection of relatively independent versions of Sociology. (Downes and Rock, 2003: 1)

To summarise, deviance is:

- Reference to behaviour that is morally or 'normatively' wrong
- Delinquency which can (but not necessarily does) lead to criminal behaviour
- Dysfunctional family background and how this may lead to criminal culture and future criminal behaviour, such as the 'yob culture' or gang violence

Criminological studies have traditionally focused on subcultures, such as punks, rockers, skinheads or the dance culture. Some of these phenomena have been linked to inequality and inner city deprivation. Cohen's (1972) definition of deviance is linked to economic deprivation – Marxist criminology – whereby not having a good career or owning consumer goods may lead some individuals to commit crime because they perceive that they are being deprived of something. Other criminogenic factors include gender – young males are more likely to offend than females – or inadequate parenting. How some agencies have taken positive steps to address particularly youth crime can be seen in Chapter 9.

One term you may have come across in your theoretical studies is anomie. This concept was first defined by the French Sociologist Émile Durkheim (1858–1917) who established the idea that when people find themselves in rapidly changing social conditions, they will lose the social guidelines (norms) of what is 'acceptable' behaviour. Durkheim's studies concentrated on how and why people break the law in society. He suggested that crime was 'normal' in a modern industrialised society and hypothesised that social change in conditions could lead to unacceptable behaviour and deviance (anomie), particularly in young people (Durkheim, 1893).

Durkheim coined the term 'anomie' or lawlessness (derived from the Greek *a-nomos* meaning 'lawless') whereby he explained that anomie resulted in the transition from the pre-industrial society to the industrial and mechanical society. He then argued that deviant and anomic behaviour can lead to exclusion from a given society and a collective punishment of that individual (see also Jones, 2006: 156ff).

Robert Merton (1938) took the anomie theory a step further, linking it to the social anomie of the post-depression years of the late 1930s in America. By looking at the 'American Dream', he portrayed the class struggle in American culture which could lead to crime. His anomic vocabulary included 'retreatism' and 'rejection'. He linked his theory to practical examples like Al Capone and the godfather-type gangster, whose rebellious and amoral behaviour became part of a celebrated culture in American society, that placed high value on economic affluence and social ascent (see Downes and Rock, 2003: 104–140).

Glueck and Glueck (1950) linked deviance and criminal behaviour to dysfunctional family background, when they compared 500 well-behaved schoolboys from a 'good' family background with 500 institutionalised delinquents from care and foster homes. The authors found that 66 per cent of the delinquents had a criminal father or brother, compared with 32 per cent in the 'goodies' control group (see Glueck, 1934: 235–237).

Bowlby (1944, 1979) concluded that maternal deprivation through rejection was linked to childhood antisocial behaviour (anomie) and delinquency and Hirschi (1969) in his 'control theory' found that children from larger families were harder to discipline and likely to receive less parental attention than small families.

The causes of crime (criminogenic factors) can be defined as:

- Deviant and criminal behaviour influenced by societal and familial factors, known as 'the environment'
- Causes of crime, largely linked to life style, life-cycle and familial conditions in which the individual lives

You may find reference to the 'broken windows' theory, a term first used in criminology by the political scientist James Q. Wilson and the criminologist George L. Kelling, in an article in *Atlantic Monthly* (March 1982). The authors used the image of 'broken windows' to explain how neighbourhood communities can decay into crime and disorder if (factory) windows are not mended and are left broken. This would suggest to passers-by that no one is in charge or cares on the estate. With time, more windows would then get broken by rock-throwing deviants. Soon, only criminals and drop-outs will be present in that neighbourhood. This, in turn, will attract more anomie, including drug dealing and prostitution, until someone might even get killed. Wilson et al.'s point was that small disorders can lead to larger disorders and to serious crime (Wilson et al., 1998: 29–38).

The following list may assist you with some criminological terms regarding deviance:

- **Norms** are social sets of specified behaviour patterns, such as religious norms, legal norms, health norms, cultural norms, etc. Norms emerge in most social situations.
- **Deviance** is a pattern of norm violation. For example, there can be class deviance or situational deviance, where the norms emerging are transgressed.

- **Stigma** (pl. stigmata) – deviance can be highlighted as a 'stigma construct' or 'label' bestowed upon certain types of behaviour at certain times. A terrorist, for example, is a political martyr or freedom fighter on the one hand and a murderer on the other.
- **Norm violation** (stigma construct) – precisely who or what is deviant depends upon a positive understanding of the norms and labelling processes in particular social contexts.

In summary, deviance is a shifting, ambiguous and volatile concept.

## 1.2 ___ The changing nature of criminal offences _____

Critical criminology asks questions on how the causes of crime vary in different social situations, societies and different periods of history. How and why do criminal acts suddenly change? Why are certain criminal acts suddenly 'legal' or decriminalised, such as homosexuality? Why do governments unexpectedly decategorise the possession of cannabis?

It is important for you to understand the social processes involved in changing the law and bringing about new legislation whereby criminal acts are defined in law, how they are prosecuted and how they lead to a conviction. This is known as the criminal process. Ultimately, law is shaped by social forces and shaped by choices and decisions made by individuals.

Beck (1999) recognises a changing relationship between social structures and social agents which, over the past 20 years, has led to the individualisation of society's decision-making and law-making process. Beck argues that, although Western societies are facing terrorism threats on a scale not previously encountered, modern societies are showing an increased sophisticated resilience and an ambitious restraint towards terrorism organisations and that life must continue as normal. Postmodernists usually examine the way in which the law has been influenced by social change over time, which, in turn, affirms the power of human beings over the making and reshaping of the law (see Roach Anleu, 2005).

Given the changes in the law over time and having looked at the reasons for social change and the law, you begin to realise how Britain has seen the most rapid changes in criminal justice policies and therein a plethora of considerable new legislation (see Appendix 1). This has been driven by the public's fear of crime, enhanced by the media (see Smartt, 2006c). The fact is that our society continues to be fascinated by crime. Just have a look at British daily newspapers, with an overabundance of daily crime stories, or TV drama series featuring human transgression, police or court scenarios. Often relatively exceptional crimes are hyped in the press, which means that members of the public tend to believe that there is ever-increasing crime 'out there'. The upshot is, communities feel unsafe and under threat (see Smartt et al., 2002).

This, in turn, increases the demand for tougher penal policies, resulting in increased criminal justice legislation; this, again, influences law enforcement priorities, such as policing. Since 9/11, there has been excessive legislation combating terrorism, with changes in PACE-Codes (*Police and Criminal Evidence Act 1984*) and terrorism acts (*Terrorism Act 2000*; *Anti-terrorism, Crime and Security Act 2001*; *Terrorism Act 2006*) (see also Chapter 6.10).

New offences have come about, such as issuing false cheques or the cloning of credit cards, yet old statutes – like the Theft Acts of 1968 and 1978 – prevail. 'Joy riding', which in law is the 'taking a vehicle without the owner's consent' (or 'TWOking'), contrary to section 12 of the *Theft Act 1968*, usually coupled with 'dangerous driving' within section 2 of the *Road Traffic Act 1988* has become increasingly unfashionable amongst criminal youths. This is due to the improved car security and may mean that TWOking could soon either be decategorised or disappear altogether from the statute books.

Most criminal offences have become statutory offences, that is, there is now an Act of Parliament in place of common law, for example, having sexual inter-course with children under the age of 16 or internet grooming (*Sexual Offences Act 2003*) (see Chapter 5.5). But many modern-day offences are still covered by aged legislation: graffiti is part of the *Criminal Damage Act 1971*; stabbing a prison officer with an Aids-infected needle comes under the ancient *Offences Against the Person Act 1861*.

Making the correct charge in cases of domestic violence can be difficult for the police and the Crown Prosecution Service, since there is no specific offence called 'domestic violence'. There are a number of offences and statutes linked to crimes of 'domestic violence' and police need to make a distinction between an 'assault' (s. 47 *Offences Against the Person Act 1861* (OAPA)) and 'common assault by beating' (or 'battery') (s. 39 *Criminal Justice Act 1988*). This can be tricky (see Smartt and Kury, 2007: 1263–1280).

The English Crown Prosecution Service (CPS) introduced statutory charging for domestic violence crimes in 2004, making this a priority crime. This means in practice, even if the victim makes a withdrawal statement at the police station or even at trial stage, prosecutors may issue witness summons to force the (hostile) witness to come to court to give evidence against the per-petrator. Alternatively, the CPS can go ahead without the victim being present in court as key witness.

> We know that domestic violence is a serious public health issue and that the statistics are shocking. For women aged 19–44 domestic violence is the leading cause of morbidity (and) ... 89% of the victims who suffer sustained domestic violence are female; however, we also know that domestic violence can affect ... male victims. (Home Office, 2005b)

But still, incorrect charging can make the difference between the perpetrator receiving a conditional discharge or a fine or a four-year custodial sentence. The distinction between a kick, a punch or a push of the woman by her tormentor is then left to magistrates or the jury to decide (see Kury and Smartt, 2006: 382–407). In this context, read the case of *Ahluwalia* at the end of this chapter.

## 1.3 —— Measuring crime and criminality

There are essentially two 'official' ways of recording crime statistics: recorded and reported crime. The British Crime Survey and the International Crime Victim Surveys help to identify those most at risk of different types of crime. They assist governments in planning new legislation in order to prevent crimes.

**Recorded crime** refers to official police reports, or 'notifiable' offences. Most of these comprise *summary* offences. Reporting a crime means that someone reports to the police that a crime has been committed or the police observe or discover a crime or crime-related incident. It is not necessarily the case that a reported crime to the police may result in the crime actually being logged or recorded. A crime report constitutes a crime record number, usually for insurance purposes. The Home Office issues 'Counting Rules for Reported Crime' to police forces; these are fairly straightforward, as most crimes are counted as 'one crime per victim' and the offence committed is obvious, such as domestic burglary. It gets more complex where more than one offence has taken place, maybe on several occasions over a period of time, or there is more than one offender or victim.

**Recorded crime** figures are important indicators of police workload in a region and their specific performance, known as 'clear-up rates'; they are then used for local crime pattern analysis. This does not mean all criminal offences are cleared up. Once a crime is recorded and investigated by the police and evidence is collected to link the crime to a suspect, it can be detected according to criteria contained in Home Office 'Detection Guidance'. In many cases, someone is charged or cautioned or the court has taken the offence into consideration (TIC) (see Chapter 6.2).

**Reported crime** involves victim surveys. Traditionally, crime victim surveys mostly concentrated on surveying traditional property crime, violent and street crime (robbery). Zedner argues that no surveys have as yet measured sexual aggression or intra-family violence (Zedner, 1999: 577–612). Since 1982, the Home Office's British Crime Survey (BCS) has measured the amount of crime in England and Wales by asking now about 40,000 people aged 16 or over anonymously about crimes they have experienced in the last year.

The British Crime Survey is considered to be the most reliable indicator of trends in violent crime as police recorded crime is susceptible to reporting and recording changes, especially in less serious offences. The BCS establishes the 'dark figure' that is unreported crime. It is an important alternative to police records. The British Crime Survey is about levels of crime and public attitudes to crime. The results play an important role in informing government policy and can be found on the Home Office and Ministry of Justice websites (see Appendix 4, useful websites). The British Crime Survey includes:

- Personal experiences of crime
- Public attitudes to the criminal justice system, including the police and the courts

- Fears about crime
- Security concerns, such as home and vehicle security measures
- Violence at work, such as bullying and harassment
- Perceptions of equality and prejudice
- Volunteering and community activities
- Experience of household fires
- Illegal drug use
- Sexual victimisation including stalking
- Domestic violence

For the first time the BCS 2007 brought together police recorded statistics and victim surveys. This most helpful combined survey estimated that there were about 11 million crimes experienced by people over the age of 16 during the year 2006; this meant 8.4 million fewer crimes than in 1995. The police recorded 6 million crimes in 2005–6, of which around 73 per cent were acquisitive crimes such as burglary or theft (a decrease of 1 per cent in 2005) (see Chapter 6.7).

Whilst crime recorded by the police showed a decrease by 2 per cent compared with the same quarter in the previous year, the BCS 2007 showed a statistically significant increase in the risk of being a victim, from 23 per cent in the year to December 2005 to 24 per cent in the year to December 2006. Though it is worth noting that the risk of being a victim of crime is still significantly lower than the peak of 40 per cent recorded by the BCS in 1995. The domestic burglary rate has been steadily falling since 1999 and there has been a steady downward trend in car crime. Since the de-regulation of alcohol and pub licensing in 2007 (from the magistrates' courts to local authority licensing), alcohol-related offences, involving 'violence against the person', have increased (ss. 47; 20 and 18 of the *Offences Against the Person Act 1861*) (see Chapter 5.4).

What about the fear of crime? The overall proportion of people who perceived a high level of anti-social behaviour in their local community remained stable (from 17 per cent in 2005 to 18 per cent in 2006). Perceived problems were noisy neighbours or loud parties, people being drunk or rowdy and people using or dealing drugs. There was a decrease in perceiving problems with abandoned or burnt out cars. The proportion of people who thought that the police in their area did an excellent or good job showed an increase from 50 to 51 per cent in the 12 months to December 2006 (Home Office, 2007c).

How has crime changed? Crime in England and Wales peaked in 1995 and since then it has fallen by 44 per cent according to the BCS 2007. There have been large falls in domestic burglary and vehicle thefts over the last 10 years (burglary down 59 per cent, vehicle thefts down 60 per cent) (Home Office, 2007c).

What about violent crime? The BCS 2007 showed violent crime as remaining stable – a fall of 43 per cent, representing 1.8 million fewer crimes since 1995. Recorded crime has shown a different pattern, with the number of violent crimes recorded by the police showing substantial increases, due to changes in recording practices, increased reporting by the public and increased police activity.

Who is most at risk? The BSC has repeatedly established that it is young males, aged between 16 and 24, rather than old people, who remain most at risk of becoming victims of violent crime.

The International Crime Victim Survey (ICVS) is the most far-reaching global victim survey programme that looks at householders' experience of crime, attitudes to policing, crime prevention and the fear of crime in a large number of countries; the results of which are internationally comparable (see Kury et al., 2002). The first round of 14 countries in the International Crime Victim Survey began in 1989 conducted by the Dutch Ministry of Justice, in cooperation with the Home Office and the Swiss University of Lausanne. The third ICVS round was conducted in 48 countries in 1996, followed by the 2004–5 round in only 15 'old Europe' countries. In total, the ICVS has surveyed over 70 different countries (see Smartt et al., 2002: 133–150).

Another way of measuring victimisation is by measuring the costs of crime. Home Office researchers Brand and Price (2000) measured the costs by using the British Crime Survey and the Commercial Victimisation Survey; the latter measures industrial crimes, industry turnover and costs and their insurance and private security costs. It is difficult, however, to measure emotional costs of the impact of crime on victims. The researchers found that the most costly property crimes are theft of or from vehicles, costing around £4,700 per incident in 1999. Burglaries cost an average of £2,300 and criminal damage around £500.

## 1.4 ___ Victims

Victimology is the study of why certain people become victims of crime, including the emotional and psychological effects of crime (see Zedner, 2007), though the word 'victim' can be rather indiscriminately used today such as cancer victim, holocaust victim, accident victim, bullying at work or hurricane victim.

The term 'victimology' was first coined by the American psychiatrist Frederick Wertham, in 1949, though the seminal text is by Hans von Hentig, *The Criminal and His Victim* (1948) which called for a study in victims. Von Hentig proposed a dynamic, interactionist approach that challenged conceptions of the victim as passive actor in the criminal justice system (see Fattah and Sacco, 1989). Von Hentig focused both on those characteristics of victims which precipitated their suffering and on the relationship between victim and offender, arguing:

> The law … makes a clear-cut distinction between the one who does and the one who suffers. Looking into the genesis of the situation, in a considerable number of cases, we meet a victim who consents tacitly, co-operates, conspires or provokes. (Von Hentig, 1948, quoted in Fattah, 1978: 198–213)

During the founding of victimology in the 1940s, victimologists such as Herrmann Mannheim (1889–1974) and Hans von Hentig (1887–1974) tended to use dictionary definitions of victims as hapless and tricked fools who instigated their own victimisations. The empirical approach of the victimological perspective in positivistic criminology became the lifetime study of Marvin Wolfgang. In his *Patterns in of Criminal Homicide* (1958), Wolfgang developed the concept of 'victim precipitation' to express the contribution of the victim in the realisation of the crime. Fattah (1999) argues that many victims of crime remain unaware of state compensation schemes and that such schemes like the Criminal Injuries Compensation Authority have made some ridiculously low awards in the past.

The subject of victim-proneness, first coined by Wolfgang and von Hentig, remains one of the most controversial sub-topics in criminology, linked to 'guilt' and 'victim blaming' and of being in the wrong location at the wrong time. By classifying victims into typologies based on psychological and social variables, Sebba (1996) suggests that certain individuals are more 'victim-prone' than others (see also Rock, 1994, 2004).

Victims were eventually put on a statutory basis by the provision of compensation or victim restitution with the *Crime and Disorder Act 1998*. There are now hundreds of victim support agencies that assist victims of crime either formally or informally to deal with the trauma and practical ways to come to court, such as:

- **A code of practice for victims** which sets out the minimum standards of service that a victim can expect from the criminal justice system
- **National standards** to meet the needs of specific groups of victims, such as victims of road traffic accidents, rail or shipping disasters or human trafficking
- **Funding** to support the development of community-based services for sexual crime victims
- **Measures to prevent repeat victimisation** in domestic violence cases
- **Victims Advisory Panels** which enable victims of crime to have their say on how victims should be supported in the justice system

Some restorative justice measures have brought victim and offender together in some form of victim–offender mediation. There are a number of restorative justice and reconciliation schemes, first introduced in Canada and the United States during the 1970s, followed by Austria and Germany, whose probation services led on victim–offender mediation ('*Täter-Opfer Ausgleich*') (see Wright, 1996; Marshall, 1999) (See Chapter 7.6).

The Home Office regularly conducts studies into the cost of victimisation, amounting to an estimated £60 billion in 2000, with personal crimes, such as offences against the person or homicides, by far the most costly (Home Office, 2000). For this reason people are spending more on private security measures, such as private car or house alarms or 'gated' communities (see Anderson, 1999: 611–641).

## 1.5 ___ Case study

___ *R v Ahluwalia* [1992] 4 All ER 889 ___

There are times when domestic violence can lead to murder. The case of Kiranjit Ahluwalia is of enormous importance to criminologists who take a particular interest in gender and crime issues. *Ahluwalia* concerns an extreme case of domestic violence where the woman killed her husband. The case is important because it sets the precedent for the 'slow-burn effect' in relation to the defence of provocation available to women, also known as 'battered woman syndrome' (see also Chapter 5.3).

---

### Facts of the case

Kiranjit Ahluwalia, aged 33 at the time of the killing, was born in India into a middle class family. She was under pressure from her family to marry. The marriage was arranged with Deepak, who came from a family of Kenyan Asians.

After their marriage in Canada when Kiranjit was 24, the couple moved to Crawley in England in 1981. Both had jobs. Their two boys were born in July 1984 and January 1986.

From the start, their marriage was a violent one. Deepak was a big man and Kiranjit was only slight. She complained to her GP about her husband's violence. She told her doctor in October 1981 that she had been hit four times on the head with a telephone and thrown to the ground; that in September 1983, she was pushed whilst pregnant sustaining a bruised hand. The GP also gave evidence at trial that Kiranjit had made several suicide attempts between 1983 and 1986.

In 1983, the Croydon County Court had granted her an injunction in the form of a restraining order, to stop the husband from hitting her, but the violence continued until 1986, when she obtained her second injunction from the court after her husband had held her throat and threatened her with a knife. She learnt in March 1989 that her husband was having an affair with a woman who worked with him at the Post Office.

On 8 May 1989, Deepak arrived home about 10.15 p.m. after seeing his girlfriend. Kiranjit tried to talk to him about their relationship, but he refused, indicating that it was over. He demanded money from her to pay a telephone bill and threatened to beat her if she did not give him £200 the next morning. He then threatened to burn Kiranjit's face with a hot iron if she did not leave him alone.

Kiranjit had bought some caustic soda and a can of petrol a few days earlier. At about 2.30 a.m. on 9 May 1989, she got up, went downstairs, poured about two pints of the petrol into a bucket – to make it easier to throw – lit a candle on the gas cooker and went upstairs, equipped with an oven glove for self-protection and a stick. She went to the husband's bedroom, threw in some petrol from the bucket, lit the stick from the candle and threw it into the room. She then went to dress her son.

The husband, now on fire, ran to immerse himself in the bath and then ran outside screaming, 'I'll kill you.' Neighbours found the door locked and saw Kiranjit standing calmly at a ground-floor window clutching her son. They shouted to her

---

to get out of the house, but she opened a window and said, 'I am waiting for my husband'. They made her hand the child out and later she emerged herself.

Fire officers extinguished the flames and found a bucket still smelling of petrol and the saucepan with caustic soda.

The husband died from severe burns on 15 May 1989 and Kiranjit Ahluwalia was charged with his murder.

At her trial at Lewes Crown Court, she gave no evidence and no medical evidence as to her mental state was adduced. Her case was that she had no intention either of killing her husband or of doing him really serious harm. She only wished to 'inflict some pain' on him. Her defence counsel, Mr Robertson QC, strongly relied on a note which she had written to her husband, begging him to come back to her. But the trial judge reminded the jury of the rules on provocation: *'Bear in mind it is a sudden and temporary loss of self-control for which you are looking, not a thought-out plan how to punish him for his wickedness.'* (RV Duffy [1949])

On 7 December 1989, the jury found Ahluwalia guilty of murder. She was sentenced to life imprisonment by Leonard J. She appealed.

Ahluwalia's appeal took nearly three years when she sought to adduce fresh medical evidence to support a plea of diminished responsibility.

Her appeal was heard in September 1992; it rested on the misdirection of the jury on the issue of provocation. But Lord Taylor of Gosforth confirmed that the trial judge had correctly directed the jury regarding the *Duffy*-defence of provocation, regarding the 'sudden and temporary loss of self-control'.

However, her defence counsel Geoffrey Robertson QC successfully argued that her mental state at the time of the offence, as well as her physical characteristics, ought to have been taken into account by the trial jury. This meant that the original trial jury should have been directed when applying the 'reasonable person' test as having the same characteristics of the accused of being a 'battered woman' over a long time and that they too would have lost their self-control given similar circumstances. Therefore the accused should have been able to avail herself to the defence of provocation. Counsel argued further that the jury direction on the phrase 'sudden and temporary loss of self-control' (the *Duffy*-defence) may have led the jury to think provocation could not arise, unless the defendant's act followed immediately upon the acts or words which constituted the alleged provocation. A retrial was ordered.

## Ahluwalia's retrial in 1992

At her retrial, Geoffrey Robertson QC adduced fresh medical evidence on the appellant's mental state and that she could not be held responsible for her actions at the time she doused her husband in petrol. He submitted that women who have been subjected frequently over a period to violent treatment may react to the final act or words by what he called a 'slow-burn' reaction rather than by an immediate loss of self-control.

Mr Robertson surmised that the appellant had been suffering from 'battered woman syndrome', stating that not only had the appellant suffered mental and physical violence, abuse and humiliation over some ten years but that the course of ill-treatment had affected her personality so as to produce a state of 'learnt helplessness'. Counsel linked these arguments to a temporary state of diminished responsibility – within the meaning of the *Homicide Act 1957* – when Ahluwalia committed the arson attack on her husband.

Kiranjit Ahluwalia's original conviction was quashed and she was found not guilty of murder by means of diminished responsibility.

When Kiranjit Ahluwalia was finally freed on appeal in 1992, her case changed the face of British justice and the fate of other women, such as Sarah Thornton[1] and Emma Humphreys[2] who were also successfully freed in 1992, following the *Ahluwalia* ruling (see Smartt and Kury, 2007).

In February 2003, Kim Galbraith walked out of Cornton Vale prison in Scotland, after serving four years for shooting her husband Ian dead at their home in Furnace, Argyll in 1999. Her release marked a victory for the 'Easterhouse Women's Aid' campaign group, who had fought tirelessly like the Southall Black Sisters had fought on behalf of Kiranjit Ahluwalia, to have the women's murder conviction changed to one of culpable homicide on the grounds of diminished responsibility.

 ■ **Exam Questions**

1  Illustrate what is meant by deviance in relation to criminological literature.
2  Give a detailed definition of what constitutes a crime and give examples from legislation and common law.
3  What is meant by 'fear of crime'? Compare from criminological literature with popular media coverage.
4  What is the difference between recorded and reported crime? Give examples by using research statistics.
5  Explain and discuss the difficulty when applying the *Duffy*-defence of provocation to women who stand trial for murder by referring to the case of *Ahluwalia*.

■ ■ **Further Resources** ■

Tim Newburn's volumous yet lively *Criminology* (2007) serves as an excellent introduction to all current themes in criminology. Chapter 1, 'Understanding crime and criminology' is as a comprehensive introduction to criminology for students who are either new or relatively new to the subject. The textbook covers all popular areas found in criminology and criminal justice, illustrated by graphics, photographs and newspaper extracts.

Philip Smith and Kristin Natalier's *Understanding Criminal Justice* (2004) addresses the question we have raised at the start of this book: Why study the law and criminal justice? The authors provide an overview of the sociological approaches to law and criminology. The book focuses on how law, as both a jurisprudential concept and a set of specific rules, and the criminal justice system interact and affect each other and the broader social aspects. The book demonstrates the relevance of both empirical research and theoretical perspectives to critical and creative thinking whilst acquainting students with contemporary issues and debates: conceptual, policy related and topical. There is useful data from the UK, USA and Australia.

John Muncie and David Wilson's comprehensive edition of the *Student Handbook of Criminal Justice and Criminology* (2004) is a 'one-stop shop' for the study of criminology and the criminal justice system. The Handbook discusses crime and criminology in relation to the media, race, Islam, gender and politics and considers all the relevant theoretical debates that dominate criminology.

David Downes and Paul Rock's comprehensive text *Understanding Deviance* (2003) provides the foundation to the sociology of crime and 'rule breaking' in society. It is an invaluable text for students studying criminology.

Geoffrey Robertson's *The Justice Game* (1999) is a good read, revealing the life of this celebrated barrister in some of the most newsworthy cases. The Australian-born lawyer defended, *inter alia*, Cynthia Payne, Salman Rushdie, Kate Adie, Arthur Scargill and *Gay News*.

## Notes

1  *R v Thornton [1992]* 1 All ER 306, Court of Appeal.
2  *R v Humphreys [1995]* unreported, *The Times*, 7 July 1995.

# 2

# THE LEGAL SYSTEM OF ENGLAND
# AND WALES

| Overview |
| --- |

Chapter 2 examines:

- The sources of English law
- The constitutional and administrative structure of the UK Parliament and its law-making powers
- The nature of the English civil and criminal court system and its key personnel
- The changing nature of other civil courts, such as the coroner's court, tribunals and inquiries

Chapter 2 introduces you to the English legal system, so that you get a good grounding in basic legal principles and sources of law. In order to understand how legislation comes about in the form of statutes (Acts of Parliament), you need to understand the set up of the UK Parliament before you embark on criminal procedure.

There has long been a heated debate in Parliament whether the UK should have a written constitution, similar to its continental European partners, but the strong arguments protecting cultural heritage and legal flexibility in a multi-cultural society have so far prevailed.

This chapter promotes greater understanding of the English court system to encourage you to participate in criminal as well as civil court proceedings as an observer, so that you can see how the law works in practice.

## 2.1 ___ Sources of law

There are four major sources of law:

- Custom
- Common law ('judge-made' or 'case law')

- Acts of Parliament ('statutes' or 'legislation')
- European Union law

## Custom

There are very few examples of customary law, but custom usually applies to local or geographical rights. Did you know, for example, that the law requiring a London taxi driver to carry a bale of hay on top of his cab to feed the horse was in force until 1976? Or that Welshmen are not allowed in the city of Chester after dark? Or that fishermen in Lowestoft have the right to dry their nets on someone else's land? (see Elliott and Quinn, 2008: 94). Custom enters a legal dispute when one party alleges that they have had a particular right to do something since 'time immemorial'. This has to be at least since 1189 (see Cawthorne, 2004).

## Common Law

This goes back to 1066 when William the Conqueror of Normandy invaded England. Judges at that time would hear and decide cases according to local custom (see above). A process then evolved, whereby the best legal practice would be recorded, which was the beginnings of the development known as 'common to all' or common law. The common law tradition is an important source of law alongside statutory provision. This is particularly important in criminal law. Continental European law, on the other hand, has a codified system, such as the French or German 'penal' codes (*Code Pénale* or *Strafgesetzbuch*) or the Italian Penal Procedural Code (*Code de Procedure Penale*). Around the twelfth century, we see the origins of the 'doctrine of precedent'. This was where a number of scholars began to record the decisions of the courts. Hereafter, justices began to rely on these reported cases to assist them in making decisions where they were faced with other similar cases. Each case not only received a case name, but also the legal texts or law reports, year and page references, so that cases could be easily found (see Smartt, 2006a).

How then do you cite common or case law? When you look up cases online, in your legal textbooks or at the back of this book (see Appendix 2), you need to know the exact case citation.

**Criminal cases** are cited: *R v Smith* (the 'v' stands for '*versus*' in Latin, meaning 'against'). The 'R' stands for *Rex* (King) or *Regina* (Queen). You pronounce this as: 'The Crown against Smith'. This means that the state (in the name of the King or Queen) is prosecuting the defendant (Mr Smith) for a criminal offence committed.

**Civil cases** are cited: *Smith v Jones*. You pronounce this as: 'Smith and Jones'. Civil actions are between two individuals, where the 'claimant' (Smith) brings an action against the other party, the 'defendant' (or 'respondent' – Jones).

*Law Reports*   Most appeal cases are recorded either in the Court of Appeal or the House of Lords; they are then recorded and cited in annual law reports. There are Weekly Law Reports, All England Law Reports, EU Law Reports and more specialist reports from the Family Court or tribunals. Each year, about 2,000 cases are recorded in law reports; the oldest dating back some 700 years. A civil case will be cited as follows: *Hill v Chief Constable of West Yorkshire* [1988] 2 WLR 1049. This means you will find this case recorded in the second volume of the Weekly Law Report of 1988 at page 1049. Have a look at the Appendix 2 of this book which gives all cases cited in this book. Here follow the most important abbreviations:

- **AC – 'Appeal Court'**   These are case decisions from the House of Lords Appeal Court, the final instance in criminal cases, but not in civil cases which would be the European Court of Justice (see Chapter 4.2)
- **Cr App R – 'Criminal Appeal Reports'**   These are decisions either from the Chancery Division, the Family Division, the Criminal Appeals Division (Crim Div.) or the Queen's Bench Division (QBD) of the High Court and their appeals to the Court of Appeal

Other law reports and citations appear like this at the end of each case name:

- WLR – 'Weekly Law Reports'
- All ER – 'All England Law Reports'
- Fam Div – 'Family Division' of the High Court
- Ch D – 'Chancery Division' of the High Court, Queens Bench Division
- QBD – 'Queen's Bench Division'
- KB – 'King's Bench Division'

A large amount of common law has now been substituted by statute (Acts of Parliament). For example: section 1 of the *Sexual Offences Act 2003* replaces the common law offence of 'rape', previously relied on in *DPP v Morgan* [1976] (see Chapter 5.5).

_____ Acts of Parliament (legislation or statute) _____

The term 'parliament' refers to the period of parliamentary time between one general election and another. Parliament is usually referred to as the 'legislature' and it is important that you do not confuse parliament with the 'government', although members of a government are also usually Members of Parliament (MPs), where there are presently 659 MPs at Westminster. Supremacy of Parliament is a fundamental constitutional principle, also known as 'parliamentary sovereignty' in the UK. Simply put, any UK parliament can make or unmake laws (see Barnett, 2006). Parliament is made up of three parts:

- The Crown
- The House of Lords
- The House of Commons

Parliament has three main functions, which are to:

- Examine proposals for new laws
- Scrutinise government policy and administration
- Debate the major issues of the day

Since 1999 some responsibility for making new laws has been devolved to the Scottish Parliament (or Government), the National Assembly for Wales (or Cynulliad Cenedlaethol Cymru) and the Northern Ireland Assembly (since May 2007). We will be discussing Scotland and Northern Ireland jurisdictions in Chapters 3 and 6.

It is worth noting that the *Government of Wales Act 2006* created five Assembly electoral regions as specified in the *Parliamentary Constituencies and Assembly Electoral Regions (Wales) Order 2006*. Like in Scotland, there is a First Minister (or Prif Weinidog). New legislative powers were conferred on the Welsh Assembly from May 2007 under Schedule 5 of the 2006 Act in the fields of agriculture, fisheries, forestry and rural development, culture, economic development, education and training. Within each field, the Assembly has the power to make 'Measures', that is a piece of law with similar effect to an Act of Parliament.

How are laws made in the UK Parliament at Westminster? Legislation goes through a number of stages before it becomes an Act of Parliament (statute). A proposed statute, known as a bill, must be agreed by both Houses of Parliament (House of Commons and House of Lords) and receive Royal Assent from the Queen (or King) before the bill becomes an Act of Parliament. A bill can be introduced into either the House of Commons or the House of Lords. In both cases it will go through a number of stages or 'readings' in the first House. This will include a general debate on the principles of the bill ('second reading'), a more detailed examination of the individual provisions ('clauses'), when changes to the bill can be made and a further final consideration of the bill as a whole. The bill is then sent to the other House where it will go through a similar process. Once the two Houses have agreed to the bill, it is sent to the Queen (or King) for Royal Assent.

*The House of Lords Bill 2007* sets out proposals to create a part-elected, part-appointed House of Lords and to end the link between the peerage and a seat in Parliament. The bill expresses the belief that an effective and credible 'Second Chamber' is essential to sustain democracy in the UK; it would play a role in the legislative process and review the work of the House of Commons.

_____ Secondary legislation (Statutory Instruments)_____

Whilst Acts of Parliament are known as 'primary legislation' or often as 'black letter law', statutory instruments (SIs) are secondary legislation.

Statutes cannot always cover every rule or regulation for every detail of the subject they deal with. In order to prevent the need for an Act of Parliament every time a detail needs to be updated or added to, statute has given the government the power to do this at a later stage. Statutory Instruments have the full force of law. About 3,000 Statutory Instruments are issued each year (see Appendix 1, Statutes).

SIs are usually drafted in government departments by civil servants who worked on the original bill to parliament. Statutory Instruments contain an explanatory note that explains their scope and purpose. For example the *Statutory Instrument 2005 No. 40: The Licensing Act 2003 (Transitional provisions) Order 2005* gave supplementary guidelines to local authorities under the *Licensing Act 2003* for the transfer of pub and liquor licensing from magistrates' courts to local authorities.

In English (but not Scottish) law, the law of **equity** provides another source of law. Equity is the name given to a set of legal principles supplementing legal rules of 'natural justice'; it is defined to be 'a correction, or qualification' of the law. Equity or 'fairness' was a principle of justice dating back to the fourteenth century; it gradually evolved to provide flexibility and refinement to the framework of common law. The Equity side of the Court of Chancery dealt with thousands of disputes over inheritance and wills, land and use of land, debts, marriage settlements and apprenticeships.

Confusingly, equity stands alone and is contrasted with legislation or statutory legislation. The most important distinction between law and equity is that they offer different sets of remedies. The most common remedy a court of law can award is money damages. Equity can also offer injunctions or decrees directed by the High Court, which stop a person from acting, like a non-contact order in domestic violence cases. Law courts also enter orders, called writs, such as the writ of habeas corpus, a remedy against unlawful detention. The most common equitable remedies are 'mandamus', 'prohibition' or 'certiorari' orders, renamed in 2004 as mandatory, prohibiting and quashing orders respectively (s. 3 of the Civil Procedure (*Modification of Supreme Court Act 1981*) Order 2004).

**European Union Law** is another source of law and will be discussed fully in Chapter 4.


## 2.2 ___ Court structure and key personnel

Some courts are 'superior courts' and others are 'inferior courts' of record. This means that superior courts record judicial judgements in law reports mentioned previously; they also have unlimited jurisdiction. These are: the House of Lords, the Court of Appeal, the High Court and the Crown Court. Inferior courts do not record any legal judgement. These are: magistrates' courts, county courts, coroners' courts or tribunals (see Figure 2.1).

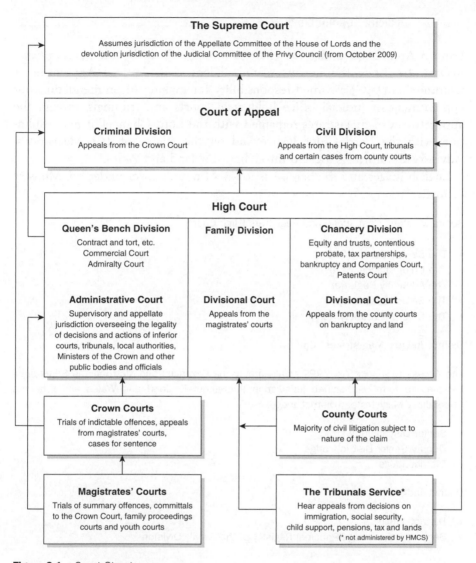

**Figure 2.1** Court Structure

*Source*: Her Majesty's Court Service (HMCS): www.hmcourts-service.gov.uk

A brief note on Queen's Counsel or QCs. Traditionally, barristers of at least 10 years standing were only eligible to apply to become QC, also referred to as 'silks', derived from the gown they wore. Only Queen's Counsel had the privilege of sitting within 'the bar' of court. QCs were traditionally selected from barristers rather than from lawyers in general. Since 1994, solicitors of England and Wales have been entitled to be admitted to the upper courts (such as the High Court) and were also permitted to apply for appointment as Queen's Counsel. A QC will be known as King's Counsel if a king assumes the throne (for Scotland, see Chapters 3.1–3.3).

From 3 April 2006 under the changes brought about by the *Constitutional Reform Act 2005*, the newly created, independent Judicial Appointments Commission (JAC) assumed responsibility for making recommendations for appointment of judicial office holders in courts and tribunals, though the appointment of magistrates remained with the Lord Chancellor in consultation with the Lord Chief Justice and on the advice of 101 Magistrates' Advisory Committees located throughout England and Wales.

English judges and the bar are as follows (in rank order under the Ministry of Justice):

Senior Masters, Cost Judge and Registrars (High Court)

- The Senior Master (QBD)
- The Chief Chancery Master
- The Admiralty Registrar
- The Senior Cost Judge
- The Chief Bankruptcy Registrar

District Judges (Magistrates' Courts)

The *Access to Justice Act 1999* amalgamated the Provincial and Metropolitan Stipendiary Benches to form one unified jurisdiction throughout England and Wales and renamed Stipendiary Magistrates, District Judge.

- Senior District Judge
- Deputy Senior District Judge
- District Judge

District Judges (Civil)

- District Judge
- Senior District Judge Principal Registry of the Family Division

_____ The Attorney General _____

The Attorney General (AG) is a barrister and usually a Queen's Counsel (QC). He or she – such as Baroness Scotland of Asthal PC QC in 2008 – almost invariably has a seat in the House of Commons. The Attorney General and the Solicitor General are known as Law Officers of the Crown and together with the Advocate General of Scotland they have three main functions:

- **Guardian of public interest**, for example, in taking action to appeal unduly lenient sentences; bringing proceedings under the *Contempt of Court Act 1981*, giving consents for prosecutions or referring to the Court of Appeal on a point of law

- **Chief legal advisor to the government**
- **Criminal justice minister**, overseeing law officers of the Crown Prosecution Service, Serious Fraud Office, Revenue and Customs Prosecutions Office and the Public Prosecution Service in Northern Ireland.

The Attorney General represents the Crown in important cases (both criminal and civil). Important case law, usually with the Attorney General's direction and reference is cited in this text, such as *Attorney General's Reference (No 2 of 1992)* [1994] that automatism must include a 'complete loss of voluntary control' (see Chapter 5.6 and Appendix 2).

## The Director of Public Prosecutions

The Director of Public Prosecutions (DPP) acts on behalf of the Crown in all criminal appeals and is in charge of the Crown Prosecution Service (CPS). The Director of Public Prosecutions (DPP) is a barrister or solicitor appointed by the Minister of Justice who acts under the supervision of the Attorney General. Certain prosecutions can only be instigated with the DPP's permission, for instance in terrorism cases. Some cases are cited in the name of the DPP, such as *DPP v Morgan* [1976] – concerning rape.

## Judicial work of the House of Lords and the Supreme Court

The House of Lords has a judicial as well as legislative function. Though the European Court of Justice is the supreme court in all civil legal matters, the House of Lords is still the highest appeal court in the UK in relation to all criminal matters. A new Supreme Court starts in 2009, separating the judiciary from the legislature. It assumes the jurisdiction of the Appellate Committee of the House of Lords and the devolution jurisdiction of the Judicial Committee of the Privy Council. The Supreme Court is an independent institution, presided over by independently appointed law lords (s. 23 *Constitutional Reform Act 2005*). The Supreme Court is a superior court of record under the auspices of the Ministry of Justice (MOJ).

The Present Lords of Appeal in Ordinary (the **Law Lords**) become the first justices of the 12-member Supreme Court and remain members of the House of Lords. A selection commission for new justices to the Supreme Court is composed of the President and Deputy President of the Supreme Court and members of the appointment bodies for England, Wales, Scotland and Northern Ireland. All new judges appointed will *not* be members of the House of Lords.

The Court of Appeal–Criminal Division (CA Crim Div) hears appeals from persons convicted at the Crown Court. An appellant appeals against either his conviction or his sentence (or both). The Court of Appeal also hears cases referred to it by the Attorney General (AG) or the Criminal Cases Review Commission (CCRC) (see Chapter 6.6). The Court of Appeal can sit anywhere in England. It is important for you to note that an appeal hearing is not a retrial and the Lords Justices of Appeal debate points of law only (please refer to Figure 2.1).

Normally, three judges hear appeals without a jury. Judges who sit in the Court of Appeal are known as Lords Justices of Appeal. The cases you see read at the end of each chapter have either come from the Court of Appeal or the House of Lords and have set the precedent in each case in common law. The jurisdiction of the Court of Appeal–Civil Division (CA Civ Div) hears civil appeals from all three divisions of the High Court and from county courts. Once again, three judges normally hear the appeal. If, in the interest of economy, only two judges hear a case and they are divided in their opinion, the case must be reargued before an uneven number of judges, no fewer than three, before any appeal can be taken to the House of Lords. The Court of Appeal is composed of the following justices:

- Lord Chancellor (LC)
- Master of the Rolls (MR)
- Lord Chief Justice (LCJ)
- President of the Queen's Bench Division (QBD)
- President of the Family Division
- Vice-President of the Court of Appeal (Civil Division)
- Plus other Lords and Ladies Justices of Appeal

From 3 April 2006, the role of Lord Chancellor changed with the *Constitutional Reform Act 2005*, thereby modifying this role. The Lord Chief Justice holds the office of President of the Courts of England and Wales and is Head of the Judiciary of England and Wales. As President of the Courts of England and Wales he is responsible:

1   for representing the views of the judiciary of England and Wales to Parliament, to the Lord Chancellor and to Ministers of the Crown generally;
2   for the maintenance of appropriate arrangements for the welfare, training and guidance of the judiciary of England and Wales within the resources made available by the Lord Chancellor;
3   for the maintenance of appropriate arrangements for the deployment of the judiciary of England and Wales and the allocation of work within courts (s. 7 *Constitutional Reform Act 2005*). The courts are:

    - The Court of Appeal
    - The High Court

- The Crown Court
- The county courts
- The magistrates' courts.

Rt Hon Jack Straw MP was appointed Lord Chancellor and Secretary of State for Justice on 28 June 2007 and heads the Ministry of Justice (see Chapter 6.1).

## The Privy Council

The Judicial Committee of the Privy Council is the court of final appeal for the UK overseas territories and Crown dependencies, and for those Commonwealth countries that have retained the appeal to Her Majesty in Council or, in the case of Republics, to the Judicial Committee (see Smartt, 1999). It is also the court of final appeal for determining 'devolution issues' within the UK. Members of the Privy Council are addressed as 'The Right Honourable' (Rt Hon).

## High Court

The High Court of Justice – to give it its full title – is principally a civil court. It comprises three divisions:

- Queen's Bench Division (QBD)
- Chancery Division
- Family Division

Apart from London, there are also high courts in Birmingham, Bristol, Caernarfon, Cardiff, Carlisle, Chelmsford, Chester, Exeter, Leeds, Lewes, Lincoln, Liverpool, Manchester, Middlesborough, Newcastle, Norwich, Nottingham, Oxford, Preston, Sheffield, Stafford, Swansea, Truro, Warwick and Winchester. High Court personnel comprises:

- The Lord Chancellor – he is the President of the Chancery Division
- The Lord Chief Justice – he presides over the Queen's Bench Division (QBD)
- The President of the Family Division
- The Vice-Chancellor (VC), who is vice-president of the Chancery Division
- The Senior Presiding Judge
- Ordinary high court judges, referred to as *puisne* judges (pronounce: 'pju-ne' meaning 'lesser' or 'assistant'), presently 98 in number

To be qualified for appointment as a puisne judge, a person must either have a 10-year high court qualification (s. 71 *Courts and Legal Services Act 1990*), or have been a circuit judge for at least 2 years. High Court judges are normally knighted as 'Knights Bachelor' or appointed as, for example, 'Dame

Commander of the Order of the British Empire', as soon as possible after their appointment and should be addressed accordingly in their private capacities. A High Court judge, or a more senior member of the judiciary, is never given the letters QC after their name, even if they had been a Queen's Counsel when they were at the bar, such as Baroness (Lady) Kennedy of the Shaws (Helena Kennedy QC) (See Preface).

## The Queen's Bench Division (QBD)

The Queen's Bench is part of the High Court and acts mainly as a civil court where a single judge tries such cases as breach of contract and actions in tort at first instance. Most actions are either settled or abandoned – only about 1 per cent result in a trial. A person who has been dealt with by the magistrates or who has appealed unsuccessfully to the crown court may also appeal on a point of law to the Queen's Bench. This procedure is also available to the prosecution. The magistrates or the crown court will be asked by the appellant to state their findings on fact and the questions of law that arose. The Queen's Bench Division of the High Court comprises the Lord Chief Justice, assisted by a number of puisne judges.

## Judicial review

Administrative or public law governs acts of public bodies, such as the Prison Service. Judicial review allows individuals, businesses, and other groups to challenge the lawfulness of decisions made by ministers, government departments, local authorities and other public bodies. The main grounds of review are that the decision maker has acted outside the scope of its statutory powers, that the decision was made using an unfair procedure or that the decision was an unreasonable one. The *Human Rights Act 1998* created an additional ground, making it unlawful for public bodies to act in a way incompatible with Convention rights.[1]

The court is now referred to as the 'Administrative Court', part of the Queen's Bench Division (QBD) of the High Court. Claims are generally heard by a single judge sitting in open court at the Royal Courts of Justice in London (The High Court) or by a Divisional Court (a court of two judges) where the court so directs. In judicial review, the court is not really concerned with the conclusions of a particular process and whether those in a public authority who made a decision were 'right' but whether the public body followed the correct procedures. When a body is described as acting *ultra vires*, it is acting beyond its prescribed powers, where the body has taken an action which is incompatible with a higher legal authority.

Judicial review remedies include:

- **a mandatory order** – that is an order requiring the public body to do something (formerly known as *mandamus*)
- **a prohibiting order** – that is an order preventing the public body from doing something (formerly known as *prohibition*)
- **a quashing order** – that is an order quashing the public body's decision (formerly known as *certiorari*)
- **a declaration**
- **Human Rights Act Damages**

To be entitled to apply for judicial review, a person must have 'sufficient interest' (or standing), referred to as *locus standi*. Lord Diplock set out the grounds for judicial review in the case of *Council of Civil Service Unions v Minister for the Civil Service* [1985], a case concerning the lawfulness of the union ban at GCHQ (Government Communication Headquarters, the UK Intelligence agencies M15 and M16).

Judicial review proceedings are brought in the name of the Crown. Post 2000, cases are cited as follows: *R (on the application of Begum) v Headteacher and Governors of Denbigh High School* [2006], a case concerning the wearing of Muslim dress by a school girl.

Pre-2000, cases are cited as follows: *R v Secretary of State for the Home Department, ex parte Venables (and ex parte Thompson)* [1998].

_____The Chancery Division_____

The Chancery Division of the High Court is purely a civil court, largely concerned with the administration of equity presided over by the Lord Chancellor, such as the famous case of Michael Douglas and Catherine Zeta-Jones over the illicit use of their wedding photographs at the Plaza Hotel in New York in November 2000 by Hello! magazine (*Douglas and others v Hello! Ltd.* [2007]).

The Chancery Division deals with the sale, exchange, partition or use of land, landcharges, mortgages, execution of trusts, administration of the estates of deceased persons, bankruptcy, dissolution of partnerships, contentious probate business and interpretation of wills, the appointment of a guardian in a minor's case and company law, at first instance. Additionally, the Chancery Division has some appellate jurisdiction in taxation or insolvency, land registration and patents.

_____The Family Division_____

The Family Division of the High Court acts in all matrimonial matters, the maintenance and protection of minors and any other proceedings with minors, adoptions, applications for consent to the marriage of a minor and child abduction (*Child Abduction and Custody Act 1985*). It is presided over by the President of the Family Division.

In *Venables and another v News Group Newspapers Ltd.* [2001] the President of the Family Court Division, Dame Elizabeth Butler-Sloss, was asked to decide whether she could grant a life-long reporting ban and anonymity order on the two convicted Bulger-killers who had by then turned 18. At issue here was whether the media could be restricted 'for life' from reporting on the boys by way of a life-long injunction once the boys were released from youth custody. The President granted the order.

## County Courts

County courts are often referred to as 'small claims' courts. Most civil legal actions start in the county court; the location depends on where you live and the claim in each case, usually for £15,000 but can go up to £50,000 (*County Courts Act 1984*). If the case is simple the county court will decide to use the small claims procedure and will allocate the case to the 'small claims track'. This can be done online. The most common types of claim in the small claims track are:

- compensation for faulty services provided (builders, dry cleaners, garages and so on)
- compensation for faulty goods (television, washing machines)
- disputes between landlords and tenants (rent arrears or compensation for not doing repairs)
- wages owed or money in lieu of notice

If a case is complex, the judge may refer it to another track for a full hearing or the High Court. The Crown Court and county courts are organised for administrative purposes into 6 circuits and 18 groups (*County Courts Act 2003*). Group boundaries are aligned to the 42 criminal justice system (CJS) areas. Court Service employees are civil servants (see also Chapter 6). The jurisdiction of a county court is limited by:

- **Financial criteria** – civil actions are limited to a value of £15,000–£50,000 including claims for damages and personal injuries
- **Geographical criteria** – like magistrates' courts each case will usually be dealt with in the area you live
- **Remedies** – the county court cannot grant equitable remedies, such as mandatory, prohibiting or quashing orders (*see 'equity'*).

## Inquests

Inquests examine unexplained deaths, such as violent, unnatural or sudden deaths and deaths in custody (police or prison cells). An Inquest is a factual inquiry to find out who has died, and how, when and where they died, together with information needed by the registrar of deaths, so that the death can be registered. An Inquest is not a trial. It is a limited inquiry into the facts surrounding a death.

In Scotland, the Procurator Fiscal and the sheriff courts investigate suspicious deaths under the *Fatal Accidents and Sudden Deaths Inquiry (Scotland) Act 1976*. Inquests are – as the name states – inquisitorial in nature, a civil process, whereby the coroner chooses and questions the witnesses for the purpose of the inquiry; this may be done with a jury (*Coroners Rules 1984*). It is then the duty of the jury or coroner to return a verdict of either accidental death or suicide; an 'open' or unexplained verdict may also be returned.

Coroners are usually lawyers but in some cases they may be doctors; they must follow the laws and regulations which apply to coroners (*Coroners Act 1988*). It is the Coroner's duty to find out the medical cause of the death, if it is not known, and to enquire about the cause of it if it was due to violence or otherwise appears to be unnatural. It is not the job of the Coroner to blame anyone for the death, as a trial would do. A Coroner normally sits alone, although the law does require a Coroner to sit with a jury in a limited number of circumstances, for example, if the death occurred in custody or if the death resulted from an incident at work.

The Coroner decides who should be called as a witness, who must have 'a proper interest'. They can be:

- a parent, spouse, child, partner and representing the estate of the deceased
- anyone who gains from a life insurance policy on the deceased (or any insurer)
- anyone whose actions may have caused or contributed to the death, accidentally or otherwise
- the chief officer of police
- any person appointed by a government department
- anyone else who the Coroner may decide also has a proper interest

The Inquests into the deaths of Diana, Princess of Wales and Emad El-Din Mohamed Abdel Moneim Fayed (Mr Dodi Al Fayed) started on 2 October 2007. Lord Justice Scott Baker was appointed as Assistant Deputy Coroner for Inner West London for the purposes of the hearings. The Jury returned a verdict of unlawful killing due to gross negligence by driver Henri Paul on 7 April 2008.

On 22 April 2005, the jury in the Harold Shipman Inquest at Leeds Crown Court returned a verdict of 'suicide'. Dr Shipman had been found hanged in his cell in Wakefield Prison on 13 January 2004, a day before his 58th birthday. Shipman was convicted in 2000, for murdering 15 patients in his care.

Fundamental changes to the coroner's system were proposed in the Coroner Reform Bill of 2006, 'Improving death investigation in England and Wales', such as a national full time chief coroner and a Coronial Council.

Tribunals are investigative places and a significant part of the British justice system where justice is done quickly and simply. They are administrative bodies or adjudications, a civil provision by the state for all its citizens to secure the just and peaceful settlement of disputes between two parties regarding their respective legal rights. In other words, they are a form of dispute resolution where ordinary citizens can go to present their grievance and obtain justice. Tribunals deal with over 500,000 cases a year, more than any other branch of the justice system. Cases often involve the most vulnerable in society, such as victims of crime, victims of persecution, of discrimination or unfair treatment where the disputes tend to be over benefit entitlement, tax, asylum or employment.

The primary function of a tribunal is to find the facts though there may be an onward appeal on a point of law, but not from a finding of fact. These principles were confirmed by the Court of Appeal in *AJ (Cameroon) v Secretary of State for the Home Department* [2007]. The judgement contains some useful guidance on fact-finding which now assists all tribunals, namely:

- The fact-finder can reject evidence without making alternative findings
- The fact-finder must survey all the relevant evidence
- The fact-finder can be selective and need not deal with every point
- Factual arguments are not a basis for asserting illegality

The most common tribunals include:

- Employment tribunals
- Rent assessment committees
- Department for Work and Pensions (DWP) appeals tribunals
- Educational services tribunals
- National Health Service tribunals
- Mental health review tribunals
- General Medical Council (GMC)
- Solicitors' disciplinary tribunals
- Bar Council
- Medical appeal tribunals
- Disability appeal tribunals
- Pension appeal tribunals

## 2.3 ___ The Legal Defence Services

The Legal Defence Services comprise the Legal Services Commission in civil matters and the Criminal Defence Service – both deal with what is commonly known as 'legal aid', first introduced by Clement Attlee's Labour Government in 1949. The idea was that the state should support the most vulnerable and disadvantaged people in society in court proceedings. Over time, the system was abused and by 2006 England had the highest per capita spend on legal aid in the world, amounting to more than £30 per head, compared with less than £5 per head each year in France or Germany. This eventually resulted in large public overspending. Criminal legal aid had possibly become the biggest 'free for all' in British society.

The *Access to Justice Act 1999* introduced a new scheme of legal defence services, whereby not everyone was entitled to 'legal aid'. All applications are now handled by the Legal Services Commission (LSC) and the Community Legal Services scheme now assists people with civil actions in the courts. The *Criminal Defence Service Act 2006* introduced means testing and abolished criminal legal aid. The Criminal Defence Service (CDS) guarantees people under police investigation or facing criminal charges *some* initial access to free legal advice and representation, usually with a duty solicitor in the police station or at first court appearance. However, there is no longer an automatic right to criminal legal aid.

## 2.4 —— Case study —————————————————————————

——————— *R v R* [1992] 1 AC 599, House of Lords ———————

This famous case established that rape can exist within marriage, because until the early 1990s there existed the general principle in English law that a husband could not be prosecuted for raping his wife, due to the fact that the marriage contract allowed him unfettered conjugal rights.

The anonymous citation of the defendant (the husband) by simply the initial 'R' means there is an automatic reporting ban by way of an anonymity order on rape and sexual offence cases, so that the victim cannot be identified; this is known in media law terms as 'jigsaw identification' (see Smartt, 2006c: 253).

---

### Facts of the case

The couple married on 11 August 1984 and their son was born in 1985. On 11 November 1987 the couple separated for two weeks before becoming reconciled. On 21 October 1989, as a result of further matrimonial difficulties, the wife left the matrimonial home with their four-year-old son and returned to live with her parents. She filed for divorce.

Shortly before 9 p.m. on 12 November 1989, R. forced his way into her parents' house, where his wife was alone that evening. R. attempted to have sexual

*(Continued)*

---

intercourse with his wife against her will. In the course of that attempt, he assaulted her sexually and physically, squeezing her neck with both hands.

R. was charged with the rape of his wife, contrary to the s. 1 *Sexual Offences Act 1956*, which states that a man commits rape if '*he has unlawful sexual intercourse with a woman who at the time of the intercourse does not consent to it .... it is felony for a man to rape a woman,*' punishable by life-long imprisonment.

R. was also charged with assault occasioning actual bodily harm (ABH) contrary to section *47 Offences Against the Person Act 1861* (OAPA). R. only pleaded guilty to 'attempted rape' and to the section 47 assault charge. He was convicted at Leicester Crown Court and sentenced to three years' imprisonment for the attempted rape of his wife and given 18 months' imprisonment concurrent for the assault.

R. appealed against his conviction on the grounds that the trial judge had erred in law by ruling that a man could rape his wife, when she did not consent. The Court of Appeal dismissed the appeal and R. appealed to the House of Lords.

## House of Lords

Lords Justices Lane C.J., Sir Stephen Brown P., Watkins, Neill and Russell considered R.'s appeal whether, despite his wife's refusal to consent to sexual intercourse with her husband, she did in fact consent by the fact she was married to him.

Their Lordships found that there could no longer be a rule of law that a wife was deemed to have consented irrevocably to sexual intercourse with her husband because she was married to him and that she could make it clear that she does not consent by simply saying 'no'. Further, that a husband can be convicted of the rape or attempted rape of his wife where she had withdrawn her consent to sexual intercourse and that in modern times the supposed marital exemption in rape could no longer form a part of English law.

In summary, the precedent set by the House of Lords in *R v R* is that it is unlawful to have sexual intercourse with *any* woman without her consent; they also declared the husband's immunity under the *Sexual Offences (Amendment) Act 1976* as invalid.

 ■ **Exam ʔuestions** ▬▬▬▬▬▬▬▬▬▬▬▬▬▬▬▬▬▬▬▬

1   What are the sources of English law? Give examples.
2   What are the advantages and disadvantages of delegated legislation? Give examples (see Appendix 1).
3   Discuss the principal function of judicial review. Provide examples in common law (see Appendix 2).
4   What is meant by alternative dispute resolution? Discuss with reference to the tribunal services in the UK.
5   Discuss developments in law in relation to rape (see also Chapter 5.5).

## ■ ■ Further Resources ■

*Glanville Williams: Learning the Law* (Williams and Smith, 2006) remains a beautifully written text and is a student classic.

Catherine Elliott and Frances Quinn have written the most user-friendly legal textbooks for students, such as their *English Legal System* (2008) and *Criminal Law* (2008).

In the Thomson-Sweet & Maxwell legal research series, you will find John Knowles and Philip Thomas' *Effective Legal Research* (2006) and Anthony Bradney et al.'s *How to Study Law* (2005) very accessible guides to legal learning and legal skills, as well as how to do online research via LexisNexis and Westlaw.

## ___ Note

1  Section 3 of the *Human Rights Act 1998* permits judicial review of Acts of Parliament, although the UK courts are not entitled to strike down legislation but instead can make rulings that legislation is incompatible with the Convention under s. 4 of the Act.

# 3

# THE LEGAL SYSTEMS OF SCOTLAND
# AND NORTHERN IRELAND

| Overview |
| --- |

Chapter 3 examines:

- Sources of Scots law
- The background to the Troubles in Northern Ireland
- Devolved governments of Scotland and Northern Ireland
- Workings of the Scottish and Northern Irish court systems and their key personnel structures
- Changes in the Northern Ireland criminal justice system

This chapter examines the devolved systems of Scotland and Northern Ireland, their separate regulatory bodies of control and progressive developments in criminal justice and law enforcement.

Scotland has a distinctly different jurisdiction to England and Wales, though it has no sovereignty power nor is it regarded as a separate nation state within the European Union. The *Acts of Union 1707* dissolved both the Scottish and English parliaments and replaced them with a new Parliament based in Westminster. Since 1999, however, some powers have been devolved to the Scottish Parliament in Edinburgh.

Northern Ireland, though part of the United Kingdom, has some of its own legislation. This chapter will highlight some of the complexities of the political situation in Northern Ireland before and after the 'Good Friday Agreement' of 10 April 1998 (The 'Belfast Agreement') and give a brief explanation of the Troubles in the province. It will also be shown how the St Andrew's Agreement of 2006 facilitated the decommissioning of paramilitary weapons and the release of paramilitary 'scheduled' prisoners from some of the Northern Irish prisons. The agreement was signed on 13 October 2006, when the British Prime Minister Tony Blair and the Irish Taoiseach Bertie Ahern formally agreed a way forward in the Northern Ireland Troubles, together with the leaders of the Democratic Unionist Party, the Reverend Dr Ian Paisley, and the Sinn Fein leader Gerry Adams.

The chapter will also explain the difference in the criminal court procedures and systems in Scotland and Northern Ireland, with specific focus on jury trials.

## 3.1 —— Sources of Scots law

The *Acts of Union* were a pair of parliamentary acts passed in 1706 and 1707 by the English and Scottish parliaments. The statues took effect from 1 May 1707 implementing the Treaty of Union negotiated between the two countries that had shared a monarch since 1603 but had retained separate and sovereign parliaments.

In 1999 parliamentary elections took place for the first Scottish Parliament. Presently, there are 129 Members of the Scottish Parliament (MSPs) in Edinburgh, dealing with devolved Scottish legislation, such as criminal law and criminal procedure, court prosecutions, legal aid, the administration of prisons and probation, most judicial appointments, health and educational services, social work, housing, the sale and use of land. MSPs are elected by an 'additional member system' (AMS), which means a voting system in which some representatives are elected from geographic constituencies and others are elected under proportional representation from party lists – very similar to the continental European voting system. Voters generally have two votes, one for the party and the second for the candidate in a constituency. The Scottish Parliament sits for a fixed term of four years in Edinburgh.

### ———— Legislation ————

Sources of Scots law are based on Roman law dating back to the Twelve Tables of 449 BC to the *Corpus Juris Civilis* of Emperor Justinian I (ca. 530). Roman law does not only describe the legal system of ancient Rome, but the law that was applied throughout most of Europe until the end of the eighteenth century. For these reasons, many modern civil legal systems in continental Europe – such as Germany – are heavily influenced by Roman law. This is particularly true in the field of private law in Scotland. So, when a Scottish lawyer refers to 'private law' he means anything that refers back to the *Acts of Union 1707*.

Statutes or legislation of the Scottish Parliament have full force of law under the *Scotland Act 1998*. For example, the *Freedom of Information (Scotland) Act 2002*, which came into force on 1 January 2005, allows any person or organisation to ask for information held by a Scottish public authority, such as the Scottish Prison Service. Acts of Sederunt and Acts of Adjournal regulate Scottish court procedure, whereby Acts of Sederunt apply to the Court of Session (civil procedure) and Acts of Adjournal to the High Court of Justiciary (High Court, criminal procedure).

## Subordinate (secondary) legislation

Subordinate legislation is Scottish-specific legislation passed by the Scottish Parliament in form of 'Orders in Council', made by the Queen (or King) in Council. There are also regulations made by the government, court procedural rules, ministerial rules, Statutory Instruments and local authority by laws.

## Precedents

Precedents are similar to English common law. They are set by judicial decisions in important cases. Just like in English law, judicial precedent prevails as a source of law in the absence of any relevant statutory provision.

## Writers and institutional texts

Writers and institutional texts are another source of Scots law. These are like *Blackstone's Commentaries*[1] in English law, that is writers are highly respected authors of law texts, mainly written during the seventeenth, eighteenth and nineteenth centuries. Here are some institutional Scottish writers:

- **Craig**: Sir Thomas Craig (ca. 1538–1608) was a lawyer (jurist), appointed in 1564 as justice-depute and presided over many criminal trials in Edinburgh. His major work was '*jus feudale*' (1603) comparing the laws of England and Scotland.
- **Stair**: James Dalrymple, 1st Viscount of Stair (1619–1695) was Lord President of the Court of Sessions from 1671 and helped shape the private legislation of Scotland. Stair's greatest work was *The Institutions of the Law of Scotland* (1681) which collated civil, canon and feudal laws with the 'customs of neighbouring nations'.
- **Erskine**: John Erskine of Carnock (1695–1768) was a Scottish law professor at the University of Edinburgh. He wrote *The Principles of the Law of Scotland and the Institutes of the Law of Scotland* (1773).

## Custom

Custom is where English and Scots law differ most notably, since Scots law is largely based on Roman law, such as continental jurisdictions of France or Italy.

## Equity

As we have already mentioned in Chapter 2, equity incorporates the principles of natural justice and fairness and is a different source of law from legislation. Unlike in England, equity is applied by the Scottish courts without distinction from the law, thereby avoiding the highly complex English construct of equity applied by the English courts – for instance in the Chancery Division of the High Court (see Ashton et al., 2003).

You will find Scottish cases cited in this format:

- **Justiciary Cases** – cited for example: 2005 JC 100; these are decisions from the Scottish High Court
- **Session Cases** – cited for example: 2005 SC 100; these are decisions of the Court of Sessions
- **Scottish Civil Law Reports** – cited for example: 2005 SCLR 100
- *Scots Law Times* – cited for example: 2005 SLT 100.

## 3.2 ___ The Scottish court structure and key personnel ___

### ___ The Court of Session ___

The Court of Session is Scotland's supreme civil court. It sits in Parliament House in Edinburgh as a Court of First Instance and a Court of Appeal. The Court's origins go back to the early sixteenth century and is headed by the Lord President. Second in rank is the Lord Justice Clerk, followed by 30 other judges. These 32 judges are designated Senators of the College of Justice or Lords of Council and Session. They are appointed to the Divisions by the Secretary of State for Scotland. The Court of Session is divided into the Outer House and the Inner House (see Figure 3.1).

The Divisions hear cases on appeal from the Outer House, the sheriff courts and tribunals. If a case is particularly important or difficult or if it is necessary to overrule a previous binding authority, a larger court of five or more judges may be convened.

The **Outer House** largely deals with all cases at first instance, including delict (tort), contract and commercial cases and judicial review. It consists of 19 Lords Ordinary sitting mostly alone and in some cases with a civil jury. Lords Ordinary cover a wide spectrum of work, but designated judges deal with intellectual property disputes and commercial cases.

The **Inner House** is in essence the Appeal Court. It is divided into the First and the Second Divisions, which, in spite of their names, are of equal authority, presided over by the Lord President and the Lord Justice Clerk respectively. Each Division is made up of four judges, but the quorum is three.

### ___ The High Court ___

The High Court of Justiciary – known simply as the High Court – is Scotland's supreme criminal court. It sits in cities and larger towns throughout Scotland and as an appeal court in Parliament House in Edinburgh. In practice the High Court deals with serious crimes such as murder, culpable homicide, armed robbery, drug trafficking and sexual offences. The High Court consists of the Lord Justice General, the Lord Justice Clerk and 25 additional judges of the Court

**CRIMINAL COURTS**

The High Court of Justiciary

|

Judge

|

Murder, rape, serious drug offences

|

No appeal to other courts

**SHERIFF COURT**

Sheriff

|

Criminal cases either with/without a jury,
depending on the seriousness of the case

**DISTRICT COURT**

Justice of the Peace/Magistrate

|

Minor criminal cases

**CIVIL COURTS**

The Court of Session

|

The Supreme Civil Court in Scotland

Only in Edinburgh

Judge

Hears cases at first instance and
cases appealed from sheriff court

|

Appeals can be made from the
Court of Session to the House of Lords

**SHERIFF COURT**

Sheriff

|

Family cases / smaller money claims etc.

SCOTTISH LAND COURT

For determination of agricultural land disputes

LAND VALUATION APPEALS COURT

For rating questions

THE COURT OF THE LORD LYON

For matters of heraldry

**Figure 3.1**   The Scottish court structure

of Session who, when sitting in the High Court, are known as Lords Commissioners of Justiciary. Appeals are heard from the high courts, sheriff and district courts. When hearing appeals against conviction, the High Court consists of at least three judges; only two judges sit when hearing sentence appeals.

The **Lord Advocate**, chief law officer in the Scottish Executive (similar to the Attorney General in England), may refer a point of law that arose in the course of a case to the High Court for its opinion. Though a case may be settled in the Scottish High Court, the Lord Advocate can appeal a decision and give an opinion setting out the law for future similar cases. The Lord Advocate's decision will then set the precedent.

## Sheriff courts

There are 49 sheriff courts, arranged into six geographical areas – known as 'Sheriffdoms'. Each is overseen by a sheriff principal. Sheriffs have limited sentencing powers, currently up to three years' imprisonment and/or an unlimited fine in solemn cases and six months imprisonment and/or £5,000 fine for summary cases. If the sheriff court considers its sentencing powers to be insufficient, it can commit a case to the High Court.

## District courts

District courts sit in each local authority area under summary jurisdiction only. Each comprises at least one justice of the peace, that is a lay magistrate, who sits alone or in threes with a qualified legal assessor as convener of court. They handle cases, such as public order offences, breach of the peace, drunkenness, minor assaults, petty theft and offences under the *Civic Government (Scotland) Act 1982*.

## Key court personnel

The Scottish legal profession is divided into advocates and solicitors. Advocates are members of the Faculty of Advocates and are referred to as 'counsel' or Queen's Counsel. Similar to changes in England, advocates – like barristers – had an exclusive right of audience with the House of Lords, the Judicial Committee of the Privy Council, the Court of Session and the High Court of Justiciary. But since 1990, they share that right with solicitor advocates (see MacQueen, 2004). Like in England, solicitors constitute the larger of the two groups; they deal with all kinds of legal matters, such as conveyancing, executry, trust work and general legal advice (*Solicitors (Scotland) Act 1980*). They are regulated by statute and are governed by the Council of the Law Society of Scotland.

Solicitor advocates are members of the Law Society of Scotland. They are experienced solicitors who have obtained an extension of their rights of audience by undergoing additional training in evidence and in the procedure of the Court of Session.

The Scottish criminal courts comprise the following personnel:

- **The Lord Advocate** (or one Advocate Depute) presents the case in the High Court against the accused
- **The Procurator Fiscal** (or one Advocate Depute) presents the case in a sheriff court or a district court
- **The Solicitor Advocate** conducts the case for the defence and provides the court with background information on the accused

Here follows the courts with the relevant key personnel:

- **High court** – normally one judge
- **Sheriff court** – normally one sheriff
- **Stipendiary magistrate's court** – normally one magistrate
- **District court** – normally one lay justice of the peace

## 3.3 ___ Scottish criminal procedure

The Crown Office and Procurator Fiscal Service (COPFS) (known as 'the Fiscal') are responsible for the prosecution of all crime in Scotland, the investigation of sudden or suspicious deaths, and the investigation of complaints against the police. COPFS is run by the Lord Advocate and the Solicitor General who, as law officers, are the only non-elected members of the Scottish Government. The Fiscal must prove a case 'beyond reasonable doubt', though an accused in Scotland may also plead 'no case to answer'. Please refer to Table 3.1 which follows, summarising the various stages in Scottish criminal procedure.

### ___ Types of offences

*Solemn* Solemn covers the most serious cases involving trial on indictment before a judge or sheriff sitting with a jury. A Scottish jury is made up of 15 people and a simple majority (8–7) is sufficient to establish guilt or innocence.

Three verdicts are available to the jury: guilty, not guilty, or not proven. A not proven verdict is the equivalent of not guilty in that it is an acquittal. The Criminal Procedure Division deals with policy on solemn criminal procedure matters (including bail) under the *Criminal Procedure (Amendment) (Scotland) Act 2004* which reformed the operation of the solemn courts.

**Table 3.1** Stages of procedure in the Scottish criminal justice system

| | |
|---|---|
| **First calling** | In *serious* cases that will be heard by a jury, this stage may involve one or two procedural hearings, which are held in private, i.e. no public access. The accused may be held in custody, or released on bail. In *less serious* cases, there may also be one or two procedural hearings, held in public. At these hearings the accused will indicate whether or not (s)he admits that (s)he committed the crimes. The accused may be ordered to be held in custody, or released, possibly on bail. |
| **Not guilty** | If the accused denies committing the crimes, a date will be fixed for hearing evidence in the case, i.e. a trial. This date is likely to be several months ahead. |
| **Guilty** | The accused can decide to admit that (s)he committed the crimes at any stage in the proceedings. This can be done on a date already fixed for hearing the case, or the accused can ask for the case to be advanced for this purpose. Once the accused has admitted to the court that (s)he committed the crimes, the case will proceed to sentence. |
| **Trial** | At the trial, the Prosecutor will call witnesses. Note: the case may not go ahead on the arranged day. This can happen for a number of reasons, for example the accused or an important witness may not appear, or some other evidence may not be available. |
| **Verdict** | After all the evidence has been presented, a decision will be taken about whether or not the accused is guilty. In the most serious cases this decision will be taken by the jury. In other cases the decision will be taken by the Sheriff/Stipendiary Magistrate/JP. |
| **Sentence** | If the accused admits (s)he is guilty, or is found guilty after a trial, the Judge/Sheriff/Stipendiary Magistrate/JP will impose a sentence. This may be done on the same day, or the case may be continued for a few weeks, to obtain background or medical reports on the accused. |
| **Appeal** | If the accused feels that some element of his/her trial was unfair, or that the sentence was unduly harsh, (s)he can appeal to the *High Court of Justiciary*. The prosecutor can also appeal if (s)he believes that the sentence was too lenient. An appeal can take several months and the accused may be released pending the appeal. |

*Summary* Summary covers less serious cases involving a trial with either a sheriff, a justice of the peace sitting or (in Glasgow) a stipendiary magistrate – all sitting alone without a jury, or a bench of three justices of the peace. Today, almost all cases which come to court in Scotland, some 96 per cent, are heard by a judge who sits without a jury. Less serious cases range from breaches of the peace to assaults and weapons offences and nearly all road traffic offences. They are those offences which are most likely to affect local people and local communities.

Which court will hear which type of case is very similar to English and Welsh proceedings, depending on the severity of the crime committed and the likely sentence to be imposed. Solemn cases may be heard in the High Court buildings in Edinburgh or Glasgow, summary cases in a sheriff courthouse in a town or city near where the crime occurred (see Chapter 3.2).

There are no committal proceedings in Scotland, this means that the accused appears in private before a sheriff on petition for judicial examination. If he is remanded in custody for further investigation and is not allowed bail, the accused cannot be detained longer than 110 days, by which time his trial must begin. If he is on bail, the trial must begin within 12 months. These sentences available to the Scottish courts are:

- **Absolute Discharge** – this is given when it is considered inappropriate to punish the accused – perhaps because of the circumstances of the crime – or the character of the accused
- **Admonition** – this is a kind of warning given to the person found guilty of the crime
- **Caution** – this requires the accused to lodge a sum of money in the court as security for his good behaviour for a certain period – up to six months in a district court or one year in sheriff court. At the end of this period, if the accused has been of good behaviour, he can apply to the court to have the money repaid
- **Fine** – what fine is given depends on the court the accused appears in. Fines can be paid in lump sum or in instalments. Fine defaulting requires the accused to appear at a fines enquiry court, where he may be given further time to pay, or be sentenced to a period of imprisonment as an alternative to a paying the fine
- **Supervised Attendance Order** – instead of imprisonment or failing to pay a fine, the court may impose Supervised Attendance Order which requires the accused to carry out a constructive activity such as unpaid work of between 10 to 100 hours to be completed in a given period
- **Compensation Order** – the court may order the accused to pay compensation to victims for loss or injury resulting from the crime. The court will consider the accused's financial circumstances. Monies are paid into court, then forwarded to the victim
- **Probation Order** – this order requires the accused to be under supervision of a local authority officer or social worker for between six months and three years
- **Community Service Order** – this order is a direct alternative to imprisonment and requires the accused to undertake between 80 and 300 hours of unpaid work in community under the supervision of a social worker
- **Imprisonment** – what sentence is given depends on the type of court the accused appears in. For example, a youth aged between 16 and 21 would be sentenced to a Young Offender Institution (YOI).

In March 2005 the Scottish Executive's White Paper *Smarter Justice, Safer Communities*, under Minister for Justice Cathy Jamieson MSP, proposed a radical reform of the summary justice system. The result was the *Criminal Proceedings etc. (Reform) (Scotland) Act 2007* with the following aims:

- Faster and more visible community justice
- Working across organisations effectively and efficiently
- Tackling lower level offending quickly and appropriately, leading to
- Reduction in reoffending
- Engaging with communities to ensure that their concerns are addressed

The outcome has been speedier justice and strict fine enforcement in the sheriff courts.

## 3.4 ___ History of the Troubles in Northern Ireland _____

It is difficult to begin this chapter without briefly mentioning some background history of the sectarian violence in Northern Ireland, universally referred to as 'The Troubles'. This was a period of communal violence involving paramilitary organisations from both sides of the community as well as the locally recruited police force, the Royal Ulster Constabulary (RUC), the British Army and others in Northern Ireland from the late 1960s until the late 1990s, ending with the 'Good Friday Agreement' (or 'Belfast Agreement') of 10 April 1998.

Hardline nationalists were known as republicans, and most of the violence on the Catholic side was caused by the Irish Republican Army (IRA). Hardline unionists were known as loyalists, and the main paramilitary groups on the Protestant side of the community were known as the Ulster Defence Association (UDA) and the Ulster Volunteer Force (UVF).

The violence was extreme and spilled over into the Republic of Ireland and the UK mainland. British troops were sent to Northern Ireland in 1969 after violent clashes between Catholics and Protestants. When the first soldiers were deployed in August 1969, commanders believed they would be in Northern Ireland for just a few weeks, commonly known as 'Operation Banner'. But it was not until 31 July 2007 that 'Operation Banner' finally came to an end. The army's support role for the police had been long and continuous. A total of 763 military personnel were killed during the campaign, and at the height of the Troubles, there were about 27,000 soldiers in Northern Ireland.

The sectarian division of Northern Ireland into unionists, largely Protestants – who favoured continued union with Britain – and the mainly Catholic nationalists, whose desire was for a united Ireland, had long been a source of strife and particularly since the partition of the island in 1921.

There have been a number of controversial killings in the Northern Irish province. One was the killing of Belfast solicitor Pat Finucane (see below). Subsequently, the Stevens Inquiry into the killing of Pat Finucane took four years, taking some 5,000 statements from people (see below). Sir John Stevens, formerly Chief Constable of the Metropolitan Police, conducted three inquiries into collaboration between members of the security forces and loyalist paramilitaries. He arrived in Northern Ireland months after the killing of Pat Finucane in 1989. The Stevens Report 2007 revealed that members of both the army and the RUC not only passed security information on republican suspects to loyalist killers, but on occasion a number of individuals actually encouraged the same gunmen to kill (for further research see the BBC's news online website on Northern Ireland at http://news.bbc.co.uk).

## The killing of Pat Finucane

Pat Finucane was shot dead in front of his family at his home in Belfast on 12 February 1989 by loyalist gunmen who accused him of being a senior IRA commander responsible for running the republican paramilitaries in the background. In fact, Finucane was simply a solicitor, famous for winning IRA defence cases, such as 23 men allegedly involved in the murder of two British soldiers during an IRA funeral in 1988; one of his most famous clients was Bobby Sands, republican hunger striker in the Maze Prison. No one was charged.

The Stevens Inquiry established that army double-agent Brian Nelson (see below) had supplied the gunmen with the intelligence needed to identify solicitor Finucane. In his evidence to the Stevens Inquiry, Nelson said he had warned army handlers that Mr Finucane was a target but they did nothing. Clearly Pat Finucane's murder could have been avoided. In May 2003 loyalist paramilitary Ken Barrett was charged with Finucane's murder. Though initially denying the charges, Barrett confessed during his trial at Belfast Crown Court in September 2004 before a single 'Diplock' judge. Barrett was sentenced to 22 years in prison, but was released early in May 2006 under the terms of the Good Friday Agreement.

## Double-agent Brian Nelson

When former loyalist paramilitary Brian Nelson returned to Belfast at the height of the Troubles to rejoin the Ulster Defence Association (UDA) he was also recruited by a team from the army's secret Northern Ireland intelligence unit, the Force Research Unit (FRU). Double-agent Nelson handed the UDA's entire target files over to the army thereby providing vital intelligence that guided killers to their targets. When the Stevens Inquiry team arrived in Belfast in 1989, Nelson attempted to flee Northern Ireland. He was arrested and jailed for ten years on conspiracy to murder in 1992. Released in 1999, he lived at a secret location in England and died on 13 April 2003 of a brain haemorrhage. Lord Stevens' Report (2007) established that Nelson had been central to the British policy of collusion and had played a crucial role in the murder of Pat Finucane; Nelson had provided a dossier on the Belfast lawyer to the UDA, who had murdered Finucane in February 1989.

There were a number of unsuccessful attempts to restore peace and establish devolved government after the outbreak of the Troubles in 1969 and the nationalist Irish Republican Army's (IRA's) declaration of a ceasefire in August 1994.

## The Good Friday Agreement

Shortly after the ceasefire was announced, the British government entered into negotiations with parties and groupings associated with the unionist and nationalist causes. Despite a period of renewed violence and the temporary exclusion and withdrawal of several of the groups, an agreement was finally signed in 1998. The 'Good Friday' or 'Belfast agreement' was signed on 10

April 1998 and approved by the Northern Ireland people in a referendum on 22 May 1998. The essence of the Good Friday agreement stated that Northern Ireland should remain part of the United Kingdom, so long as that was the wish of the people living there. The agreement made provisions for devolved government with an Assembly at Stormont, Belfast (*Northern Ireland (Elections) Act 1998*). Fay et al. (1999) summarise the casualties during the period of the Troubles as follows:

- 3,225 people were killed between 1969 and 1994
- 1,896 of these were killed by republican paramilitaries
- 935 were killed by loyalist paramilitaries
- 316 were killed by the British Army
- 52 were killed by the RUC

## 3.5 ___ Institutions in Northern Ireland _____

The power sharing that followed the supposed ending of hostilities was not smooth. The Northern Ireland Assembly was suspended on a number of occasions as unionists insisted on greater assurances from republicans that violence would end. On 1 August 2005, the then Secretary of State for Northern Ireland, Peter Hain, announced a programme of security normalisation, including a commitment to repeal all counter-terrorist legislation. Eventually, the IRA announced that it was unequivocally giving up its armed struggle and that it had decommissioned all its weapons, and in October 2006, all political parties agreed to fix a timetable to restore the Northern Ireland Assembly and to enter a power-sharing government.

The *Northern Ireland Act 2006* – known as the 'St Andrews Agreement' – provided for a 'Transitional Assembly'. A crucial part of the St Andrew's agreement was that Sinn Féin would support the new Police Service of Northern Ireland (PSNI) – Sinn Féin had historically been opposed to the PSNI.

On 3 May 2007, the Protestant paramilitary Ulster Volunteer Force (UVF) declared an end to its terror campaign; during the height of the Troubles, the UVF is said to have murdered more than 500 people including 33 lives lost in bomb attacks in Dublin and Monaghan in 1974. Though the UVF had previously declared a ceasefire some 13 years before, the group was blamed for more than 20 murders since.

_____The Northern Ireland Assembly_____

On 26 March 2007, the Northern Irish people voted for a power-sharing executive, and on 9 May 2007, the new Northern Ireland Assembly was sworn in. The power-sharing political line-up comprised the First Minister Ian Paisley (Democratic Unionists) and his Deputy First Minister, Martin McGuinness – a former IRA Commander (Sinn Féin). This was an extraordinary and historic moment since it meant unity of former arch-enemies who now represented a cross-party Assembly at Stormont.

The Northern Ireland Assembly has legislative powers, though they are different to those found in the National Assembly for Wales and the Scottish Parliament. The Assembly represents devolved government for Northern Ireland at Stormont, Belfast. It deals with Executive Bills and secondary legislation for Northern Ireland ('Orders in Council'). Northern Ireland legislation deals with matters of criminal justice, agriculture and rural development, education and employment (see Taylor, p. 1998).

There are now 108 representatives for Northern Ireland in the Assembly; they are split into two camps, dominated by the big four unionist and nationalist parties. Key decisions need to have the support of at least 40 per cent in each 'camp'.

## Primary legislation in Northern Ireland

Primary legislation is brought about by way of a bill through the UK Parliament at Westminster but with Northern Ireland-specific reference, such as the *Police (Northern Ireland) Act 2000*.

The Speaker of the Northern Ireland Assembly has a scrutiny role in relation to the competence of legislation prior to the first and final stages of a bill. A copy of the proposed bill goes to the Northern Ireland Human Rights Commission. A bill becomes an Act of Parliament when it has been passed by the Assembly and has received Royal Assent by the Queen (or King) in Parliament.

## Subordinate (Secondary) legislation

Orders are subordinate legislation similar to Statutory Instruments, regulations or bylaws. Generally speaking, primary legislation provides the framework and subordinate legislation contains the details.

## 3.6 ___ Northern Ireland court structure and key personnel

The court system of Northern Ireland is similar to that of England and Wales with the **Advocate General for Northern Ireland** as the chief law officer of the Crown. He is part of the Assembly and – like his English counterpart – acts in the public interest.

### The High Court

The High Court normally sits at the Royal Courts of Justice in Belfast. The High Court has three divisions, each handling different types of work

The House of Lords

Final Court of Appeal in the United Kingdom. Hears appeals on points of law in cases of major Importance.

The Court of Appeal

Hears appeals on points of law in criminal and civil cases from all courts.

The High Court

Hears complex or important civil cases in three Divisions and also appeals from county courts.

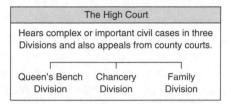

Queen's Bench Division    Chancery Division    Family Division

County Courts (including Family Care Centres) (7 Divisions)

Hear a wide range of civil actions and also appeals from magistrate's courts.
**Small Claims Court**
Hears consumer claims and minor civil cases.

The Crown Court

Hears all serious criminal cases.

Magistrates' Courts (including Youth Courts and Family Proceedings Courts) (21 Petty Sessions Districts)

Conduct preliminary hearings in more serious criminal cases.
Hear and determine less serious criminal cases, cases involving juveniles and some civil and domestic cases, including family proceedings.

Coroners' Courts

Investigate the circumstances of sudden, violent or unnatural deaths.

The Enforcement of Judgments Office

Enforces money and other judgments.

**Figure 3.2**   The Northern Ireland court structure
*Source*: Northern Ireland Court Service

(see Figure 3.2). Its chief law officers are the Lord Chief Justice, known as the President, three Lord Justices of Appeal and nine other judges (*puisne* judges).

Actions are usually commenced in the High Court by a writ of summons and the Masters of the Supreme Court deal with all applications. Two Masters are assigned to assist in Chancery Division and deal with matters such as bankruptcy. Two Masters are assigned to the Queen's Bench Division, one of whom also assists the Court of Appeal. Two are assigned to Family Division, dealing with probate, matrimonial matters or the care and protection of children.

A single judge of the Belfast High Court normally deals with trials. There is a right of trial before judge and jury in fraud, libel, slander, malicious prosecution or false imprisonment cases. Special arrangements can be made to allow a claimant to obtain a speedy judgement, known as summary judgement, either where the other party does not dispute the claim or where the plaintiff can establish at an early stage that the other party has no real defence to the action (*The Rules of the Supreme Court (Northern Ireland) 1980* [SR No. 346] as amended). Like in England, judicial review is a statutory remedy, provided for by section 18 of *The Judicature (Northern Ireland) Act 1978*.

### County courts in Northern Ireland and key personnel

There are seven county court divisions, divided into regional sections. These are: Belfast, Ards, Antrim, Londonderry, Omagh, Craigavon and Armagh. Within these regions there are 21 courthouses across Northern Ireland. There are about 17 county court judges (excluding the Chief Social Security Commissioner) and four district judges. The county court judges also sit in the crown court to hear criminal cases.

District judges deal exclusively with civil cases. They hear uncontested matters up to £15,000 and contested cases up to a value of £5,000. Essentially, district judges deal with 'small claims' business, primarily designed to resolve simple consumer disputes – the maximum amount claimable under this legislation is currently £2,000. If the value of the case or land is above these limits, the case will be commenced in the High Court.

The county court also has jurisdiction to hear applications for adoptions, undefended divorces and proceedings for libel or slander. The county court has jurisdiction to determine appeals against decisions made by the Secretary of State for Northern Ireland by claimants for compensation under the criminal injuries and criminal damage legislation.

### The Crown Court

Like in England and Wales, the crown court deals with all cases committed for trial by magistrates' courts. Cases for trial are usually heard before a judge and jury, with the exception of judge-only or juryless courts in scheduled offences (see 'Diplock Courts' below). The crown court sits in seven divisions.

The Lord Chief Justice is President of the crown court. From time to time, the Lords Justices of Appeal, high court judges and county court judges all sit in the crown court. The most senior judges preside over indictable and scheduled offences (see below).

All appeals from the crown court are heard by the Court of Appeal. A defendant in a non-scheduled case may appeal against conviction on a point of fact, on a point of law or on any other ground. The right of appeal is, in certain cases, subject to obtaining the leave of the court first. In addition to an appeal against conviction, a defendant may also appeal against sentence unless it is one fixed by law and the leave of the court is always required for an appeal against sentence.

## Magistrates' courts

The magistrates' courts are administered in the same way as in England and Wales where criminal proceedings are commenced and more serious (indictable) crimes are committed to the crown court for trial (*Schedule 2 Magistrates' Courts (Northern Ireland) Order 1981*). It also has civil jurisdiction, such as family courts. There are 21 Petty Sessions Districts, which are spread throughout the seven county court divisions.

The main difference between an English or Welsh and a Northern Irish magistrates' court is that there are no longer lay magistrates in Northern Ireland. On 1 April 2005, lay magistrates were abolished. Magistrates' courts in Northern Ireland are largely staffed by salaried professional resident and deputy magistrates similar to English district judges. Lay magistrates now only preside over first remand hearings, deal with warrants or simple youth justice matters (*Justice (Northern Ireland) Act 2002*; Commencement No.8 of 2005).

One of the main reasons for changing over to a professional magistracy was that sentencing someone to custody was seen as a possible infringement of human rights, where a non-legally qualified lay person was instrumental in ordering the custody of an offender.

Here follow Northern Irish criminal court proceedings at a glance:

- **Remand** – In adjourning a case the court will require the defendant to appear again on the next date fixed. This requirement to appear is referred to as a remand and may be either on bail or in custody
- **Committal** – The procedure by which a person is returned for trial to the crown court by the magistrates' court
- **Arraignment** – The procedure by which the defendant has the charges formally put to him before the judge at the crown court and he enters his plea of 'guilty' or 'not guilty'
- **Plea** – The defendant's admission of guilt or denial of guilt in response to the charges put to the defendant at arraignment

## Scheduled offences

Scheduled offences cover terrorist as well as other offences arising from public order situations and serious sectarian violence (Schedule 9 of the *Terrorism Act 2000*). Scheduled offences are heard separately in crown courts, and until 2005 were heard in Diplock Courts (see below).

The Diplock court system or 'juryless courts' was established after an inquiry and report by Lord Diplock in 1972. The essence of Diplock Courts was that they protected jurors from the risk of intimidation, ensuring that those charged with 'scheduled' offences received fair trials so that justice could be seen to be done fairly and effectively. This meant that a trial on indictment of a 'scheduled offence' was heard by a single judge sitting without a jury, normally at Belfast Crown Court (see McKittrick and McVea, 2001).

Following the Diplock Report, the *Northern Ireland (Emergency Provisions) Act 1973* became the basis for 'anti-terrorist' legislation in the province. This legislation marked the period known as 'criminalisation' of political violence and paramilitary prisoners were treated as common criminals (as opposed to freedom fighters).

This led to a number of prisoner protest hunger strikes in the Maze Prison in 1981, led by Bobby Sands (see Davies, 2004; Lister, 2004; Barker, 2006), enabling Sinn Féin to become a serious political force (see Taylor, 1998).

On 1 August 2005, Secretary of State for Northern Ireland, Peter Hain, formally announced an end to the armed campaign and sectarian violence. There followed the abolition of all counter-terrorist legislation and the abolition of the Diplock Courts, following Lord Carlisle's 'Report on the Government's Independent Review of Terrorism Legislation'. From 2005 onwards, the number of scheduled cases at Diplock Court hearings had drastically decreased to about 60 each year from about 300 in 2004.

_____ Juries in Northern Ireland _____

With the introduction of ordinary jury courts from 2006 onwards, criminal record checks had become routine to prevent disqualified persons from serving as jurors.[2] Jury-vetting is carried out by the centralised Northern Ireland Court Service and the Criminal Justice Secretariat, responsible for supporting the Criminal Justice Board. Reasons for such stringent jury checks lie in the polarised nature of the Northern Ireland society, in as much as some jurors may be unduly influenced by their political and religious backgrounds and beliefs in reaching a verdict. In this context, jury checks limit the defendant's ability to 'pack a jury', thereby reducing the risk of perverse verdicts. A range of jury protection measures were put in place to reduce jury intimidation or fear of intimidation.

The *Justice and Security (Northern Ireland) Act 2007* makes it clear that there will be circumstances when juryless courts may still be necessary. Section 1(2) of the 2007 Act states that the Director of Public Prosecutions of Northern Ireland may issue a certificate that a trial on indictment of a defendant can be conducted without a jury if it is felt that either the defendant or witnesses (or both) are associated with a proscribed organisation or have been members in the past.

The practical reality includes some juryless courts for scheduled offences to date. Where a jury is constituted in such cases, special measures will be put into place, such as the jury will sit behind a screen so that they are entirely shielded from members of the public for their own protection. Jurors are routinely balloted by number only and some jurors receive special police protection during or even after a trial. The same goes for public inquiries.

You may wish to read and research the case regarding the Robert Hamill Inquiry, where former RUC officers requested total anonymity in court: Re. Officer L [2007] UKHL 36.

## 3.7 ___ Case study

___ *R v Clegg* [1995] 1 AC 482 ___

The case of Private Lee Clegg is presented here to give you a socio-legal insight at the height of the Troubles in Northern Ireland during the early 1990s. The case has as its background the controversial situation regarding the British army's presence in the province.

The question in law concerns the notion of self-defence: can a trained army officer avail himself of this defence to murder?

---

### Facts of the case

Private Lee Clegg, a British soldier stationed in Northern Ireland, was on night patrol with members of his Parachute Regiment, when a member of his patrol stopped a car at a vehicle checkpoint some distance down the road. Unbeknown to the soldiers at the time, the car had been stolen and was joyridden by some youngsters. The car had accelerated away from the patrol and was driving in the centre of the road towards Clegg with its full headlights on. Someone at the checkpoint had shouted at Clegg to stop the car and Clegg and three colleagues opened fire at the approaching car. The driver and a rear-seat female passenger were killed.

Clegg was charged with the murder of the female passenger. At his trial before a single judge, Clegg's defence was that he thought that the life of a colleague on the other side of the road was in danger and that, in self-defence, he had fired three shots at the windscreen and a fourth shot into the side of the car as it was passing. However, scientific evidence showed that the fourth shot was fired *after* the car had passed and was already over 50 feet down the road.

The judge accepted that the first three shots had been fired by Clegg in self-defence and that of another colleague but that the fourth shot could not have

*(Continued)*

---

been fired in self-defence, since, once the car had passed, the soldiers were no longer in any danger. Clegg was convicted of murder, on the basis that he had used unreasonable and excessive force.

Clegg appealed to the Court of Appeal for Northern Ireland, but his appeal was dismissed. He appealed to the House of Lords.

### The House of Lords

The question before their Lordships, Lords Keith of Kinkel, Browne-Wilkinson, Slynn of Hadley, Lloyd of Berwick and Nicholls of Birkenhead, concerned the law regarding self-defence. Could a soldier on duty use the defence of self-defence (or defence of another)? Was the force used by the appellant excessive or unreasonable in self-defence? And if so had Clegg used excessive and unreasonable force? Their Lordships upheld his murder conviction. It was a finding of fact that the appellant had *intended* to cause death or serious bodily harm or GBH under s. 18 OAPA and that he had not acted in self-defence or in the defence of his colleagues, because he had fired the fourth shot when the car had ceased to pose a threat to his patrol group. Moreover, there was no suggestion that Clegg believed that the driver of the car was a terrorist or that he would have carried out terrorist offences if allowed to escape.

It followed that a soldier or police officer who, in the course of his duty, kills a person by firing a shot which constitutes the use of *excessive* and *unreasonable* force in self-defence, was guilty of murder, not manslaughter.

The case of Clegg stirred up heated public debate at the time and caused controversy in both houses of Parliament. The final House of Lords' decision set a higher standard on the use of 'reasonable force' in self-defence cases for those serving in the army or the police services, confirming the *Attorney General for Northern Ireland's Reference No. 1 of 1975* [1977] in that the test for self-defence is greater for those in the armed forces or the police.

 **Exam Questions**

1 What are the main differences between the English, Scottish and Northern Irish criminal proceedings? Discuss with reference to relevant legislation and common law.
2 Compare and contrast the sentencing powers of English and Northern Irish magistrates and Scottish sheriffs by reference to criminal procedure in each of the three jurisdictions.
3 What was the main purpose of Diplock Courts in Northern Ireland? Discuss with reference to historical and socio-legal developments in the province.
4 Explain the difference between juries in England and Wales, Northern Ireland and Scotland.
5 In the light of *Clegg* [1995], discuss the notion of self-defence and the use of 'reasonable' force (see also Chapter 5).

# ■ ■ Further Resources ■

## Scotland

Hector MacQueen's *Studying Scots Law* (2004) provides a useful background to the Scottish legal profession.

Nicole Busby et al.'s *Scots Law* (2003) serves as a good students' guide with specific reference to the *Human Rights Act 1998* and its impact in Scotland.

Christina Ashton et al.'s *Fundamentals of Scots Law* (2003) gives a comprehensive account of the Scottish legal system.

## Northern Ireland

Television journalist Peter Taylor (1998) provides an excellent socio-political background to 30 years of the Troubles. He begins with partition in 1921 and charts the IRA's bombing campaign during the 1950s. The book concludes with the 'normalisation' process and decommissioning.

Ireland correspondent for the *Independent*, David McKittrick and historian David McVea (2001) provide an excellent account of the Troubles, referring to more than 3,500 deaths in 43 years of Northern Irish history.

Marie Therese Fay et al. (1999) provide superb insight into the Northern Ireland conflict with reference to tragic human costs at the height of the Troubles.

David Lister (2004) describes the dangerous and turbulent life of loyalist 'Mad Dog' Johnny Adair, from a glue-sniffing boy from Belfast's Shankill Road to becoming a merciless, outlawed Ulster freedom fighter and terrorist killing machine.

In *Dead Men Talking* (2004), Nicholas Davies reveals some uncomfortable truths surrounding the Sir John Stevens Inquiry, detailing covert killing operations by the RUC Special Branch and MI5, authorised by the British Government and carried out by loyalist terror groups.

## Notes

1  Sir William Blackstone originally published legal commentaries on English common law from the mid-eighteenth century with Clarendon Press, Oxford (1765–1769). Blackstone's commentaries remain the leading works on the English law precedent.

2  Though Art. 3 and Schedule 1 of the *Juries (Northern Ireland) Order 1996* had previously set out those persons who were disqualified for jury service by virtue of their criminal record.

# 4

# EUROPEAN UNION LAW AND EU LAW
# ENFORCEMENT

| Overview |
| :--- |

Chapter 4 examines:

- The relevance of EU law to criminologists
- History and development of the European Union
- The sources of EU law
- The EU institutions
- The role of the European Court of Justice
- European and international law enforcement

Though it may not be immediately clear to criminologists why you should have to study European Union (EU) law, this chapter alerts you to the fact that crime is now a global issue across all European and international borders, involving all governments and their law enforcement agencies of the present 27 member states of the European Union.

The Al Qaida attacks of 9/11 in the USA, 11 March 2004 in Madrid and 5 and 21 July 2005 in London did not only change the law enforcement landscape in the United States but also within Europe. They demonstrated the scale on which Al Qaida was prepared to operate, its desire for 'high impact' attacks with a worldwide resonance, its indifference to causing mass civilian casualties of any background or religion and its ability to deploy ambitious, innovative methods of attack, using planes rather than explosives as weapons. This also meant that the European states had to work more closely together in terms of law enforcement and governmental security strategies.

All 27 EU governments are now well aware that terrorism requires a global response. The Council of Europe's *Convention on the Prevention of Terrorism* of 2005 broadened international cooperation in the fight against terrorism (*Council of Europe Convention on the Prevention of Terrorism*, Warsaw, 16.V.2005). Furthermore, the EU works closely with the United Nations (UN) in the fight against terrorism whilst continuing to defend human rights. As a framework for providing collective security, there are now some 13 international conventions against terrorism, combined with several UN Security Council Resolutions; together, they provide a strong basis for enhancing international cooperation against terrorism. The same is true for the international agreements against the proliferation of weapons of mass destruction and their means of delivery.

After the initial historical and legal introduction, this chapter will alert you to the workings of European Union law and the significance of EU institutions. We will then move on to some practical law enforcement examples made possible by the European Arrest Warrant. The third pillar of the European Union has now been strengthened to enable national police forces and prosecutors to infiltrate today's ever-emerging new terrorism networks. Had it not been for the European Arrest Warrant (EAW) some of the wanted Al Qaida terrorist suspects of the Madrid or London bombings would never have been extradited so quickly back to stand trial at British, Italian or Spanish courts. The EAW has facilitated substantial judicial cooperation within the European Union on the basis of the principle of mutual recognition of judicial decisions and judgements (see Andreas and Nadelmann, 2006).

Finally, we will be looking at Britain's security services, MI5 and MI6, in their cooperation with Europol and Interpol and give some examples of law enforcement and prosecutions across transnational borders.

## 4.1 ___ History of the European Union ___

The idea of a united federal Europe – also known as the 'European idea' – and of establishing some body representative for Europe goes back to the 1930s with the Briand Plan which brought about the Council of Europe. Twice during the Second World War, Winston Churchill publicly expressed his conviction that Europe, when hostilities had ceased, must join together under a 'Council of Europe' (cited in Churchill's Zürich speech of 19 September 1946).

The European Economic Community (EEC) or 'common market' as it was called then was created by the Treaty of Rome on 25 March 1957, when the great leaders from six European countries, France, West Germany, Italy, The Netherlands, Belgium and Luxembourg, met in the grand hall of Rome's Capitoline museum to sign the EC Treaty ('Treaty of Rome').

Britain chose not to join the EEC at that time, maybe because it disliked the political integration implicit in the new grouping or maybe because it wanted to preserve its neutrality within Europe. Britain applied for membership four years later, but was blocked by the French President, Charles de Gaulle's veto. Britain eventually joined the EEC in 1973 along with Denmark and Ireland. Spain and Portugal joined in 1986.

With the *Treaty on European Union 1992* (TEU), also known as the 'Maastricht Treaty', the EEC became the European Union (EU) and it is fair to say that the EU metamorphosed far beyond its economic sphere, with the single market successfully completed by then. Here follows a summary of accession countries to the European Union:

- 1957: France, West Germany, Italy, The Netherlands, Belgium and Luxembourg
- 1972: The UK, The Republic of Ireland (Éire) and Denmark
- 1981: Norway and Greece
- 1986: Spain and Portugal
- 1990: Former East Germany (The German Democratic Republic)
- 1995: Sweden
- 2004: Cyprus, the Czech Republic, Estonia, Hungary, Latvia, Lithuania, Malta, Poland, Slovenia and Slovakia
- 2007: Bulgaria and Romania
- Possibly Turkey in 2012

By the beginning of the new millennium, the EU institutions had moved into new policy areas such as social policy, welfare and the environment. Most member states adopted a single currency, the Euro, in 2001 but not the UK, Sweden and Denmark. A common foreign policy emerged with a passport-free travel zone under the 'Schengen' agreement (except the UK). There were new policies on justice and home affairs, plus a promising defence alliance with its own military-planning staff. The European Union sent troops as far afield as Aceh and the Congo and coordinated national deployments in Lebanon in 2006–07.

## 4.2 ___ European Union institutions

The five major institutions of the Community are:

- The Commission
- The European Council ('Council of Ministers')
- The European Parliament
- The European Court of Justice and the Court of First Instance
- The Court of Auditors

### ___ The Commission (Brussels and Luxembourg) ___

The Commission is politically the most powerful EU institution. It is the Community's executive, responsible for implementing the decisions of the European Parliament and the Council of Ministers, a kind of 'civil service' of the European Union. It manages the day-to-day business of the EU by implementing its policies and running its spending programmes. Confusingly, some of its administration is based in Brussels and some in Luxembourg. The main functions of the Commission are to:

- propose and draft legislation
- manage and implement EU policies and the budget
- enforce EU law
- represent the EU in international matters

Until 2006, there was one Commissioner from each member state. When Bulgaria and Romania joined in January 2007, the Council fixed the maximum number of Commissioners to 27. Elections are held every five years.

_____ The European Council (or Council of Ministers) (Brussels) _____

Officially known as the 'Council of the European Union' the Council of Ministers is the EU's second decision-making body alongside the Commission. It passes laws and legislates jointly with the EU Parliament. The Council coordinates the broad economic policies of all member states. It defines and implements the European Union's common foreign and security policy and seals international agreements between the EU and other international organisations, on behalf of the Community. The main functions of the Council of Minsters are:

- **Legislative** – to pass EU laws jointly with the European Parliament
- **Economic policy** – to coordinate economic policies of member states
- **Foreign policy and home affairs** – to conclude international agreements
- **Budgetary** – to approve the EU's budget jointly with the EP
- **Security and common foreign policy** – to develop the EU's Common Foreign and Security Policy (CFSP)
- **Justice and home affairs** – to coordinate cooperation between the national courts and police forces in criminal matters

The Council of Ministers coordinates the actions of all member states and adopts measures in the area of police and judicial cooperation in criminal matters. Together with the European Parliament, the Council constitutes the budgetary authority that adopts the Community's budget. Council of Ministers' meetings are usually attended by one minister from each member state, depending on the agenda set. Presently, the presidency of the European Union rotates every six months amongst its member states; the country with the presidency is responsible for setting the agenda, promoting legislation and formulating EU policy. This will change with the new Reform Treaty (the *Lisbon Treaty 2007* – see below). The Treaty of Lisbon was signed by all heads of state of the 27 member states in Lisbon on 13 December 2007. Once ratified by all 27 EU states, the treaty will provide the EU with more modern and efficient institutions and unify all existing EU treaties. The target date for ratification is set on 1 January 2009 followed by the elections to the European Parliament.

_____ The European Parliament (Brussels; Luxembourg; Strasbourg) _____

Though initially the European Parliament only had a consultative role, the Parliament's main function is now to guarantee the democratic legitimacy of European Union law. The European Parliament can amend and adopt legislation and shares the decision-making power with the Council of Ministers. The

Parliament exercises overall political supervision of all EU policies and monitors expenditure and has overall responsibility over budgetary control. Though mainly in Brussels, the European Parliament confusingly also works from Luxembourg and Strasbourg. The main functions of the EU Parliament are:

- **Legislative** – to pass EU laws jointly with the Council of Ministers
- **Supervisory** – to supervise the democratic process of EU institutions, such as the Commission
- **Budgetary** – to adopt or reject the EU budget in its entirety

Members of the European Parliament (MEPs) sit in political groups; that is they are not organised by nationality but by political affiliation. The two largest groups are the European People's Party (Christian Democrats) and European Democrats (EPP-ED) and the Socialist Group (PES).

## The European Court of Justice and Court of First Instance (Luxembourg)

The European Court of Justice (ECJ) – also known as the Court of Justice of the European Communities – was established under Art. 220 EC. Its main function is to ensure that all treaty functions are observed and adhered to by all member states. The European Court of Justice is located in Luxembourg and can sit as a full court in a Grand Chamber of 13 judges, or in smaller chambers of three or five judges. In total, the European Court of Justice has 27 judges and eight Advocates General from all 27 member states. They are chosen from the highest judicial offices in their respective countries and are appointed for a term of six years (renewable). Advocates General are responsible for presenting the final 'opinion' in the cases assigned to them. The European Court of Justice cooperates with all the national courts on matters of Community law. The European Court of Justice does not have the English court structure or its legal hierarchy; there is no appeal system. European Court of Justice opinions are legally binding on all member states – known as the doctrine of direct effect. The Court of First Instance's main function is to sift through the cases in advance before they reach the European Court of Justice. The Court of First Instance is made up of at least one judge from each member state, appointed for six years. The President is appointed for a period of three years.

*Preliminary Rulings*   What it is important to remember is that the European Court of Justice does not decide or rule on a particular case transferred to it either from a national court or an individual. It merely gives 'Preliminary Rulings' or opinions and interprets treaty provision which is subsequently translated into 21 'official' EU languages. Judgements are always given in the language of the referring country.

The Court of Auditors was set up in 1975. Its primary function is to check that funds from member states' taxpayers are properly collected and spent economically; second, to avoid any fraudulent actions by EU institutions. Such was the case with some scandalous 'misappropriations' by certain Commissioners during the late 1990s. There are 27 auditors, appointed by the Council of Ministers, for a renewable term of six years. The Court of Auditors has no legal powers of its own. If auditors discover fraud or irregularities, they have to inform the European Anti-Fraud Office (OLAF).

_____ The European Central Bank (Frankfurt) _____

What some regard as the sixth EU institution, the European Central Bank (ECB), was created by the Maastricht Treaty in 1992 under Art.105 (1) EC. Its main objective is to maintain EU monetary policy and price stability within the Eurosystem. The main functions of the European Central Bank are to:

- Define and implement the monetary policy for the Euro area
- Conduct and control foreign exchange operations
- Manage the foreign reserves of all Euro area countries
- Print Euro notes and coins

In summary, the main function of the European Union has been to restore peace and prosperity to its citizens after the two world wars. But there are problems, the biggest being economy stability, particularly in the former socialist-communist countries that joined the EU during the early twenty-first century.

## 4.3 ____ Sources of European Union law _____

_____ Primary legislation: the treaties _____

The EU treaties – such as the *Treaty of Rome 1957* – are primary sources of law and supreme to all laws of the 27 member states. There is no European criminal law (yet), neither is there a European criminal court. In essence, European Union law and its treaties deal with civil law, such as free movement and non-discrimination of workers (Art 39 EC), free movement of goods (Arts 23–26 EC), competition law and state monopolies (Arts 81–82 EC).

The *Maastricht Treaty 1992* brought about the Single European Market with the European Community (EC) and from 1993 onwards those travelling to and from EU member states were able to purchase seemingly unlimited amounts of goods for personal use, established under the 'free movement of goods' principle (Arts 23–26 EC). The Maastricht Treaty of 1992 also established the **Three Pillar** structure, which comprises:

1 **The Community pillar** – the EC (European Community), the ECSC (European Coal and Steel Community) and Euratom (European atomic energy). It concerns economic, social and environmental policies
2 **The Common Foreign and Security Policy (CFSP) pillar** – it deals with social, political and foreign affairs as well as military matters
3 **The Police and Judicial Cooperation in Criminal Matters (PJCC) pillar** – it is concerned with law enforcement and the fight against global crime and terrorism (originally named 'Justice and Home Affairs')

Though there are numerous treaties, one of the more important ones was the Treaty of Nice in 2001, facilitating the admission of ten new member states to the EU. This included many ex-communist central European states with their accession to the European Union on 1 May 2004, including the Baltic States and Poland. By way of the *EU (Accessions) Act 2006*, Romania and Bulgaria became the European Union's 26th and 27th member states on 1 January 2007.

Plenty of other countries are seeking membership in the near future, the most controversial one being the accession of Turkey. Others have chosen to stay out even though they would instantly qualify for membership, such as Iceland, Norway and Switzerland. With the German presidency of the European Union in early 2007, a seven-year budget was agreed by the Council of Ministers, to set out plans for an energy policy and for tackling climate change. At the same time, Ministers rejected the 'Constitution' and decided to draft a new 'Reform Treaty' which became the *Lisbon Treaty* in December 2007. Major EU Treaties are:

- Treaty of Rome 1957 (the 'EC Treaty')
- Treaty on European Union 1992 (TEU) ('Maastricht Treaty')
- Treaty of Amsterdam 1997 – this re-numbered all original EC treaty articles
- Treaty of Nice 2001 – it approved the accession of ten further member states
- Athens Treaty 2003 – ten new member states signed the accession to the EU
- Rome Treaty 2004 (The Constitutional Treaty or 'EU Constitution')
- Lisbon Treaty 2007

*The Lisbon Treaty 2007 ('The Reform Treaty')*   The original EU's Constitution of 2004 was meant to harmonise the functions of the institutions and all existing treaties into one piece of legislation. So what were the problems? Euroscepticism had spread across even the 'old' EU countries: France, The Netherlands and Denmark rejected the Constitution in their national referendums in 2003–04, whilst ten other states had ratified the Constitution by then. Confusingly, the Constitution had been fully ratified by 16 of the 27 member states on 29 October 2004 in Rome, but could not come into force unless it was ratified by all 27. The mistrust in the Constitution was probably most pronounced in Britain, where the government wanted to keep its labour market free of unnecessary EU regulations and directives on working time or job security.

On 23 June 2007 at a Brussels summit, all EU leaders eventually agreed a format for a new 'Reform Treaty' driven by the German Presidency under Chancellor Angela Merkel. Eurosceptics argued that the Reform Treaty would preserve much of the draft Constitution. The *Lisbon Treaty 2007* was finally signed by all 27 leaders of the EU on 12 December 2007, which would come into full force in 2009. The *Lisbon Treaty* comprises:

- Increased powers for the European Parliament
- A smaller European Commission
- Fewer Commissioners (from 27 to 18 in 2014)
- An EU Council President
- A High Representative for Foreign Affairs
- Double majority voting (from 2014)
- Removal of national veto powers in 50 policy areas

The Lisbon Treaty creates a new legal identity of the European Union and replaces all earlier treaties. However, the Lisbon Treaty still needs to be ratified and adopted by all 27 member states. On 12 June 2008 Ireland rejected the Treaty in a referendum. On 17 July 2008 the UK ratified the Treaty.

_____ Secondary legislation _____

Secondary sources of law take the form of regulations, directives, decisions, recommendations or opinions all enshrined in Art. 249 EC.

*Regulations*   Regulations are the most important sources of secondary legislation in that they are of general application in the national laws of all member states, like a statute. They take immediate effect without the need for further implementation at a national level and Regulations are directly applicable, as Article 249 EC (Treaty of Rome) states:

A Regulation shall have general application. It shall be binding in its entirety and directly applicable to all member states.

For example, when the Council of Ministers issued *Council Regulation No 1612/68* on 15 October 1968, on the 'Freedom of movement for workers within the Community', it gave all Community workers, including their immediate families, the right to travel freely between member states, to seek or take up work without a work permit.

Regrettably, this marvellous opportunity of 'free movement' has been abused by some. It is for this reason that some 'old European' governments, like Germany,

France or the UK, have implemented restrictions on migrant workers recently, particularly those seeking work from the relatively new Eastern European states, such as Romania or Bulgaria. They are prohibited from claiming immediate social benefits when migrating to the more prosperous member states. Arguably, this contravenes the spirit of the Treaty of Rome, as Advocate General Trabucchi stated in *Mr and Mrs F v Belgian State* [1975], that, 'the migrant worker is not to be viewed as a mere source of labour, but as a human being.'

*Directives*    Directives specify a legal obligation on specific member states 'to whom they are addressed', as Art. 249 EC states:

> A Directive shall be binding, as to the result to be achieved, upon each member State to whom it is addressed, but shall leave to the national authorities the choice of form and methods.

Once the Council of Ministers have issued a Directive, it is up to the individual member state to decide how best to achieve that objective in form of national legislation (statute). An example is *Directive 2004/38/EC* of 29 April 2004, 'On the right of citizens of the Union and their family members to move and reside freely within the territory of the member states'.[1] The Directive provides for families of member states' workers to travel and reside with an EU worker. This means that family members do not necessarily have to originate from the European Union.

*Decisions*    These are administrative acts addressed specifically to individuals, which can be an individual of a member state or a company. Decisions are binding in their entirety on those to whom they are addressed and there is no need for implementing legislation. An example can be for an airline to give an undertaking not to breach EU competition policy. One such decision concerned competition law within the EU and British Airways (BA). The EU Commission had imposed a fine of 6.8 million Euro on BA in December 2003 for its 'abuse of dominant position' in competition law, originally initiated following a complaint by Virgin Atlantic Airways in 1999 (*British Airways plc v Commission* [2007]).[2] The subsequent appeal by BA was dismissed in June 2007 (European Commission, 2007).

*Recommendations and Opinions*    Article 249 EC states that Recommendations and Opinions are not legally binding and are simply a 'recommend' decision made by the Council of Ministers or the Commission. Asylum and immigration issues are a common example, such as the *Council Recommendation of 22 December 1995* on 'Harmonizing means of combating illegal immigration and illegal employment and improving the relevant means of control' (see Steiner et al., 2007).

## 4.4 ___ EU law enforcement, asylum and immigration policy ___

Is there a criminal law for Europe? The short answer is: no. But, with the strengthening of the third pillar – 'Police and Judicial Cooperation in Criminal Matters' (PJCC) (see above) – the EU now focuses specifically on drug trafficking, organised crime, such as cigarette smuggling, terrorism, human trafficking or money laundering.

How EU law and treaty principles can be abused by organised criminals, such as the 'free movement of goods' principle, can be seen by the example of cigarette bootlegging as researched by Hornsby and Hobbs (2007).

The EU Commission has also focused increasingly on the strength of its asylum and immigration policy. The *Dublin Convention* of 15 June 1990 provides a mechanism for determining the state responsible for examining applications for asylum lodged in one of the member states of the European Union. In view of the difficulties the member states anticipated in identifying aliens who had already lodged an asylum application in another member state, the ministers responsible for immigration agreed in 1991 to establish a Community-wide system for the comparison of the fingerprints of asylum applicants – known as the 'Dublin system'.[3] Organisations working with refugees describe the present 'Dublin' system as an asylum 'lottery'. There is large scale 'asylum shopping', which means some asylum seekers lodge applications in more than one EU country. Eurodac has been matching fingerprints from asylum seekers across the EU and found that 12 per cent of asylum seekers between 2003 and 2005 had already made a claim in another member state.

The 1999 Tampere summit in Finland further addressed the first pillar, the European Communities and EU asylum policy. Thereafter, asylum applications to EU member states dropped: whilst there were 405,455 applications in 2002, there was a significant drop by more than 50 per cent in 2006, down to 181,770. In Britain, the number of asylum applications has dropped by about a quarter, from 103,080 in 2002 down to 27,850 in 2006.

The difficulty remains in that all 27 member states have different policies on immigration and asylum, though even the more liberal countries, like Denmark and the Netherlands, have recently tightened their policies. Spain was the only EU country until recently to grant large-scale amnesties to illegal immigrants, including a tribe of Embera-katio Indians from Colombia in April 1999, from the north-east territory of Alto Sinu, who had been victims of the conflict between Colombia and armed groups.

With the Canary Islands only 100 km (60 miles) off Africa's west coast, Tenerife is now on the frontline of illegal African migration into Europe. Since the beginning of 2006, up to 10,000 Africans have boarded handmade boats in the hope of getting into Europe, ready to risk death. Spanish officials reported that more than 1,700 have died along the way and coastguards working off the Canary Islands have rescued hundreds of men, women and children. Apart from

Spain, the 'Dublin system' has created additional burdens for frontline southern states, such as Malta, Italy and Greece.

The Council's Hague Programme of 2004 further discussed common asylum and immigration policies; its main aim was to bring the 'Geneva Convention on Refugees' in line with EU policy and to harmonise border controls and police cooperation. The Hague Programme includes:

- Regulation of migration flows
- External border control
- Combating organised cross-border crime
- Repressing the threat of terrorism
- Fighting human trafficking (see also s. 31 *UK Borders Act 2007*)

Section 32 of the *UK Borders Act 2007* includes the automatic deportation of 'foreign criminals', that is non-British citizens who are convicted in the UK of an offence where the person has been sentenced to a period of at least 12 months.

## The European Arrest Warrant

The European Arrest Warrant (EAW) was brought about by EU Council secondary legislation of 13 June 2002 (Decision 2002/584/JHA), regulating the surrender procedures between member states. From 1 July 2004, the EAW replaced and unified the existing extradition system. This means that each national judicial authority now recognises requests for the surrender of a suspect or criminal person made by the judicial authority of another member state. The Treaty of Amsterdam 1997 had already introduced a pan-European judicial network and legal database, known as 'Eurojust', on 1 May 1999, to assist all member states' law enforcement agencies and prosecution services with the pursuance of serious cross-border and organised crime.

The primary purpose of the European Arrest Warrant was to facilitate easier legal cooperation and law enforcement cooperation between these member states, in order to extradite suspects from one country to another where they were wanted on criminal charges. The EAW can be summarised as follows:

- **Provides a faster extradition procedure** – the state in which the person is arrested has to return the suspect or convicted criminal to the state where the EAW was issued within three months or 90 days of the arrest
- **Simplifies extradition procedures** – criminal suspects cannot escape arrest and are returned to the country where the crime took place
- **Abolished the dual criminality principle** – that is the principle of 'double jeopardy' (*ne bis in idem*) for 32 serious offences including terrorism; human trafficking; sexual exploitation of children; child pornography; money laundering; counterfeiting; illicit trafficking in arms and ammunition
- **Pursues offences that carry imprisonment of three years or more** in the member state that issued the warrant

How then does the EU tackle global terrorism threats? On 11 March 2004, ten bombs exploded on four packed early-morning commuter trains in Madrid, killing 191 people and leaving 1,800 injured. At first, the Spanish government suspected the Basque separatist group Eta, but evidence quickly emerged that Islamic militants were behind the attacks. On 26 April 2004, the Spanish interior ministry issued five arrest warrants on Moroccan and Indian nationals linked to the Madrid bombings via the European Arrest Warrant in cooperation with Italy. On 6 November 2006, Rabei Osman Sayed Ahmed and Yahia Ragheh were found guilty of being connected to major Al Qaida terrorist cells that extended throughout Europe to Iraq.

The *Extradition Act 2003* facilitated extradition to and from the UK, such as the London 7 July 2005 bombers from Italy. Only two weeks after the 7 July London bombings, on 21 July 2005, London was spared a second bomb outrage. One of the main terrorist suspects, Hussain Osman, wanted for the attempted bomb attacks on the Shepherd's Bush Underground station, had fled to Rome by Eurostar. Born Hamdi Issac Adus in Ethiopia in 1978, Osman had moved to Italy at the age of 14 in 1992, and from there had travelled to Britain in 1996, later recruited by Al Quaida to plan the bomb attack on London.

On 30 July, Hussain Osman, Ramzi Issac and his brother Fati Issac, were arrested in Rome on charges of possessing and destroying false documents in the Northern Italian province of Brescia. Following these arrests by Italian police, Scotland Yard demanded the extradition of Hussain Osman to London under the European Arrest Warrant. But Osman's outspoken Italian defence lawyer, Antonetta Sonnessa, told the world media on 1 August 2005 that Osman categorically refused his extradition on the grounds that the whole bomb attack idea had been an elaborate hoax and that the European Arrest Warrant contravened his human rights. However, Osman lost his appeal and was extradited to London on 22 September 2005. As his plane touched down at RAF Northolt, Osman was immediately arrested by anti-terror police officers. Hussain Osman, 28, was convicted at Woolwich Crown Court on 9 July 2007, and given a life sentence, together with Muktar Ibrahim, 29, Yassin Omar, 26, and Ramzi Mohammed, 25. Their plot to detonate explosives on three Tube trains and a bus in London on 21 July 2005 was a viable attempt at mass murder, Mr Justice Fulford said. Two other men, Manfo Kwaku Asiedu and Adel Yahya, faced a retrial after the first jury failed to reach a verdict.

So, does the European Arrest Warrant contravene human rights legislation? On 18 July 2005, the German Constitutional Court (*Bundesgerichtshof*) ruled in the case of Mamoun Darkazanli, that the European Arrest Warrant was 'unconstitutional'. This case concerned a Syrian-born German, suspected of being an Al Qaida operative. Darkazanli had been held in custody for extradition to Spain under the EAW procedure. On appeal, the German Bundesgerichtshof held that the European Arrest Warrant did not respect fundamental human rights, nor did it grant procedural guarantees. However, the EU Commission held in 2006 that German legislation was at fault and not the

European Arrest Warrant. Therefore, Germany reinstated the EAW in 2006 (see also Blekxtoon, 2004).

In conclusion, the European Arrest Warrant has replaced lengthy extradition procedures with a new efficient way of bringing to justice suspected criminals who have absconded abroad and for people convicted of a serious crime who have fled the country. EU-wide inter-agency collaboration between police and intelligence services is now well developed as a result of the universal appreciation that terrorism is a common threat.

## Europol

The 'European Police Office', Europol, was set up by the *Europol Convention 1998*, based in The Hague and comprises the EU's principal law enforcement and intelligence organisation. Europol's original mandate started in 1995 with the 'Europol Drugs Unit' (EDU) and was expanded in January 2002. The agency now deals with all serious forms of international organised crime and terrorism, including fraud and money laundering, cybercrime and human trafficking (see also Santiago, 2000).

In July 2006, Austrian and Croatian Police successfully prevented a Serbian criminal gang from distributing 2,400 pieces of counterfeited 500 Euro banknotes through the European Union at a face value 1.2 million Euros. The Austrian Criminal Intelligence Service and the National Central Office of the Federal Ministry of the Interior of the Republic of Croatia arrested three suspects in Zagreb. Europol had provided analytical support to the investigators in both countries.

There have been some atrocious human trafficking violations which Europol has sought to combat. Human traffickers target, deceive and exploit vulnerable individuals with the promises of well-paid employment opportunities and improved social conditions. Their victims are subjected to various forms of exploitation, be it sexual, forced labour of children, or forms of physical and psychological abuse. In May 2007, a Maltese skipper refused to pick up 26 African migrants clinging to a tuna net in the Mediterranean because they were in Libyan waters. The migrants were eventually rescued by an Italian vessel instead. In June 2007, a French naval frigate found the bodies of 18 people, thought to be African migrants trying to get to Europe, who had drowned in the Mediterranean.

On 18 July 2006, a number of arrests were made in Italy and Poland, as a result of a successful joint operation by the Italian Carabinieri and the Polish Police. With the help of Europol intelligence, the joint police forces dismantled an international network of criminals who had engaged in human trafficking for the purpose of labour and prostitution across EU borders. Twenty-five suspects were arrested and 120 Polish victims were found in forced labour farm-camps in Italy; all had been promised well-paid jobs. There were allegations of serious physical abuse and counterfeiting Euros (see also Milke, 2003).

Europol assisted the German footballing authorities during the FIFA Football World Cup in Germany in 2006. The Europol information exchange monitored all member states' criminal intelligence databases for known football hooligans. Europol coordinated EU police forces, such as the German and the British police, thereby offering strong security support at all German stadiums. Intelligence had been gathered during several other major sports events in previous years, such as the 'Confederations Cup' in Germany 2005.

## Interpol

The 'International Criminal Police Organisation' (Interpol) was created in 1923 and remains the world's largest international police organisation and intelligence base, with presently 184 member countries. Interpol's General Secretariat is located in Lyon, France. Interpol's mission is to prevent or combat international crime within the governance of the UN's Universal Declaration of Human Rights. The Secretariat has six regional offices: Argentina, Côte d'Ivoire, El Salvador, Kenya, Thailand and Zimbabwe and a liaison office at the United Nations in New York. Officials from more than 80 countries work side-by-side in Interpol's four official languages: Arabic, English, French and Spanish. Interpol cannot intervene in political, military, religious or racial activities. Interpol's remit is to:

* Prevent or combat international crime
* Facilitate cross-border police cooperation
* Operate within existing laws of member countries

## MI5

The work of the British Intelligence Service, known as MI5, includes the protection of the UK against international threats and threats to national security. Before the collapse of Soviet communism, MI5's investigations largely centred on espionage. Since the early 1990s, MI5's work principally involves investigating Al Qaida networks in the UK.

## MI6

The British Secret Intelligence Service (SIS), or MI6, was established in 1909. Its origins lie in the foreign section of the Secret Service Bureau, first headed by Captain Sir Mansfield Cumming. MI6 was put on a statutory basis with the Intelligence Services Act (ISA) 1994, with chief authority of the Foreign Secretary.

The Crown Prosecution Service (CPS) now conducts its international work with the help of Europol, Interpol and Eurojust. One such example was a case of international human trafficking in early 2006, when London's CPS obtained strong evidence regarding trafficking by Turkish gang-members into the UK via Belgium, Italy, the Netherlands and Austria. Forty-seven people had been smuggled into the UK and attempts had been made to smuggle a further 400 immigrants illegally into the country. The CPS learnt that ringleaders Ramazan Zorlu and Riza Gun had been operating a commercial venture to facilitate the illegal trafficking of Turkish immigrants; for each person smuggled, they were earning a fee of about £14,000. Intercept evidence from Belgian, Italian and Austrian prosecution services had found in October 2005 that 414 illegal immigrants, including some pregnant women and several children, had attempted to enter the UK in lorries, cars, vans, trains and aeroplanes. When the people smuggling gang members were eventually convicted at Croydon Crown Court in October 2006, Prosecutor Hilary Bradfield gave the following statement:

> The gang's 'customers' were subjected to some appalling conditions, including being without food for several days, transported in coffin-like compartments under lorries and being delayed at various locations waiting for transport, without means of support. The size and complexities of this case required very skilled co-ordination at all stages of the prosecution by the police, CPS, counsel and the court, as well as our colleagues abroad, leading to the closure of this highly lucrative network. ('Work in Europe helps convict people smuggling ring', CPS press release, 4 October 2006)

## 4.5 ___ Case study

_____ *R v Henn; R v Darby [1980]* _____

We said earlier in the chapter that there is no body of criminal law for Europe yet. But to show how the UK criminal courts have included EU law, we have included the Henn and Darby case which was first heard at the Ipswich Crown Court in 1975. The case/demonstrates how two criminal 'entrepreneurs', Maurice Donald Henn and John Frederick Ernest Darby, manipulated the 'free movement of goods' principle in order to import pornographic materials into the UK. Both defendants argued that they were merely bringing in the merchandise from the European mainland for their 'friends' and that the UK Customs and Excise had contravened the spirit of the Treaty of Rome (Article 30 EC (ex. 28)) by not allowing foreign 'goods' into the country. The UK argued that Henn and Darby had offended against the *Customs Consolidation Act 1876* and the *Customs and Excise Act 1952*. Since the House of Lords could not decide it referred the case to the European Court of Justice for a preliminary ruling.

## Facts of the case

Maurice Henn and John Darby were operating a mail order business in the UK, trading in pornographic films and 'top shelf' magazines imported from Denmark, Germany and Sweden into the UK. On 14 October 1975, a truck load arrived at the port of Felixstowe from the Dutch Europoort at Rotterdam, containing a large consignment of films and magazines of a 'sexually explicit nature'. HM Customs and Excise officers had been monitoring Henn and Darby's operations. On this date, customs had observed how Henn had met the lorry consignment on the road from Felixstowe to Ipswich, had collected the boxes and put them into his car to London.

Henn was arrested on 15 October. All boxes were seized and Henn was charged with importing 'indecent and obscene' goods contrary to section 42 of the *Customs Consolidation Act 1876* and section 304 of the *Customs and Excise Act 1952*. Darby was arrested and charged on the same day in London as he collected and sought to distribute the films and magazines. Both were indicted to the Crown Court at Ipswich, where their trial started nearly two years later, on 17 May 1977. The charge read that Henn and Darby were knowingly involved in the fraudulent evasion of the prohibition of the importation of indecent or obscene articles contrary the 1876 and 1952 Acts. Henn and Darby pleaded 'not guilty' to the charges at the local magistrates' court, arguing that the old *Customs Consolidation Act 1876* contravened the 'free movement of goods' principle of EU law, namely Article 30 EC (ex 28).

The Ipswich Crown Court heard that the imported films and magazines depicted detailed and explicit sexual activities with scenes of violence. Two of the magazines contained photographs of naked girls between about five and 14 years old, engaging in sexual activity with an adult man. Five of the magazines contained advertisements, inviting readers to apply to a 'Model Contract'. One magazine advertised for models for acts of buggery.

Both men were convicted. Henn was sentenced to 18 months' imprisonment and Darby to two years' imprisonment. Both were ordered to pay substantial fines. They appealed against conviction and sentence. Their appeals were heard by the Court of Appeal Criminal Division on 4 to 7 July 1978. Their appeals failed and on 9 November 1978, they were granted leave to appeal to the House of Lords.

On 29 January 1979, the House of Lords referred the case to the European Court of Justice to seek clarification as to the conflict of laws between existing English customs and excise law and EU law concerning the principle of free movement of goods.

At the **European Court of Justice**, Advocate General Warner gave the opinion that the UK had contravened EU law under Art. 30 EC in that it had prohibited and restricted imported goods. He stated that a member state should apply the same criteria to 'home-produced' goods, such as pornography, as to foreign imports. The UK appeared to tolerate 'home produced' pornographic literature and yet prohibited Danish, Swedish or German imports. This clearly amounted to a 'quantitative restriction' on imports and thereby a discrimination in EU law, contra Art. 30 EC.

However, the European Court of Justice allowed an exception in this case, in that a country may lawfully prohibit imported articles, such as pornographic material, if these were deemed 'indecent or obscene' in domestic law. And since that was

*(Continued)*

the case, the UK could derogate from the 'free movement of goods' principle. But then, the UK would have to apply this legislation to nationally published goods too. And for this reason, Henn and Darby's appeals were dismissed and their convictions were upheld.

 ## ■ Exam Questions

1 What are the main sources of EU law? Discuss with reference to specific legislation and case law.
2 What are the main principles enshrined in the Treaty of Rome?
3 What are the principal EU institutions? What are the proposed changes with the Lisbon Treaty 2007?
4 Discuss the consequences of the European Court of Justice's ruling in *Henn and Darby* and explain why the two defendants' convictions were eventually upheld.
5 Discuss the way in which the European Arrest Warrant has provided law enforcement and prosecution support to EU member states.

## ■ ■ Further Resources ■

John Fairhurst's book, *Law of the European Union* (2007) and Josephine Steiner et al.'s *Textbook on EC Law* (2007) provide authoritative reading and concise treatment of EU institutions in this rather complex area of law.

*Race Against Evil* (2003) charts David Race Bannon's chilling autobiography as a former Interpol agent with the 'Archangel' team. As an assassin, he was rumoured to be responsible for more than a hundred killings.

Peter Andreas and Ethan Nadelmann's *Policing the Globe* (2006) covers the history of crime control on a global perspective and offers a controversial, yet enlightening view of international policing, prosecutions and criminal justice agencies.

## Notes

1 Amending Regulation (EEC) No 1612/68 and repealing Directives 64/221/EEC.
2 Decisions by the European Court of Justice (2/93).
3 Council Regulation (EC) No 2725/2000 of 11 December 2000, established by Eurodac for the comparison of fingerprints for the effective application of the Dublin Convention (Official Journal L 316 of 15.12.2000).

# 5

# ESSENTIAL CRIMINAL LAW

---

| **Overview** |

Chapter 5 examines:

- The building blocks of a criminal offence: the *actus reus* and the *mens rea*
- The concept of causation
- The constituent elements of homicide
- The concept of an act of omission
- The concept of recklessness
- The distinctions between non-fatal offences against the person
- The changing nature of sex crimes and legislation

---

Chapter 5 provides you with the basic building blocks to a criminal offence: the *actus reus* and the *mens rea* elements to a crime. We will focus on the meanings of causation and highlight the developments in recklessness.

The multifaceted area of homicide will be discussed as to how the law differentiates between murder, voluntary manslaughter and involuntary manslaughter. A resulting conviction will determine whether the defendant is given a determinate or a life sentence.

There then follows a discussion on the topic of non-fatal offences against the person and whether present legislation might be outdated for the courts to deal with modern-day offences.

The chapter closes with recent sexual offences legislation where it will be demonstrated that common law in this area has largely been 'codified' in definitions of structured statutory legislation within the *Sexual Offences Act 2003*.

## 5.1 —— Elements of a crime: *actus reus* and *mens rea* ——

In establishing liability for a criminal offence, the prosecution must prove that the defendant possessed both the *actus reus* and the *mens rea* to the criminal offence.

*Actus non facit reum, nisi mens sit rea* (An act does not make a man guilty of a crime unless his mind is also guilty)[1]

The 'actual criminal act' – in Latin, *actus reus* – describes the conduct element of a criminal offence. It must be proved that the defendant has performed a harmful conduct or behaviour towards a victim. In other words, it must be proved that the defendant committed the offence, in particular circumstances and with specific consequences.

Each criminal offence carries its own *actus reus* which will be demonstrated in the following sections with the various offences.

Definition of *actus reus*:

- The **external** element of a crime
- The **activity** on the part of the accused

_____Mens rea_ – the mental element_____

*Mens rea* is the state of mind and defines the intention of the defendant at the time he committed the *actus reus*. 'Rea' refers to the criminal act and not to some moral quality. For this reason, it's best not to use the common translation of 'guilty mind' which can be misleading. Have a look at the case of *R v Miller* (James) [1983] 2 AC 161 and see how difficult it was for the House of Lords to decide on the coincidence of *actus reus* and *mens rea*. In *Miller*, Lord Diplock referred to *mens rea* as 'the conduct of the accused and his state of mind.'

*Causation*   The prosecution must show that the defendant *caused* the death of the victim – this is known as causation. The prosecution must also prove that the defendant *intended* to kill the victim or cause grievous bodily harm (GBH) to the victim under section 18 of the *Offences Against the Person Act 1861*. The *mens rea* for murder is an intention to kill or cause GBH.

Lord Parker CJ's famous judgement in *Smith* [1959] set the precedent for causation, whereby the defendant's appeal was allowed, in that the victim did not die from the result of the defendant's stab wound but from poor medical treatment which was 'palpably wrong' and had broken the chain of causation.

When faced with a problem question that involves homicide, you should apply the *but-for-test*; that is, death would not have occurred 'but for the act' of the accused (*Cheshire* [1991]; *Malcherek and Steel* [1981]).

In an exam question involving 'causation' you may wish to adopt the following step-by-step approach when deciding on 'who caused the victim's death?'

**Step 1**   Was the death of the victim a *direct* result of the defendant's actions?

**Step 2**   Apply the 'but-for-test' ... had it not been for the defendant's shooting or stabbing the victim, he would have lived...or not needed hospital treatment.

**Step 3** Was the death of the victim caused by things done 'palpably wrong' in a hospital, such as poor or insufficient treatment, MRSA, tuberculosis or food poisoning? Then this may amount to a *novus actus interveniens*, but only if the treatment was *palpably wrong* to break the chain of causation.

**Step 4** Was death caused by an omission, for example the doctor did not put the victim on life support or the anaesthetist performed the wrong anaesthetic or a father did not feed his child for months? Then the defendant is not guilty of murder or GBH.

And remember: only if both – the *actus reus* and the *mens rea* – are proved, will the defendant be found guilty. Simply put, if the defendant's actions are not premeditated then the intention (*mens rea*) element of the crime is not present.

Definition of mens rea:

- The **state of mind** of the accused
- The **mental element** of a crime
- The defendant's **intention** ('purpose' or 'aim')

*Intention*   You may wish to read Lord Bridge's detailed definition of intention in Moloney [1985], before looking at the miners' strike case of Hancock and Shankland (below). In all cases, the finding of 'intention' should be left to the jury to decide.

---

### R v Hancock; R v Shankland [1986] AC 455.

Hancock and Shankland were participating in the miners' strike. H and S pushed a concrete block off a motorway bridge in order to stop a strike-breaker travelling in a taxi to the mine. The taxi was driven by the victim, who was killed in the collision as the concrete hit the taxi. H and S were found guilty of murder and appealed.

Lord Scarman addressed the issue of intent and the probability regarding death or serious injury as a 'natural consequence' of the appellants' actions by referring to the House of Lords' guidelines in *Moloney*: that they had been unsafe and misleading since the test involved probability. That is, the greater the probability (of the brick hitting the travelling car) the more likely the foreseeable consequence that serious injury or death would occur and therefore the greater probability that such consequence was also intended.

Hancock and Shankland's appeals were allowed and manslaughter charges were substituted.

---

Generally, juries are directed as follows regarding 'intent': The greater the probability of consequences that death or grievous bodily harm can be foreseen, the more likely it is that harm was therefore intended.

*Inferred (oblique) intention*   The law moves at a fast pace and each year new developments in common law present fresh challenges to the courts, particularly in the area of intention (*mens rea*). One such case was the contentious House of Lords' decision in *Woollin* [1999].

The facts concerned an angry father who threw his three-month-old son on to a hard surface. The baby suffered a fractured skull and died. Woollin was convicted of murder but because of a misdirection of the jury, the House of Lords allowed Woollin's appeal and substituted the murder verdict with one of manslaughter.

*Woollin* set the precedent for 'inferred intention', meaning that the judge *may* direct a jury as to the possible consequence of the defendant's actions and whether these could have been foreseen as natural consequences of his actions:

> Where a man realises that it is for all practical purposes inevitable that his actions will result in death or serious harm, the inference may be irresistible that he intended that result, however little he may have desired or wished it to happen. (Woollin at 113)

_____The burden of proof_____

In every case – unless statute tells us otherwise – the prosecution must prove the defendant's guilt. In *Woolmington v DPP* [1935], Lord Sankey established the 'golden thread theory' which established the following principles:

- The burden of proof lies with the **prosecution**
- The defendant does not have to prove anything (unless statute says so)

*Standard of proof*   It is normal for a trial judge to direct a jury on the standard of proof by using the phrase 'beyond reasonable doubt', for example: 'The prosecution must convince you of the defendant's guilt, which is the same as proving the case beyond reasonable doubt'. This means, once the jury has considered all the evidence and are sure that the defendant is guilty, they must return a verdict of 'guilty'. If they are not sure, they must return a verdict of 'not guilty'. This must be achieved 'beyond reasonable doubt'.

*The reverse burden of proof*   If an issue arises on which the defendant bears the burden of proof, it is normally ordered by statute, such as all terrorism legislation and most driving offences. This is known as the 'reverse burden of proof' and the defence bears the legal or persuasive burden of proof. It then follows that the jury must decide whether the defendant had a reasonable excuse for doing what he did. If they then decide that the accused 'probably' had a reasonable excuse for doing what he did, they must find him 'not guilty'. If however, the jury decides that the defendant did not have a reasonable excuse, then they must find him 'guilty' (*Lynch v DPP* [2002]).

You have seen that the law on homicide offences can be convoluted and confusing because we presently have no specific definition of 'intent'. We are then left with a plethora of common law examples giving us confusing messages especially on inferred intent (*Woollin*). Same facts with different jury verdicts may often produce either a murder conviction, a manslaughter verdict or an acquittal.

_____ Crimes of basic and specific intent _____

There are regrettably no specific legal definitions in statute to define these types of crime. Therefore, we have to rely on common law. It is important for a criminologist to recognise the significant distinction between offences of specific intent and basic intent: a lack of *mens rea*, resulting from voluntary intoxication (alcohol or drugs) will excuse the defendant in the case of an offence of specific intent. But, intoxication will not excuse a defendant for a crime of basic intent.

*Specific intent crimes*    An offence of 'specific intent' is where the defendant commits a criminal act and at the time has an *intention* to bring about specific consequences. Specific intent crimes include:

* Murder
* Attempted murder (*Criminal Attempts Act 1981*)
* Wounding (GBH) with intent (s.18 OAPA 1861; *Bratty* 1963)
* Theft (s.1 *Theft Act 1968*)
* Burglary with intent to steal (s.9 *Theft Act 1968*)
* Blackmail

An offence of specific intent is one for which the prosecution must prove intention with respect to one or more of the elements in the *actus reus*. Recklessness will not suffice. Specific intent crimes require proof of some purposive element.

*Basic intent crimes*    An offence of 'basic intent' is one where the *mens rea* of the offence is no more than an intention, as defined by Lord Simon in *Morgan* (a rape case):

> A *basic intent* crime is one whose definition specifies *mens rea* that does not go beyond the *actus reus*, that is the act and its consequences. (*DPP v Morgan* [1976])

With basic intent crime, the prosecution does not have to prove that the accused foresaw any consequence or harm beyond the *actus reus* of the offence.

Basic intent crimes include:

- Involuntary manslaughter (*Lipman* 1970)
- Rape (s. 1 *Sexual Offences Act 2003*)
- Malicious wounding (GBH – s. 20 OAPA 1861; *Majewski* 1977)
- Criminal damage (s. 1(1) *Criminal Damage Act 1971*; *R v G* 2003)
- Assault (ABH – s. 47 OAPA 1861)
- Common assault/battery (s. 39 CJA 1988)
- Drink driving offences

## 5.2 ____ Recklessness

The concept of 'recklessness' has been a complex subject in common law. Over time, each new case set a new precedent and confused students. The final decision was given by the House of Lords in *R v G* [2004] (Re. G). Please make some time and read the cases of *Cunningham*, *Caldwell* and *Re. G* and note the socio-legal developments relating to recklessness and why the courts finally changed their minds, especially regarding young offenders and criminal damage (including arson).

### _____ Subjective recklessness (*Cunningham*) _____

'Subjective' or *Cunningham* [1957] recklessness means that a person is reckless when he carries out the deliberate act, appreciating that there is a risk that damage to property may result from his act. The risk must be one, which it is in all the circumstances, unreasonable for him to take.

However, the subjective *Cunningham* approach was rejected by the House of Lords in *Caldwell*.

### _____ Objective recklessness (*Caldwell*) _____

In *Caldwell* [1982], concerning charges of arson and criminal damage, Lord Diplock established the *objective* standard for recklessness, applying the 'ordinary prudent individual' test:

1 If the defendant does an act which in fact creates an *obvious risk* that property will be destroyed or damaged and
2 When the defendant does the act he either has not given any thought to the possibility of there being any such risk or has recognised that there was some risk involved and has nonetheless gone on to do it.

Then the defendant is guilty of the offence. Caldwell was duly convicted. Which brings us to the ruling in *Re. G* [2003], where the House of Lords reviewed the whole process regarding 'recklessness'. The case involves two young boys, aged 11 and 12, who caused large damage to a Coop-building by fire. The boys were charged with reckless criminal damage and arson. But, had they given any thought as to whether the premises would be destroyed or damaged by the fire? Did they intend to destroy or damage the building? Where they perhaps too young to appreciate the ensuing fire damage?

Their Lordships made it clear in *Re. G* that the *Caldwell*-objective test of recklessness had led to unfairness and misinterpretation, particularly where children were involved, referring back to the harsh decision in *Elliott* [1983]. Lord Bingham of Cornhill summed up that it was somewhat unjust to convict children under the objective test, stating that the House of Lords was abolishing *Caldwell*-recklessness, therefore allowing the boys' appeal.

This means that in cases involving criminal damage, the subjective *Cunningham*-test is the correct one to apply.


## 5.3 ___ Homicide: murder and manslaughter _____

Presently, the law divides homicide offences into these categories:

- Murder
- Voluntary manslaughter
- Involuntary manslaughter
- Unlawful act manslaughter
- Gross negligence manslaughter

This can be perplexing and you are advised to stick with the basics: you need to remember that the *actus reus* for murder is the killing of a human being by another human being in the 'Queen's (or King's) peace'. The *mens rea* for murder requires both:

1  The **intent** to kill or cause serious bodily harm (or grievous bodily harm by wounding with intent – GBH) and
2  The **foresight** that death or GBH would occur as a virtual consequence of the defendant's actions

The problem then remains for juries to decide whether the circumstances of a case demand a murder conviction. What if they find that the degree of foresight did not amount to intention? If in doubt, they should acquit the defendant.

Earlier, you learnt that the prosecution has to show both the *actus reus* of a crime and the intention (*mens rea*) to prove the defendant's guilt. But it is also necessary to show that the defendant actually performed the act and that he *caused* the death of the victim (causation). Following on, the law then requires proof of the relationship between an act and its consequences as an element of responsibility and that the death of the victim was as a *direct* result of the defendant's actions (*Smith* [1959]).

Voluntary manslaughter was constructed by Parliament in form of the *Homicide Act of 1957*, which created three categories of manslaughter:

- Diminished responsibility
- Provocation
- Suicide pact

*Diminished Responsibility (Murder)* Diminished responsibility exists where the defendant is suffering from an abnormality of mind, arising from an arrested or retarded development, which substantially impairs the defendant's responsibility for his actions. Diminished responsibility is only a *partial* defence, which, if pleaded successfully, reduces liability from murder to manslaughter. Section 2(3) *Homicide Act 1957* states that it is for the defendant to prove that his responsibility is diminished when he committed the offence ('reverse burden of proof').

There are three elements which the defence must prove before they can establish diminished responsibility. All three elements must be present:

1 At the time of the killing, the defendant suffered from an abnormality of mind; this means a state of mind so different from that of an ordinary human being that a reasonable person would judge it to be abnormal.
2 The abnormality of mind must arise from either: a condition of arrested or retarded development of mind; or any inherent cause; or it must be induced by disease or injury. This requires medical and/or psychiatric evidence.
3 The abnormality of mind must have substantially impaired the defendant's mental responsibility for what he did which caused death.

The jury must conclude that the defendant's abnormality of mind was a real cause of his conduct. Abnormality of mind can be defined in common law as:

- Arrested or retarded development of mind (*Egan* [1992])
- Any inherent causes or functional disorders (*Sanderson* [1994])
- Induced by disease or injury (including battered woman syndrome (*Hobson* [1998]); premenstrual syndrome or post-natal depression (*Smith* [Sandie] [1982])

*Provocation (murder)* Provocation is defined under s. 3 *Homicide Act 1957*, and asks whether the provocation was 'enough to make a reasonable man do as he did?' In answering that question the jury must take into account everything both done and said according to the effect it would have had on a 'reasonable man'.

Provocation simply put means where the accused was provoked to lose his self-control and killed someone. And if successful, provocation is only a partial defence to murder and not a defence to attempted murder (*Bruzas* [1972]).

The verdict would then be 'guilty of manslaughter by reason of provocation' (*Cawthorne* [1996]).

Given such a problem question in the exam, you should cite Lord Devlin's classic definition of 'provocation' in *Duffy* [1949]:

> Provocation is some act, or series of acts, done – or words spoken ... which would cause in any reasonable person and actually causes in the accused, a sudden and temporary loss of self-control, rendering the accused so subject to passion as to make him for the moment not master of his mind.

Then, try this step-by-step *Duffy* guide:

**Step 1** The defendant must suffer 'sudden and temporary' loss of self-control. A desire for revenge does not constitute provocation, because a person has time to think and reflect (*Duffy*)

**Step 2** The defendant must be provoked. It is not enough to argue in D's defence that he suddenly 'flipped' and lost his temper (*Acott* [1997])

**Step 3** The defendant must have been provoked by something said or done to him or immediate 'other', which triggered the sudden loss of self-control (*Doughty* [1986])

**Step 4** The defendant must still have the *mens rea* to kill and be unable to restrain himself (*Cocker* [1989])

With the reasonable-man-test left up to the jury, the prosecution will then try its hardest to prove the defendant's guilt by making sure that his excuse for killing was *not* one of provocation.

*Battered woman syndrome: provocation*   To understand battered woman syndrome, a term from psychology, one must first understand how someone becomes a 'battered woman'. According to Walker (2008) one of the leading experts on battered women, a woman must experience at least two complete battering cycles before she can be labelled 'battered woman'. The term was successfully used relating to the defence of provocation in *Ahluwalia* [1992] – see Chapter 1.5).

The background to this is based on the general assumption that women are 'naturally' less criminal than men and when they kill – usually their partners – they have the necessary *mens rea* (intention) to do so.

Early criminological works argued that it was more 'natural' for a man to have criminal tendencies or to be physically violent, argued very emotionally by Lombroso and Ferrero (1895, 2004). In *The Female Offender* the Italian criminologists argued that the reason why the 'weaker sex' was less 'criminal' or aggressive was due to female hormones. Women who did indulge in crime, were seen as non-female and inherently masculine (Carlen, 1985; Heidensohn, 1985). Accordingly, it was highly 'abnormal' for women to kill:

Women are big children ... their moral sense is deficient. If women did commit crime, they had masculine hormones and showed virile tendencies, displaying 'an inversion of all the qualities which specially distinguish the normal woman', such as 'reserve, docility and sexual apathy' (cited in Heidensohn, 1996: 114)

In more recent years, purely biological explanations for criminal behaviour have fallen out of favour. Worrall (1990) argues that women who offend are not 'proper women' and female aggression is often judged more harshly by justices than aggression by males because it reflects a greater departure from female social norms.

Heidensohn (1968, 2002, 2006) believes that it is not that women commit fewer crimes than their male counterparts, but it is often the attitude of justices and those who run the criminal justice system that women are treated differently by the system. It then follows that violent women – as was the case with Kiranjit Ahluwalia – must plead mental illness (diminished responsibility) when standing trial for murder (Campbell, 1993) since in the eyes of the justices, this is not how nice girls should behave (McCullough, 1996; Batchelor, 2001).

Though the defence of 'the provoked woman' was established in *Ahluwalia*, it can generally be argued that the defence of provocation is still largely afforded to men when standing trial for murder (see also McIvor, 2004; Walklate, 2004).

*Suicide Pact*   A suicide pact is an agreement between two or more persons, whose aim it is to die together. A failed suicide pact then becomes problematical for the surviving person – who, at that time would be accused of murder, unless a suicide note had been communicated (*R v Krause* [1902]).

Section 4 of the *Homicide Act 1957* changed the law on suicide pacts, where the burden of proof lies on the (surviving) accused to show that a suicide pact was intended by way of communication (e.g. suicide note). Only then will the accused be acquitted of murder and will be convicted of manslaughter.

This then leads us to the controversial area in law of 'mercy killing' and assisted dying (euthanasia), illegal in English law. This question was addressed in *Bland* [1993], where doctors had to establish whether they were legally permitted to switch off life support for the Hillsborough football stadium disaster (1989) victim Antony Bland, aged 17. The House of Lords' decision in *Bland* set the precedent: if medical experts declared that the patient's brainstem is dead, life support may be switched off.

A similar question arose in Diane Pretty's case. Neither the House of Lords nor the European Court of Human Rights in Strasbourg were willing to allow her to die by way of her husband administering a lethal dose.[2] Though Diane Pretty was suffering from Motor Neuron Disease, the courts ruled that her intellect and capacity to make decisions were unimpaired.

Involuntary manslaughter has always been an uncertain area of law. Is it not wrong in principle that a person should be liable to be convicted of murder, when he neither intended nor was reckless as to the most important element in the offence, namely death? With the involuntary manslaughter offence, the defendant's conduct falls only just short of murder. The main element of this type of offence is that the intention to cause serious bodily harm or death was not present when death of the victim occurred. In *Lamb* (1967), the defendant in jest pointed a revolver at his friend, who had also been treating the incident as a joke. The Smith & Wesson had two bullets in chambers, neither being opposite the barrel. Without intending to fire the revolver, Lamb pulled the trigger and his friend was killed. Lamb was charged with manslaughter. His defence was that he had accidentally killed his friend by mistakenly thinking that the striking pin could not hit the bullets; he had not known that pulling the trigger rotated the cylinder thereby bringing one of the bullets into the firing position. Being directed by the trial judge as to the 'unlawful killing', the jury returned a verdict of manslaughter. Lamb received a three year prison sentence and appealed against his conviction. The Court of Appeal held that the judge had misdirected the jury and that the *mens rea* element had been missing, this being an essential ingredient for manslaughter. Accordingly, the appeal was allowed and Lamb's conviction was quashed. For involuntary manslaughter to succeed, it must be proved that:

- There must be an unlawful act
- There must be a dangerous act where any reasonable person would realise that some harm would be caused
- That the act caused the victim's death

## Unlawful act manslaughter (killing by an _____ unlawful and dangerous act) _____

There is a vast amount of confusing case law surrounding the administering of illegal substances, usually by injecting heroin into another person at their request (consent); and that person then dies as a result.

Section 23 of the *Offences Against the Person Act 1861* (OAPA) deals with the offence of 'maliciously administering poison ... so as to endanger life or inflict grievous bodily harm'. The offence of 'unlawful act manslaughter' is very serious. If convicted the accused can expect a ten-year prison sentence.

For the jury to convict of this offence, they must first find an unlawful act on the part of the accused. This means, not only the supply of the illegal substance but also the injecting of the victim, for example with a mixture containing heroin (*Cato* [1976]).

In *Dalby* [1982], the Court of Appeal decided that administering heroin by injecting a heroin-syringe to the other person, who then voluntarily injected himself and died, did *not* constitute the offence of 'unlawful act manslaughter' because the defendant had committed the unlawful act by supplying the illegal drug though the unlawful act had stopped with the supply.

How does then does the ruling in *Kennedy* (Nr 1 and 2) differ from *Dalby*? In *Kennedy* (Nr 1) [1999], the Court of Appeal held that self-injection was an *unlawful* act and that by supplying the victim with the syringe, the defendant had committed an unlawful act which had led to the victim's death (s. 23 OAPA 1861). For this reason, Kennedy was convicted of manslaughter.

Subsequently however, the Criminal Cases Review Commission referred the conviction in Kennedy back to the Court of Appeal which dismissed the appeal, stating that the original judge had failed to inform the jury that the victim by injecting himself with heroin had broken the chain of causation (*novus actus interveniens*) between the appellant's act of supplying the drugs and the victim's death. The case was referred to the House of Lords (*Kennedy Nr 2* [2007]).

Their Lordships held in *Kennedy Nr 2* that it would be helpful as a direction to the jury to find someone guilty of 'unlawful act manslaughter', where:

1  the defendant was involved in the supply of a class A controlled drug (the unlawful act)
2  which was then *voluntarily* self-administered by the person to whom it had been supplied (the victim), and the administration of the drug caused the death of the victim

If you are faced with a similar problem in the exam, you should identify the unlawful act at the beginning of your legal argument (s. 23 OAPA 1861). You should then cite the House of Lords reasoning in *Kennedy Nr 2* where they allowed his appeal, because the deceased had had a choice whether to inject himself or not. The accused had 'only' supplied the heroin and prepared the syringe. In *Kennedy* the heroin was described as having been 'freely and voluntarily self-administered' by the deceased.

The ruling in *Kennedy* is important. It means that the criminal law generally assumes the existence of free will and that informed adults of sound mind are treated as autonomous beings, able to make their own decisions as to how they will act. It follows, where the deceased was a fully informed and responsible adult, it was never appropriate to find a person who had been involved in the supply to the deceased of a class A controlled drug, which had then been freely and voluntarily self-administered by the deceased and the administration of the drug had caused his death, guilty of manslaughter.

_____ Gross negligence manslaughter _____

The final homicide category, possibly the most unambiguous, is gross negligence manslaughter, where it must be proved that the accused had a duty of care towards his victim, such as a doctor or nurse. The leading case is *Adomako* [1995], whereby the anaesthetist Dr John Asare Adomako caused a patient in a routine eye operation to die because he did not realise that a disconnection of the endotracheal tube had occurred.

Giving judgement on behalf of the criminal Appeal Committee of the House of Lords in *Adomako*, Lord Mackay applied the test for gross negligence manslaughter, involving a breach of duty of care. There was no longer a necessity to refer to 'recklessness' (*Lawrence* [1981]). Adomako was convicted of gross negligence manslaughter.

To find the defendant guilty of *gross negligence manslaughter* the prosecution must prove that:

- the defendant owed a duty of care to the victim
- the defendant breached that duty of care
- the breach caused the death of the victim
- The defendant's conduct '*departed from the proper standard of care incumbent upon him, involving as it must have done a risk of death... was such that it should be judged criminal*' (Lord Mackay in *Adomako*)

The jury should consider, having regard to the risk of death involved, the conduct of the defendant was so bad in all the circumstances that it amounted to a criminal act or omission. This means, where the accused – a doctor for instance – should have acted to save a patient but failed to act (omission) and thereby caused the victim's death.

Have a look at the case of *Wacker* [2002] concerning the trafficking of human beings in his truck whilst crossing the English Channel. What offence was Perry Wacker actually charged with?

## 5.4 ____ Offences against the person

Offences against the person make up a large part of the criminal courts' work today. The *Offences Against the Person Act 1861* (OAPA) provides the bulk of these statutory offences, dealing in the main with offences of assault, such as 'assault occasioning actual bodily harm' (ABH) under section 47 OAPA, or serious wounding by grievous bodily harm (GBH) under section 20 OAPA.

Criminology students tend to be confused regarding the various types of 'assault', whereby the 1861 Act contains mixed and muddled messages of the punishment terms. Both the section 47 (ABH) and the section 20 (GBH) offences, carry a maximum punishment of five years' imprisonment. Is it not surprising that the law in this area has been widely criticised as archaic and unclear? Only common law gives us some indications as to the practical differences between what makes up injuries under a section 47, a section 20 and a section 18 offence. And how do these offences differ from common assault and battery under the *Criminal Justice Act 1988*?

Technically, assault and battery are two separate crimes, though in *Lynsey* [1995] the Court of Appeal left the question open as to whether assault and battery should be regarded as separate statutory offences. Both are summary offences – often found in domestic violence situations – with the punishment being either a fine or six months' imprisonment. Let's have a look at the *actus reus* and *mens rea* of both:

- **Actus reus of assault**: The defendant caused the victim to apprehend imminent unlawful force
- **Mens rea of assault**: The defendant *indented* or was *Cunningham*-reckless that the victim would apprehend *imminent unlawful force*
- **Actus reus of battery**: The defendant touched or applied force to the victim
- **Mens rea of battery**: The defendant intended or was Cunningham-reckless as to touching or applying force to the victim

Since both offences appear very similar, we need to look at common law to give us some practical guidance.

An **assault** (by beating) can be defined as:

- Unlawful force on the victim (*Fagan v Metropolitan Police Commissioner* [1969])
- There must be imminent harm or fear of harm
- Words such as harassing telephone calls or text messages (including silent phone calls – *Ireland* [1998])
- Emails which include threats of violence

**Battery** can be defined as:

- Actually hitting the victim
- Unlawful touching or spitting

The *Protection from Harassment Act 1997* also incorporates verbal assaults and threats, whereby racially aggravated harassment becomes an either-way offence.

Section 47 of *Offences Against the Person Act 1861* states that ABH is an either-way offence and can be tried at the magistrates' or the crown court, depending on the seriousness of harm caused. Whether the victim was pushed or kicked, for example, rests in common law, such as *Roberts* [1972]. If the offence is tried at the crown court the maximum punishment can be five years in custody.

- **Actus reus of ABH** (s. 47 OAPA): The defendant must commit an assault or battery which causes the victim to suffer actual bodily harm
- **Mens rea**: The defendant must *intend* or be *Cunningham*-reckless as to the assault or battery. There is no need to show that the defendant intended or foresaw actual bodily harm (*Savage and Parmenter* [1992]

The House of Lords in *Ireland* [1998] held that psychological harm in the form of silent or harassing phone calls can amount to actual bodily harm. Medical and/or psychiatric evidence must be provided.

The definition of ABH-type offences can be very broad:

- Bruising or grazing
- Psychological or mental harm
- It is more than mere touching (such as battery)
- Causing tenderness to the skin
- Injury to the body, internal organs or the brain

## Malicious wounding (GBH) ('grievous bodily harm' – s. 20 OAPA)

In order to distinguish a section 47 from the more serious section 20 offence, the jury has to be convinced that the accused had a large degree of foreseeability of harm (*mens rea*) which then comprises 'maliciousness' and would make up the section 20 offence of 'wounding' (Lord Lane CJ in *Sullivan* [1984]).

'Wounding' means to 'break the continuity of the skin' (*JJC v Eisenhower* [1984]). A rupture of a blood vessel is not 'wounding', but the breaking of the outer skin is (*M'Loughlin* [1838]). Wounding usually involves an unlawful act such as the carrying or use of an illegal and dangerous weapon in public (knife or gun).

- **Actus reus of GBH** (s. 20 OAPA): The defendant unlawfully either i) wounded or ii) inflicted grievous bodily harm to the victim
- **Mens rea**: The defendant *foresaw* that the victim might suffer some harm. It is not necessary to show that the defendant intended or foresaw that the victim would suffer grievous bodily harm.

GBH (malicious wounding) can include:

- Breaking of the outer layer of the skin (*Savage and Parmenter* [1992])
- Injury inside the mouth
- Drawing blood
- Serious psychological harm (*Chan Fook* [1994])
- Infecting someone with HIV through unprotected sexual intercourse (*Dica* [2004]) (see below)
- Setting a pit bull dog on a person

The case that made modern legal history is *Dica* Nr 1 [2004] and Nr 2 [2005], where a Somalian refugee who knowingly infected two women with the human immunodeficiency virus (HIV), became the first person in more than a century since *Clarence* [1888] to be convicted of inflicting biological grievous bodily harm.

In *Dica* Nr 1, the defendant was found guilty of 'wounding' (s. 20 OAPA 1861) by infecting two women with HIV through having consensual sexual intercourse. The Court of Appeal allowed his defence in that both complainants had *consented* to sexual intercourse, thereby consenting to the risk of contracting the disease. A retrial was ordered. At his second trial, Dica (Nr 2, 2005) was once again convicted; his application for leave to appeal to the House of Lords for the second time was granted.

*Dica* sends a confusing message. Is it reckless to conceal one's condition of HIV when the complainant nevertheless gives his or her informed consent to sexual intercourse and therefore to the risk of contracting the HIV virus? What is the difference between a section 20 and a section 18 charge in this type of case?

The answer lies in the question of informed consent: did the defendant honestly believe that his sexual partner (the victim) was aware of his condition? Is it then open to the jury to infer that the defendant was reckless, if the victim did not, in fact, consent? Some answers are provided in *Konzani* [2005]:

- The defendant is guilty of **GBH** (s. 20 OAPA 1861) by having sexual relations if he causes the victim to suffer some harm, that is the victim becomes HIV positive and the victim has not given consent to run the risk of becoming HIV positive
- The defendant is guilty of **GBH with intent** (s. 18 OAPA 1861) if he *intends* to cause the victim to suffer GBH as a result of sexual intercourse, even if the victim consents to running the risk of acquiring the HIV virus

In this respect you may wish to consult the case of *Brown* [1994] which involved sexual rituals performed by consenting homosexual adults in the course of sado-masochistic practices and convictions of assault and wounding.

### Malicious wounding with intend to cause grievous bodily harm (GBH with intent) (s. 18 OAPA)

What then is the difference between a section 20 and a section 18 offence? The answer lies in the word 'intent'. It has been argued that a person who *intends* to cause serious bodily harm must also realise that there is a risk of causing death and will be guilty of a section 18 offence. The jury must be sure that there was an intention to do serious injury and that the defendant's actions might have killed the victim. If the jury finds the defendant guilty of GBH with intent he will be sentenced to life imprisonment.

- ***Actus reus* of GBH with intent s. 18 OAPA**: The defendant unlawfully wounded or caused grievous bodily harm to the victim
- ***Mens rea***: Either i) the defendant intended to cause grievous bodily harm; or ii) the defendant intended to resist or prevent the lawful arrest or detention of any person

GBH with intent (s. 18 OAPA) can include:

- The injury must be 'directly' inflicted
- Breaking bones
- Stabbing
- Loss of an ?
- Stabbing with an AIDS-infected needle
- Shot gun wound
- The defendant had the *intention* to resist arrest

In all cases, there must be the *intent* present as part of the wounding offence.

## 5.5 ____ The *Sexual Offences Act 2003* and its implications ____

The aim of the *Sexual Offences Act 2003* (SOA) was to strengthen and modernise the law relating to sexual offences. The 2003 Act is split into two parts, the first devoted to sexual offences, creating new offences and widening the scope of existing ones, and the second covering offenders with an emphasis on the protection of vulnerable individuals. The Act came into force on 1 May 2004 and contains over 50 sexual offences; here are just a few examples and you will find more in Chapter 9.3:

- Trafficking persons into, within and out of the country for the purposes of sexual exploitation
- Preventing children from being abused through prostitution and pornography
- Protecting vulnerable persons with a mental disorder from sexual abuse (e.g. by care workers)
- Voyeurism, which criminalises those who observe for sexual gratification people engaged in a private act who do not consent to being observed
- Exposure, where a man or woman exposes their genitalia with intent to cause alarm or distress
- Committing any offence with intent to commit a sexual offence
- Engaging in sexual activity in a public lavatory

_____ Rape _____

Lord Hope of Craighead described rape as, '*the most humiliating, distressing and cynical of crimes*' (*R v A* [2001]). Rape can be accompanied by acts of extreme violence, such as punching in the face or threats to kill. The sole issue for the prosecution in rape cases is whether it can be proved that the complainant did *not* consent to sexual intercourse. Section 74 SOA 2003 provides a statutory definition on the issue of consent:

If s/he agrees by choice and has the freedom and capacity to make that choice.

With the new definition under s. 1 *Sexual Offences Act 2003* (SOA), rape is redefined to include penetration of the mouth as well as penetration of the vagina or anus by the penis. Rape is indictable only and carries a maximum penalty of life imprisonment. The crime is constituted by proof of the fact of sexual intercourse with a person, who, at the time of the intercourse, did not consent to it, accompanied by proof that at the time the defendant either knew that the person did not consent to the intercourse or was reckless as to whether that person consented to it. The absence of consent is, in these cases, the crucial issue. This is a question of fact, which must be resolved in the light of the evidence and is for the jury to decide.

The clear definition of 'consent' in relation to rape then refers to the 'capacity to make that choice' to have sexual intercourse or in the context of voluntariness. This then becomes more complex when rape is alleged after the complainant has voluntarily consumed alcohol and then entered into a sexual encounter. Or if there has been an allegation of date-rape or spiked drinks – what does consent mean then? The jury should be directed as follows:

- A person consents if s/he agrees by choice to the sexual activity and has the freedom and mental capacity to make that choice
- All the circumstances at the time of the offence must be looked at in determining whether the defendant reasonably believed that the complainant consented
- Did the victim only agree to have sexual activity because s/he was subject to threats or fear of serious harm, unconscious, drugged, abducted, or unable to communicate because of a physical disability?

In rape trials, the jury must be given a clear direction as to the meaning of 'capacity' in the given circumstances (*Bree* [2007]).

───────── Child sex abuse ──────────────────────────────────

The law prior to the 2003 SOA was very confusing in relation to sexual offences involving children under the age of 16 and those under the age of 14. You may wish to compare two conflicting cases: *R v K* [2001] and *B v DPP* [2000]. In *B v DPP*, the House of Lords ruled that the offence under section 1 of the *Indecency with Children Act 1960*, of 'incitement of a child under 14 to an act of gross indecency', does not carry a strict liability offence. This meant that a defendant who mistakenly believed, albeit unreasonably, that the child is over the age of 14 was entitled to an acquittal. This now means that any sexual offence with a young person under the age of 16 is an offence. This case involved a sexual offence against a 13-year-old girl by a 15-year-old boy on a bus. A unanimous House of Lords' decision quashed B's conviction, stating that nothing in the 1960 Act displaced the common law presumption of *mens rea* so as to create an offence of strict liability. The boy had genuinely believed – though mistakenly – that the girl was at least 14.

The *Sexual Offences Act 2003* closed this loophole where the defendant would usually argue that he genuinely believed that the girl was over the age of sixteen. This defence had previously been allowed to those accused of 'child rape' and they escaped proper punishment (*Re. K* [2001]). Now, *any* sexual intercourse with a child under 13 is treated as statutory rape.

## 5.6 ___ General defences

There are a number of defences available to the accused for specific offences. These defences exist on the one hand to excuse the criminal conduct (duress), whilst on the other to provide a justification for such conduct (self-defence). They include:

- Self-defence
- Intoxication
- Duress
- Insanity
- Automatism

### ___ Self-defence (murder and assault) ___

This defence is also known as a 'private defence', usually raised to prevent a crime, like an assault. The prosecution has the burden of satisfying the jury to ensure that the defendant was *not* acting in self-defence, as per *Martin*:

---

### *R v Martin (Anthony Edward)* [2003] QB 1.

Tony Martin shot and killed 16-year-old Fred Barras and wounded the teenager's accomplice Brendan Fearon at his Norfolk farm 'Bleak House' in August 1999. Both intruders had broken into Martin's isolated farmhouse for the purpose of burglary. Martin, fearful of crime and a recluse, had told his friends that he was prepared to defend his property; he had rigged lookout posts in trees and had a stair removed as a makeshift booby trap.

The jury decided that Martin had not defended his property but had taken the law into his own hands by using excessive force to shoot the intruders. Martin was convicted of murder in April 2000. He appealed.

The Court of Appeal decided that Martin had been suffering from paranoid personality disorder and his murder sentence was converted into manslaughter by diminished responsibility in October 2001. Martin's life sentence was reduced to five years' imprisonment. Martin, 55 at the time, had served 18 months inside.

---

Following the ruling in *Martin*, Lord Chief Justice Woolf issued the following sentencing guidelines. You may find these useful when deciding on a similar problem question in an exam regarding self-defence:

- Did the defendant kill the victim by defending himself or other?
- Did the victim pose an immediate threat?
- Was the threat unjustified? and if so
- Did the defendant use reasonable force? or
- Did the defendant use disproportionate and unreasonable force?
- Was the use of force necessary?
- The jury should take into account the physical characteristics of the defendant and his mental state

The 'reasonable man test' must be applied and if you decide that the accused used unreasonable and excessive force you should find the defendant guilty of murder (see *Clegg* [1995] – Chapter 3.7).


_____ Intoxication _____

Drunkenness in itself is not that problematic: the law is quite clear that 'drunken intent is nevertheless an intent' and juries are directed on this basis (*Sheehan and Moore* [1975]). If successful, a defence of intoxication negates the element of *mens rea*. The issue becomes more complex when intoxication is inextricably linked to other defences. Criminal law recognises and distinguishes between two types of intoxication:

- **Voluntary intoxication** – getting drunk or taking illegal drugs
- **Involuntary intoxication** – spiked drinks

It gets more complicated when we are dealing with crimes of intent and elements of recklessness. In 'date rape', for instance, a drug or strong alcoholic spirit is administered illegally to a person's drink which makes them more amenable to sexual intercourse. This means that the victim appears to have consented to sexual intercourse at the time. The jury will then have to decide whether under sober circumstances the victim may not have consented (see Herring, 2007, 172 ff). The leading case on intoxication is *Majewski* (1977) further extended to intoxication by drugs in *Kingston* [1994].

Voluntary (self-induced) intoxication is defined as follows:

- Voluntary intoxication cannot be used as a defence to crimes of basic intent, such as an assault (*Majewski* [1977])
- Where the defendant says that he had consumed a lot of alcohol but knew what he was doing, the defendant has the *mens rea* to commit the offence (*McKnight and Groark* [1999])
- Voluntary intoxication can be used as defence to crimes of specific intent, such as murder, but

- If the *mens rea* exists the defendant is guilty as charged despite the intoxication
- The jury need not be given a direction as to intoxication in specific intent cases in which alcohol played a part (*McKnight* [2000])

*Drunken mistake (murder and manslaughter)*   In *Hatton*, the Court of Appeal confirmed that a defendant could not rely on a belief of a 'drunken mistake' when being attacked:

---

### R v Hatton (Jonathan) [2005] EWCA 2951

Hatton, who had drunk more than 20 pints of beer, killed the victim, who was found with seven blows from a sledgehammer. Hatton stated that he could not recall the victim's death but that he had a vague recollection that a stick fashioned in the shape of a Samurai sword had been involved. Hatton raised the self-defence, based on his own mistaken belief that he thought he was being attacked by an SAS officer (as the victim had earlier pretended to be) with a Samurai sword. The judge ruled that self-defence was not available to the defendant to rely on a mistake induced by drunkenness and the jury convicted him of murder.

The Court of Appeal affirmed *O'Grady* [1987] that an act done in self-defence when the defendant is heavily intoxicated may well be regarded as a grossly negligent mistake sufficient to find liability for manslaughter. Hatton's appeal was dismissed.

---

When you are tackling an exam question on intoxication, you should first work out whether the crime committed is one of basic or specific intent; then take the following step-by-step approach:

**Step 1**   Did the defendant realise that his act might cause *some* injury to a person or that some property may be destroyed?

**Step 2**   Would the defendant have realised this had he not been taking drugs or drink?

**Step 3**   Did the defendant have the necessary intention because of drink? (*Alden and Jones* [2001])

Then your conclusion should be:

- Self-induced intoxication (alcohol or drugs) is no defence to crimes of basic intent (e.g. assault; rape)
- Self-induced intoxication is a defence to crimes of specific intent (murder)
- It is not a defence to say that the accused would not have behaved in this way had he not been taking drugs or been drinking or that he failed to foresee the consequences of his act because he had been taking drugs or been drinking

Your final argument should be: did the drunkenness cause the mistake? Would the defendant have made the same mistake, had he been sober? If the prosecution can prove that 'but for' the intoxication, the defendant would not have made the mistake, the defendant is guilty of the crime (*O'Grady* [1987]).

Simply put, duress means: 'I had no choice but to commit the crime.' Duress is a defence to all crimes *except* murder and attempted murder (*Pommell* [1995]). Duress can be available, for instance, in relation to hijacking aircraft (see *Abdul-Hussain* below). If successful, a plea of duress exonerates the defendant altogether (not like with provocation where a successful plea reduces the charge from murder to manslaughter). The duress defence has become increasingly controversial, due to the fact that the courts have taken an inconsistent approach (*DPP v Lynch* [1975] AC 653; *Willer* [1987] 83 Cr App R 225; *Conway* [1989] QB 290).

In the absence of any statutory codification, the courts have developed the defence of duress on a case-by-case basis (*Howe* [1987]; *Hurst* [1995]). The most controversial case concerns Shiite Muslims who hijacked an aircraft when fleeing from Iraq. In *Abdul-Hussain* [1999], the jury had to consider the terror induced in the innocent passengers and weigh this up proportionately to the plight of the hijackers. The defence of duress was allowed and the defendants acquitted.

Generally, the courts will only allow the defence of duress where imminent peril of death or serious injury to the defendant, or those to whom he has responsibility, is an essential element of duress (*Cole* [1994]). Duress of circumstances can be seen as a third or residual category of necessity, along with self-defence and duress by threats.

When tackling an exam question on duress, you need to stress that this defence is only available where the defendant's criminal conduct has been *directly* caused by the threats which he seeks to rely on. These threats must be directed against the defendant or someone close to him (*Wright* [2000]). When faced with a problem question on duress, you may wish to follow these step-by-step guidelines:

**Step 1**   Was the defendant driven or forced to act as he did by threats which he genuinely believed that if he did not commit the offence, his family would be seriously harmed or killed? If you are sure that he was not forced by threats to act as he did, the defence fails and he is guilty. But if you are not sure go on to step 2

**Step 2**   Would a reasonable person of the defendant's age and background have been forced to act as the defendant did? If you are sure that a reasonable person would not have been forced to act as the defendant did, then the defence fails and he is guilty. If you are not sure, then go on to step 3

**Step 3**   Could the defendant have avoided acting as he did without harm coming to him or his family or immediate other? If you are sure he could, the defence fails and he is guilty. If you are not sure go on to step 4

**Step 4**   Did the defendant voluntarily put himself in the position in which he knew he was likely to be subjected to threats? If you are sure he did, the defence fails and he is guilty. If you are not sure, he is *not* guilty.

The defence of 'necessity' has a close affinity with duress, where the force or compulsion is exerted not by human threats but by extraneous circumstances. For example, if a defendant does the lesser of two evils, he may be able to rely on the defence of necessity.

## Insanity (fitness to plead)

An individual, who lacks control over his criminal actions, is regarded in law as 'insane' and is generally not regarded as being responsible for the consequences of his actions. A successful defence of insanity requires the satisfaction of the *M'Naghten*-rules[3] in that the defect of reason either caused the defendant to be unaware of the nature of his act or not to know the act was wrong. If so he incurs no criminal liability and cannot stand trial. The jury must then decide, given all the medical and psychiatric evidence, whether the accused suffered from a 'disability of mind'. The reverse burden of proof is on the defence on the balance of probabilities, meaning the defence must show that it is more likely than not that the defendant was unfit to stand trial.

In such cases, the jury should ask itself:

- Can the defendant challenge a juror to whom he might have cause to object?
- Can the defendant give instructions to his lawyers?
- Can the defendant agree or disagree with what the witnesses have to say?

If the defendant can do all of these things, the jury must find the defendant 'fit to plead', that is he can be tried by judge and jury. The mere fact that the defendant is highly abnormal or seemingly not capable of acting in his own best interests is not conclusive that he is unfit to be tried, although it is a factor which the jury may take into account.

The question was put to the jury in the Yorkshire Ripper case, where Peter Sutcliffe stood trial in 1981, charged with the murder of 13 women in Yorkshire between 1975 and 1980 (*Sutcliffe* [1982]). At his trial, the jury was presented with the psychiatric evidence on Sutcliffe and they refused to accept his plea of insanity. Sutcliffe stood trial and was found guilty of murdering the women. However, Sutcliffe was sectioned post conviction and is still at Broadmoor special secure hospital.

Ian Huntley, the Soham murderer, also claimed mental incapacity to stand trial for the killing of two ten-year-old girls when he was due to appear before Peterborough Magistrates' Court on 21 August 2002. Under the provisions of the *Mental Health Act 1983*, the police detained Huntley, then 28, for the maximum 28 days, during which his mental condition was assessed by psychiatrists at Rampton high-security hospital. Huntley was found 'sane' and stood trial and was found guilty of the murder of Holly Wells and Jessica Chapman in December 2003. He was sentenced to a minimum 40-year life sentence by Mr Justice Moses under new whole-life tariff of the *Criminal Justice Act 2003* because the offences involved a high degree of sadistic and sexual premeditation.

────────── Automatism ──────────────────────────────────

Automatism describes an involuntary criminal act and distinguishes between self-induced (insane) automatism and non-self induced or 'external' automatism. If successful, the latter will lead to a complete acquittal in that the accused could claim his body became that of an automaton.

The evidential burden of proof lies on the defendant (reverse burden of proof) in that he has to prove his state of automatism at the time he committed the offence.

Here follow some example of non-insane automatism (external factors):

- The after-effects of an anaesthetic
- A prescribed drug taken for the first time (e.g. Valium; Prozac)
- The after-effects of hypnosis
- Concussion

*Self-induced 'insane' automatism*   This is where the accused brought about the condition himself. One such example is committing a driving offence whilst suffering a hypoglycaemic fit, knowing that you have diabetes. Only if the defendant can prove that his condition of hypoglycaemia was caused by the wrongful or first time administration of insulin, plus the fact that he had nothing to eat, would this amount to an 'external factor'.

The best possible legal definition is provided by the Court of Appeal in the *Attorney General's Reference (No. 2 of 1992)* that automatism must include a 'complete loss of voluntary control':

---

### Attorney-General's Reference (No. 2 of 1992) QB 91.

A lorry driver who had driven for 12 hours some 343 miles without stopping had veered onto the hard shoulder of the motorway and crashed into a stationary van. Two people were killed. At his trial for manslaughter by reckless driving expert evidence showed that the truck driver had only braked at the very last minute. The accused claimed automatism as his defence, backed by medical expert Professor Brown, who argued that he had driven 'without awareness' in a 'trance-like state'. The jury acquitted him. But the Attorney-General referred the case to the Court of Appeal for clarification.

Lord Taylor of Gosforth CJ referred to a number of automatism cases which had failed in their claim of automatism, referring to 'insane' or 'internal' automatism (*Bratty* [1963] or *Sullivan* [1984] on epilepsy; *Hennessy* [1989] and *Burgess* [1991] on sleepwalking).

---

The Court of Appeal reversed the original trial judge's decision: 'The learned recorder ought not to have left the issue of automatism to the jury', because there must be the requirement of *complete loss of self-control*. In the lorry driver's case, there had been evidence of some awareness of what was happening, therefore, he had some control over his actions. He was found guilty of reckless driving.

In summary, the defence of automatism has very narrow limits as a form of defence. Criminal acts committed must be medically proven by the accused of being unconscious, either during spasms, sudden reflex actions or convulsions.

## 5.7 ___ Case study ___

___ *Woolmington v Director of Public Prosecution* [1935] AC 462 ___

In *Woolmington* the House of Lords formulated with great rhetoric that the fundamental principle in criminal law concerning the burden of proof lies with the prosecution to prove the prisoner's guilt beyond reasonable doubt (unless the accused raises the *M'Naghten* insanity defence – see above). Viscount Sankey LC pronounced the 'golden thread' theory on behalf of the House of Lords in this case, in that the Crown must prove beyond reasonable doubt that:

1  death resulted from a voluntary act of the accused (the *actus reus*), and
2  malice aforethought (*mens rea*) of the accused was established.

Bear in mind, when 21-year-old Reginald Woolmington was found guilty of the murder of his young wife, Britain still had the death penalty (see also Chapter 8.6).

### Facts of the case

Reginald Woolmington was 21 years old and his wife Violet was 17 years old when she was killed by her husband on 10 December 1934. They had known each other for some time and on 25 August 1934 they were married. Violet gave birth on 14 October that year. Reginald was a farm labourer and the couple lived at Castleton, near Sherborne, Dorset, on the farm of Woolmington's employer, Mr Cheeseman. On 22 November 1934, Woolmington's wife left him and went to live with her mother, Lilian Smith, a widow, at 24 Newtown, Milborne Port.

On the morning of 10 December 1934, Violet's aunt, Mrs Daisy Brine, of 25 Newtown, heard voices around 9.15 a.m. coming from next door, at 24, when

*(Continued)*

she was hanging out her washing. Next door, 24 Newtown, lived her sister; she also knew that Violet had moved back there with her baby to live with her mother. Mrs Brine recognised the voice of Reginald Woolmington saying: 'Are you going to come back home?' – there was no answer. Then Mrs Brine heard the sound of a gun. Upon that she looked out of the front window and saw Reginald Woolmington leave No. 24, get on his bicycle and ride away. Mrs Brine went into No. 24 and found her niece lying on the mat. She had been shot through the heart. Reginald Woolmington was charged with the murder of his wife.

## Woolmington's first trial at Taunton Somerset Assizes, 23 January 1935

Woolmington told the jury that he had had a sleepless night on 9 December and decided to frighten his wife into obedience by threatening to shoot himself. The next day, 10 December, he went to the farm around 8.20 a.m. and took a gun belonging to Mr Cheeseman. He sawed off part of the barrels and loaded the gun with the two cartridges. His wife Violet opened the front door. She was alone and they went into the back room. Woolmington said: 'Are you coming back or not, Vi?' but got no answer. He told her, if she would not come back to him he would shoot himself; he lifted the gun from under his coat. The gun went off and she fell to the ground.

A note by Woolmington was later found; it read: *'Good bye all. It is agonies to carry on any longer. I have kept true hoping she would return; this is the only way out. They ruined me and I'll have my revenge. May God forgive me for doing this but it is the Best thing. Ask Jess to call for the money paid on motor bike (Wed.). Her mother is no good on this earth but have no more cartridges only 2 one for her and one for me. I am of a sound mind now. Forgive me for all trouble caused. Good bye. I love Violet with all my heart Reg.'*

Mister Justice Finlay directed the Taunton jury that they must be satisfied *'beyond any reasonable doubt'* that Woolmington killed his wife. The jury could not agree a verdict and a retrial was ordered.

## Woolmington's second trial at Bristol Assizes, 14 February 1935

Summing up, Mister Justice Swift directed the jury to consider 'wilful murder' and they found Woolmington guilty. He was sentenced to death and appealed. The Court of Criminal Appeal refused his application on 18 March 1935. But the Attorney General appealed, arguing that the case involved an exceptional point of law which needed to be addressed in the public interest.

> **House of Lords:** Their Lordships ruled that the judge had misdirected the [Taunton] jury: *'It might have been better had the learned judge who tried the case said to the jury that if they entertained reasonable doubt whether they could accept his explanation they should either acquit him altogether or convict him of manslaughter only.'*

Their Lordships re-examined all the facts in this case, including the controversy surrounding the suicide note left by Woolmington before he had confronted his wife, and at the point of his arrest on 10 December at 7.30 p.m. he had chosen to say nothing. The trial judge had considered 'Foster's Crown Law' of 1762 on the direction and discourse of homicide. Their Lordships ruled that Sir Michael Foster's article had possibly misled the original judge and that Foster's law on homicide was not 'correct law' which led the trial judge in *Woolmington* to imply to the jury that the accused had used 'barbarous and unintentional violence'. The trial judge's reference to the jury to Woolmington's express and implied malice then meant that if a man acts calculated to kill and actually does kill, that, in turn, was evidence of malice or intent.

The House of Lords held, summed up by Viscount Lord Sankey, that the onus of proving the prisoner's guilt must lie on the prosecution and that the defendant has the right to adduce any evidence, but does not have to prove anything. The jury must convict only beyond reasonable doubt which is the standard of proof in a criminal trial (known as the 'golden rule'). The House of Lords allowed the Attorney General's appeal. Woolmington's murder conviction and death penalty were quashed, substituted by a manslaughter conviction.

## ■ Exam Questions

In this section you are asked to solve a number of problem questions typical in criminal law exams. Discuss the criminal liability of each perpetrator and the likely outcome in each case scenario.

1  McNab hails a taxi. When it stops, another man, Druleite, gets into the taxi before McNab, yelling: 'Get back, this is my cab!' McNab also leaps into the cab, swearing at Druleite: 'You'll pay for this' – and draws a knife, lunging towards Druleite inside the taxi. Druleite fears for his life, believing that he is about to be stabbed. In a mad panic, Druleite jumps from the taxi, straddles a fence and leaps into the river that runs alongside the road. Druleite can't swim and is swept away by the current. Though he is pulled from the river by a passer-by and taken by ambulance to the nearest hospital, doctors discover that he has suffered permanent brain damage, though he does not die. Discuss the criminal liability of McNab.

2  During a pub fight over their boyfriend, Karin threatens Iram with a beer bottle, then punches her in the face so that Iram's nose is bleeding. Iram, fearing further violence, stumbles backwards, falls and hits her head on a table. Unbeknown to Karin, Iram suffers from a thin skull and dies. Is Karin guilty of Iram's murder?

3  Does the *Woolmington* principle, as set out by Viscount Sankey's 'golden thread' theory, also apply to statutory crimes? Explain by reference to the reverse burden of proof.

Why not research the following cases online:

- *R v Lambert (Steven)* [2002] 2 AC 545
- *Attorney General's Reference (No. 4 of 2004)* [2005] 1 AC 264
- *Sheldrake v DPP* [2005] 1 AC 264

## ■ ■ Further Resources ■

Jonathan Herring's *Criminal Law* (2008) provides a stimulating text with a critical perspective. Case law is made particularly accessible by Herring's engaging writing style. His case referencing is exceptional.

David Ormerod's 2008 edition of *Smith and Hogan's Criminal Law* remains the essential reference guide for students of substantial criminal law.

Frances Heidensohn's *Gender and Justice* (2006) provides key issues of gendered perspectives in criminal justice and the law.

Helena Kennedy's *Eve was framed* (1992) is a must-read for everyone. Baroness Kennedy focuses on the treatment of women in British courts and gives examples of judges' prejudices in rape cases. Her chapter 'Man-slaughter' on the trial of Sarah Thornton is particularly powerful and explains 'battered woman syndrome' very well in relation to a woman's defence of provocation.

## Notes

1  This maxim is found in Sir Edward Cooke's *Institutes of the Law of England*, dating back to the early seventeeth century, but the concept is implicit in the laws of Henry I (1100–1135).

2  *Pretty v UK* [2002] FCR 97; *R (Pretty) v DPP* [2002].

3  In Daniel M'Naghten's case (26 May–19 June 1843), the House of Lords ruled that in all cases of this kind the jurors ought to be told that every man is presumed to be sane and to possess a sufficient degree of reason to be responsible for his crimes, until the contrary be proved to their satisfaction: and that to establish a defence on the ground of insanity, it must be clearly proved that at the time of committing the act the party accused was labouring under such a defect of reason, from disease of the mind, as not to know the nature and quality of the act he was doing, or as not to know that what he was doing was wrong.

# 6

# THE CRIMINAL PROCESS

| **Overview** | |
| --- |

Chapter 6 examines:

- The functions and powers of the police under the *Police and Criminal Evidence Act 1984* (PACE)
- The work of the Scottish police force
- From the RUC to the Northern Irish Police Force
- The charging responsibilities of the Crown Prosecution Service (CPS)
- Mode of trial and bail procedures in the magistrates' courts
- Crown court trial and the function of juries
- Evidential rules on bad character and hearsay
- The work and function of the Serious Organised Crime Agency (SOCA)

What is the criminal process? It links the purpose of the criminal law with the process of inquiry into a crime committed with the rules of evidence, the powers of investigation by the police, the prosecution agencies and finally with the courts (see Ashworth and Redmayne, 2005: 19ff).

What should we expect from the criminal process? Some systems are inquisitorial – like most continental jurisdictions – and some adversarial – like England and Wales. Some systems use juries and some use professional inquisitorial magistrates, like France, Portugal or Italy.

This chapter looks at new forms of policing, from 'incident-oriented', reactive policing to greater local involvement, known as community policing by employing Police Community Support Officers (PCSOs). Mixed-economy policing strategies now offer imaginative solutions to keeping law and order in our pluralist society. Local councils jointly with the police now provide reassurance policing schemes, acknowledging the diversity and multiplicity within our society (more in Chapter 7.2).

This chapter will focus on policing and the criminal process in all three jurisdictions, England and Wales, Scotland and Northern Ireland and highlight recent changes in criminal procedure.

## 6.1 ___ The functions of the Home Office and the Ministry of Justice _____

On 9 May 2007, the Rt Hon Jack Straw MP became Lord Chancellor and Secretary of State for Justice at the new Ministry of Justice. The Rt Hon Baroness (Lady) Scotland of Asthal PC QC became Home Office Minister for Crime Reduction at the Home Office, and was appointed Attorney General in June 2007. Some functions formerly held by the Home Office were transferred to the Ministry of Justice, such as prisons and probation (see Gibson, 2007a and b).

The Ministry of Justice (MOJ) comprises:

- **The National Offender Management Service** (NOMS) – Her Majesty's Prison Service and the National Probation Service (NPS)
- **Youth Justice and the Youth Justice Board** (YJB)
- **The Parole Board**
- **Her Majesty's Inspectorates of Prison and Probation**, Independent Monitoring Boards (IMB), the Prison and Probation Ombudsmen
- **Criminal, civil, family and administrative law**: criminal law and sentencing policy; the Sentencing Guidelines Council and the Sentencing Advisory Panel and the Law Commission
- **The Office for Criminal Justice Reform**: comprising the Ministry of Justice, the Home Office and the Attorney General's Office
- **Her Majesty's Courts Service**: administration of the civil, family and criminal courts in England and Wales
- **The UK Tribunals Service**
- **The Community Legal Service** and Legal Services Commission ('legal aid')
- **The Judicial Appointments Commission**
- **The Privy Council Secretariat**
- **Constitutional affairs**: including electoral reform, human rights and freedom of information.

The Home Office comprises:

- **The Office for Security and Counter-Terrorism**
- **The Crime Reduction and Community Safety Group**
- **The Border and Immigration Agency**
- **The Identity and Passport Service**
- **The Criminal Records Bureau**
- **The Police Service in England and Wales**
- **HM Inspectorate of Constabulary**

## 6.2 ___ Policing in England and Wales _____

Whilst the British 'Bobby' has often been described as the 'secret social service', introduced by Robert Peel in the nineteenth century, 'reassurance' police work today differs substantially from police work of the early twentieth century, undertaken principally by the 'thief catchers' (see Taylor, 1998; Rawlings, 2001). The popular notion of the English Bobby is well depicted in Charles Dickens' novels such as *Bleak House* (1853), where he bases his police characters on the real life inspector Charles Frederick Field of the Bow Street Runners in 1829.

Historically the police sub-culture has been described as a 'canteen' culture, where officers act differently amongst their peers where deals are done 'off the record' (Waddington, 1999: 287–309). McLaughlin (2007) explains how police governance has changed from traditional 'thief catchers' to community policing by Police Community Support Officers (PCSOs). Reiner (2000) demystifies the rise and fall of police legitimacy from the mid-nineteenth century to twentieth century 'cop culture' and how new styles of reassurance policing have made the force more accountable to the popular media. Wilson and Kelling (1982) argued that policing in 'bad' neighbourhoods should be based on a clear understanding of the connection between order-maintenance and crime prevention. In his view the best way to fight crime was to fight the disorder that precedes it and to 'mend the broken windows' (see Chapter 1.1). This analysis implies that if disorderly behaviour in public places is controlled, then a significant drop in serious crime would follow (see Hopkins Burke, 2005: 31ff).

With the *Crime and Disorder Act 1998* and revised PACE legislation in 2002, policing activity became more targeted towards drug dealing rather than drug addiction because of the strong links between drug use and crime, acquisitional crime (theft and robbery) and drug abuse. By 2007, around three-quarters of crack and heroin users claimed they committed crime to feed their habit. Due to the complex nature and problems related to drug misuse and crime, the government tried to find more integrated solution strategies in its criminal justice policies in order to deliver a more coordinated service involving education, intelligence and enforcement, social and economic policy and health (see Wilson et al., 1998).

Situated at the gateway to the criminal justice process, policing today has a major impact on what becomes defined as 'priority' crime, that is, which offences are prioritised and which sections of the community are portrayed as 'dangerous' or 'troublesome'. You may well ask, which areas of the community are 'over policed' (see Bowling and Phillips, 2002: 128–9)?

Policing today can be summarised as dealing with:

- Responses to crime
- Maintaining public order
- Crowd control
- Patrolling public spaces
- Reassurance policing
- Intelligence gathering
- Security issues and the prevention of terrorism

Hopkins Burke (2004) concludes that policing in our contemporary society has to be a finely struck balance between 'soft' and 'hard' policing: from Bobby on the beat to machine gun carrier at Heathrow Airport, especially after the terrorism attacks of 9/11 and the London bombings of 7 July 2005 and attempted attacks on 21 July 2005 (2004: 242ff). Crawford et al. (2005) argue that we now live in a society governed by 'plural policing', part of governmental penal policy with ever-changing law enforcement legislation.

Today's police force has to be more accountable whereby each force is measured by 'key performance indicators' (KPI) as management performance tools and targets. Police KPIs, for instance, deal with 'clear-up rates', where a suspect is caught and charged. Most forces' clear-up rates remain very low where only about a quarter of suspects are caught and charged each year; some forces' clear-up rates are as low as 10 per cent (see McLaughlin, 2007).

Each of the 43 regular police forces in England and Wales is regulated by a Police Authority, with the London Metropolitan Police (the Met) being overseen by the Home Office. Though the British police have been one of the few remaining forces in the world not to carry guns, this tradition is fast disappearing. Each force now has trained firearms squads as part of their critical response teams. All forces are subject to inspections by HM Inspectors of Constabulary (HMIC), who report to the Home Secretary and whose reports are published. Each force also has a Special Constabulary, a part-time volunteer force with full policing powers under PACE.

_____ The *Police and Criminal Evidence Act 1984* (PACE) _____

The main idea behind the introduction of the *Police and Criminal Evidence Act 1984* (known as PACE), which came into force in 1988, was to modernise police legislation and regulate the way police constables conducted themselves in public, particularly with regard to stop and search and arrest procedures. PACE and its codes of practice are key elements of the framework of legislation providing the police with the powers they need to combat crime. PACE dictates when a suspect is stopped, searched or questioned in public and each police constable must keep a record of this.

In summary, the principal idea behind PACE was to strike the right balance between the powers of the police and the rights and freedoms of the public. The amended version of the codes came into effect on 24 July 2006 with new legislation such as the *Serious Organised Crime and Police Act* 2005, the *Drugs Act 2005* and supplemented further by the *Terrorism Act 2006*.

The PACE Code presently are as follows:

- **Code A** deals with the exercise by police officers of statutory powers to stop and search a person, or a vehicle, without first making an arrest. It also deals with the need for a police officer to make a record of a stop or encounter

- **Code B** deals with police powers to search premises and to seize and retain property found on premises and persons
- **Code C** sets out the requirements for the detention, treatment and questioning of suspects not related to terrorism in police custody by police officers (e.g. custody records)
- **Code D** concerns the main methods used by the police to identify people in connection with the investigation of offences and the keeping of accurate and reliable criminal records (e.g. ID Parades)
- **Code E** deals with the tape recording of interviews with suspects in the police station
- **Code F** deals with the visual recording and sound of interviews with suspects at the police station
- **Code G** deals with statutory powers of arrest (s. 24 PACE, as amended by s. 110 *Serious Organised Crime and Police Act 2005*)
- **Code H** sets out the requirements for the detention, treatment and questioning of suspects related to terrorism in police custody by police officers

## 6.3 ___ Community policing

Wilson and Kelling's 'broken windows' paradigm of the early 1980s was once again pursued in the late 1990s by the American sociologist Amitai Etzioni, who linked the theory to the phenomenon of 'fear of crime' (see Chapter 1.1). Etzioni's research examined the notion of what makes a 'good society', relating to Etzioni's (*The New Golden Rule*-1997), arguing that advanced Western industrialised capitalist societies suffer from 'rampant moral confusion and social anarchy', because individuals have been given too much freedom and not enough responsibilities.

A staunch defender of communitarianism,[1] Etzioni was preoccupied with the individual's rights and his social responsibilities. He claimed that youth crime, for instance, was created by a 'parenting deficit', which prevents 'effective personality formation' of children whom he called the 'kennel kids'. Arguably, Etzioni's communitarianism theory formed the basis for legislation, such as the *Crime and Disorder Act 1998*, promoting community justice and welfare by empowering local authorities with policing and prosecution powers and increasing community policing, thereby improving the local and environmental quality of life (see Home Office, 2004b).

The *Criminal Justice Act 2003* introduced new measures which can be issued by police constables, such as the 'Penalty Notice of Disorder' (PNDs) or 'Conditional Cautions' for offences which can be dealt with by on the spot fines. They are targeted at low level offending, such as drunk and disorderly behaviour or minor shoplifting to a value not exceeding £200. PNDs usually amount to an £80 on the spot fine. Between January and September 2005, 97,297 PNDs were issued by the police, of which 14,062 (14 per cent) were issued for retail theft of goods (Sentencing Guidelines Council, 24 August 2006).

Conditional cautions are used in suitable cases where the defendant admits guilt. Offenders who are given a conditional caution have to comply with specific requirements, such as 'Acceptable Behaviour Contracts' (ABCs), which require compliance with rehabilitative or reparative conditions as an alternative to prosecution (see Chapter 7.2).

The *Police and Justice Act 2006* introduced further safer communities concepts by driving forward key elements of a government police reform programme, including measures such as:

- The 'National Policing Improvement Agency' (NPIA) which replaced 'Centrex', the police training and development unit
- Increased powers for Police Community Support Officers (PCSOs) to tackle anti-social behaviour and low level crime
- New police powers to stop, search and question *any* person or vehicle in *any* area of an airport, where Police Constables (PCs) have reasonable grounds to suspect that criminal activity has, or is about to take place
- 'Crime and Disorder Reduction Partnerships' (CDRPs), 'Community Safety Partnerships' in Wales and 'Community Call for Action' teams, to tackle vehicle crime, anti-social behaviour and substance misuse, including extended powers to Youth Offending Teams, local councils and social landlords (*Anti-Social Behaviour Act 2003*)

## 6.4 ___ Policing in Scotland

Scotland's first constables were appointed in 1617 during the reign of James VI, though 'burgh' police forces were not established until the nineteenth century, largely replacing 'town guards' made up of ordinary citizens or retired soldiers under the *Burgh Police (Scotland) Act 1833*.

The *Police (Scotland) Act 1967* provided for the sharing of legal responsibility for policing between Scottish Ministers, police authorities and Chief Constables and from 1969 onwards, the Scottish Crime Squad provided a ready means for tackling major crime; in 1986, a dedicated drugs unit was added to the squad, with branches in Glasgow and Edinburgh. Extensive police restructuring followed in 1996 by the Scottish Office which incorporated the Scottish Crime Squad into the National Criminal Intelligence Service (NCIS).

Since the inception of the Scottish Parliament in 1999, a tripartite arrangement exists for the accountability of the Scottish Police Service with most police powers and functions devolved to the Scottish Parliament (see Chapter 3.1). Six regional Joint Police Boards (police authorities) are responsible for setting police budgets and chief constables are responsible for the operational aspects of policing within their force areas. Areas for which legislative responsibility remains with the UK Government at Westminster include national security, terrorism, firearms and drugs.

## 6.5 ___ Policing in Northern Ireland

Policing in Northern Ireland has changed dramatically over recent years after the Belfast Agreement in 1998. In 2001, the Royal Ulster Constabulary (RUC) ceased to exist and the Police Service of Northern Ireland (PSNI) came about. Smyth and Ellison (1999) provide a sound historical background surrounding the controversies of policing in the province. Here follow some of the main policing events:

- 1905 – Arthur Griffith forms *Sinn Féin*; Southern Ireland is still part of the UK. The party wants Irish independence and refuses 'Home Rule'
- 1919 – 'Irish Republican Army' (IRA) is formed by Michael Collins
- 1922 – the Royal Irish Constabulary (RIC) is abolished
- 'Garda Siochana' (Civic Guards) in Southern Ireland
- Royal Ulster Constabulary (RUC) in the Northern Province
- 1960s – increase of IRA activity in the North
- 1969 – Scarman Report recommends the reorganisation of policing in Northern Ireland
- Home Secretary James Calaghan sends British troops to Northern Ireland (the Ulster Defence Regiment – UDR)
- The RUC 'Reserve' becomes an auxiliary police force
- The Patten Report 1999 recommends a new police force

In June 2003, a Policing Board, the Police Ombudsman's Office and 29 District Policing Partnerships were put in place under the *Police (Northern Ireland) Act 2000*. Lord Clyde became the Justice Oversight Commissioner (JOC) (see Barker, 2006). The workings of the RUC came under close scrutiny when the Northern Irish Police Ombudsman, Nuala O'Loan, published her report on 22 January 2007. The Report focused on the period of 1991 to 2003 and specifically on the murder of six Catholics and four Protestants in the province. The Ombudsman's report concluded that there had been long-standing collusion between the UK Special Branch police officers and members of the loyalist para-military Ulster Volunteer Force (UVF). Between them they had carried out at least 16 murders plus at least a thousand serious crimes, an estimated 30 per cent of the total death-toll committed by loyalists during the Troubles.

The Northern Irish police services came under further attack, following the acquittal of Sean Hoey, 38, at the Omagh bomb trial on 20 December 2007 at Belfast Crown Court. Trial judge Mr Justice Weir referred to 'a most disturbing situation' whereby the police forces had handled the aftermath of the Omagh bomb attack in August 1998 in a most atrocious and disorgan-ised fashion. Hoey had faced 58 charges resulting from the Omagh bomb attack.[2]

## 6.6 ___ The Crown Prosecution Service (CPS) in England and Wales _____

The Crown Prosecution Service (CPS) is responsible for prosecuting all crimi-nal cases investigated by the police in England and Wales. The head of the CPS is the Director of Public Prosecutions (DPP). The DPP is answerable to

Parliament through the Attorney General (AG) – the main legal advisor to the government (see Chapter 2.2).

How then are charges selected? Each of the 42 CPS areas – commensurate with police areas – has a Criminal Justice Unit (CJU) where a case worker, together with a prosecutor, examines the evidence in each case file. This must be enough to charge a suspect with a criminal offence. The case is then processed to the first court hearing in the magistrates' court. Charges must:

- Reflect the seriousness and extent of offending
- Give the court adequate powers to sentence
- Enable the case to be presented in a clear and simple way to court

The CPS regularly deals with the following offence types (in alphabetical order):

- Breach of anti-social behaviour orders
- Burglary
- Child abuse
- Child pornography (incl. the internet)
- Criminal damage
- Cross-border crime
- Domestic violence (incl. assault, criminal damage, etc.)
- Firearms offences
- Fraud and forgery
- Hi-tech crime
- Homophobic and hate crimes
- IT-related crime
- Murder
- Racial and religiously motivated crimes
- Rape
- Robbery
- Sexual offences
- Vehicle crimes and theft
- Violence against the person
- Violent disorder offences

_____ Code for Crown Prosecutors and General Principles_____

The CPS is responsible for deciding whether a suspect should be charged with a criminal offence. This advice starts in the police station. Prosecutors must not let their personal views influence their decisions, such as ethnic or national origin, sexual orientation, religious beliefs or political views. Strict guidelines are laid down under the 'Code for Crown Prosecutors' (s. 10 *Prosecution of Offences Act 1985*) including:

- General principles and the decision to prosecute
- Review
- The threshold test
- The full code test
- Chapter of charges
- Diversion from prosecution (simple caution or conditional caution)
- Dealing with youths (up to age 18)
- Mode of trial
- Accepting guilty pleas
- Re-starting a prosecution

*The Threshold Test*   The threshold test is applied where the CPS has not yet obtained full evidence from the police but, because of the seriousness of the allegations, needs to keep the accused on remand in custody (charge without bail). The threshold test requires the crown prosecutor to decide whether there is at least a *reasonable suspicion* that the suspect has committed an offence, and if there is, whether it is in the public interest to charge that suspect. It is applied to those cases in which it would not be appropriate to release a suspect on bail after charge, but the evidence to apply the full code test is not yet available.

There are statutory limits that restrict the time a suspect may remain in police custody before a decision has to be made whether to charge or release the suspect (normally 28 days – this is under review). There will be cases where the suspect in custody presents a *substantial bail risk* if released, but much of the evidence may not be available at the time the charging decision has to be made. The evidential decision in each case will require consideration of a number of factors including:

- the evidence available at the time
- the likelihood and nature of further evidence being obtained
- the reasonableness for believing that evidence will become available
- the time it will take to gather that evidence and the steps being taken to do so
- the impact the expected evidence will have on the case
- the charges that the evidence will support

The full code test must be applied as soon as reasonably practicable (see below).

*The Full Code Test*   The full code test has two stages. The first stage is the evidential test: if the case does not pass the evidential stage it must not go ahead no matter how important or serious. However, Crown Prosecutors must consider the second stage, the public interest test.

In the evidential test stage Crown Prosecutors must be satisfied that there is enough evidence to provide a *realistic prospect of conviction* against the defendant on each charge. This is an objective test which means that a jury or bench of magistrates or judge hearing a case alone, properly directed in accordance with the law, is more likely than not to convict the defendant of the charge alleged. You have learnt in Chapter 5 that a jury or bench of magistrates should only convict if they are satisfied beyond reasonable doubt that the defendant is guilty of the offence. So, what evidence can be used in court? Prosecutors should ask:

1 Is it likely that the evidence will be excluded by the court? Rules of evidence will dictate this; for example, will evidence be excluded because of the way in which it was gathered? If so, is there enough other evidence for a realistic prospect of conviction? Is the evidence reliable?
2 Is there evidence which might support or detract from the reliability of a confession? Is the reliability affected by factors such as the defendant's age, intelligence or level of understanding?
3 What explanation has the defendant given? Will the court believe the evidence as a whole? Does it support an innocent explanation?
4 Is the identity of the defendant in question?
5 Is the witness reliable? Will it weaken the prosecution case?

In the public interest test stage the public interest must be considered in each case where there is enough evidence to provide a realistic prospect of conviction. A prosecution will usually take place unless there are public interest factors tending against prosecution which clearly outweigh those tending in favour, or it appears more appropriate in all the circumstances of the case to divert the person from prosecution (see below). Public interest factors that can affect the decision to prosecute usually depend on the seriousness of the offence or the circumstances of the suspect. The factors that apply will depend on the facts in each case. The more serious the offence, the more likely it is that a prosecution will be needed in the public interest.

Some common public interest factors when a prosecution is likely to be needed include, if:

a a conviction is likely to result in a significant sentence
b a conviction is likely to result in a confiscation or any other order
c a weapon was used or violence was threatened during the commission of the offence
d the offence was committed against a person serving the public, for example, a police or prison officer, or a nurse
e the defendant was in a position of authority or trust, such as a teacher or care assistant
f the evidence shows that the defendant was a ringleader or an organiser of the offence
g there is evidence that the offence was premeditated
h there is evidence that the offence was carried out by a group
i the victim of the offence was vulnerable, has been put in considerable fear, or suffered personal attack, damage or disturbance
j the offence was committed in the presence of, or in close proximity to, a child
k the offence was motivated by any form of discrimination against the victim's ethnic or national origin, disability, sex, religious beliefs, political views or sexual orientation, or the suspect demonstrated hostility towards the victim based on any of those characteristics

l   there is a marked difference between the actual or mental ages of the defendant and the victim, or if there is any element of corruption

m  the defendant's previous convictions or cautions are relevant to the present offence

n   the defendant is alleged to have committed the offence while under an order of the court, such as whilst on bail

o   there are grounds for believing that the offence is likely to be continued or repeated (history of antecedents and bad character)

p   the offence, although not serious in itself, is widespread in the area where it was committed; or

q   a prosecution would have a significant positive impact on maintaining community confidence.

Some common public interest factors when a prosecution is less likely to be needed included where:

a   the court is likely to impose a nominal penalty, such as an absolute discharge

b   the defendant has already been made the subject of a sentence and any further conviction would be unlikely to result in the imposition of an additional sentence

c   the offence was committed as a result of a genuine mistake or misunderstanding

d   the loss or harm can be described as minor and was the result of a single incident, particularly if it was caused by a misjudgement

e   there has been a long delay between the offence taking place and the date of the trial, unless:

- the offence is serious
- the delay has been caused in part by the defendant
- the offence has only recently come to light, or
- the complexity of the offence has meant that there has been a long investigation

f   a prosecution is likely to have a bad effect on the victim's physical or mental health, bearing in mind the seriousness of the offence

g   the defendant is elderly or is, or was at the time of the offence, suffering from significant mental or physical ill health, unless the offence is serious or there is real possibility that it may be repeated

h   the defendant has put right the loss or harm that was caused (but defendants must not avoid prosecution or diversion solely because they pay compensation), or

i   details may be made public that could harm sources of information, international relations or national security

## Diversion from prosecution (adults only)

*Simple caution*   The Crown Prosecutor may decide to give the accused a simple caution if the public interest justifies it; the police must be informed.

*Conditional caution*   A conditional caution may be appropriate where a Crown Prosecutor considers that while the public interest justifies a prosecution, the interests of the suspect, victim and community may be better served by the suspect complying with suitable conditions aimed at rehabilitation or reparation. These may include restorative justice processes.

*Guilty pleas*   Defendants may wish to plead guilty to some, but not all, of the charges. Alternatively, they may want to plead guilty to a different, possibly lesser charge, by admitting only part of the crime. Crown Prosecutors should only accept the defendant's plea if they think the court is able to pass a sentence that matches the seriousness of the offence, particularly where there are aggravating features. Prosecutors must never simply accept a guilty plea because it is speedy or convenient. Prosecutors should always ensure that the interests of victims are served when accepting a guilty plea and the court should be invited to hear all the evidence. Particular care must be taken when considering pleas which would enable the defendant to avoid the imposition of a mandatory minimum sentence. When pleas are offered, prosecutors must bear in mind the fact that ancillary orders can be made with some offences but not with others – such as anti-social behaviour orders (ASBOs).

_____The doctrine of double jeopardy: restarting a prosecution_____

The doctrine of double jeopardy, known also as *autrefois acquit*, was developed over centuries as a protection against oppressive prosecution, where a person once acquitted of a crime could not be tried twice for the same offence. Part 10 of the *Criminal Justice Act 2003* abolished the 800-year-old doctrine; this now means that the CPS can restart a prosecution at any time.

It was the Macpherson Report of 1999, the inquiry into the murder of Stephen Lawrence in 1993, which subjected the double jeopardy rule to scrutiny and recommended that prosecution after an acquittal should be allowed, where 'fresh and viable' evidence was presented to the CPS. Failures by the London 'Met' to secure convictions in the Lawrence killing were severely criticised in the Report and the Met was accused of being institutionally racist.

Now the CPS can restart a prosecution at any time, sometimes decades after the original offence. Reasons must include that more or new evidence has become available in the form of DNA (deoxyribonucleic acid). These exceptional cases, usually following an acquittal of a serious offence, require the consent from the Director of Public Prosecution (DPP). Restarting a prosecution is relatively rare. Cases for review are brought by either the Director of Public Prosecutions or the Criminal Cases Review Commission (CCRC), an independent body that investigates suspected miscarriages of justice in England, Wales and Northern Ireland.

## 6.7 ____ Summary trial in the magistrates' courts and mode of trial _____

Well over 95 per cent of all criminal cases are heard in the English magistrates' courts – with the exception of violent, serious and homicide offences and serious fraud (*indictable* offences). Magistrates' courts also deal with civil matters, but to a much lesser degree.

Who are the magistrates? There are about 30,000 lay justices of the peace (JP), ordinary members of the public who serve at least 52 days a year as unremunerated magistrates in the local criminal courts of England and Wales.

There are an additional 130 District Judges (DJs), qualified barristers or solicitors, who sit on their own in local magistrates' courts. Increasingly, as new unified court houses are built, it is envisaged that they will be staffed by District Judges in order to speed up the justice system.

All crimes – no matter how serious – are first heard at the magistrates' court and the CPS applies strict guidelines to assist the court with the option where the defendant's case should be heard – either at the magistrates' or the crown court.

Types of offences comprise:

1  **Indictable offences** (heard/tried only at the crown court)
2  **Summary offences** (heard/tried only at the magistrates' court)
3  **Offences triable-either-way** (either-way offence) (heard/tried either at the magistrates' or crown court)

Summary offences are:

• Less serious offences, such as driving offences, harassment, common assault or battery or theft from a shop
• Only adults over the age of 18 are tried 'summarily'

Indictable offences are:

• Serious offences tried on indictment at the crown court, such as section 20 OAPA 1861 'wounding' (GBH); section 18 OAPA 1861 'wounding with intent'; section 8 *Theft Act 1968* 'robbery'; section 1 *Sexual Offences Act 2003* 'rape'
• Serious common law offences, such as murder, attempted murder or manslaughter
• Any offence punishable by long or life imprisonment

The most interesting, yet tricky, category of crimes constitutes triable-either-way offences. If the accused is charged with an 'either-way' offence (adults only), the prosecution must provide the magistrates' bench with advice as to where the case should be heard (magistrates' or crown court). Technically, the defendant chooses whether he wants to be tried *summarily* (magistrates) or *on indictment* (crown court). The magistrates however have the last say and decide upon the jurisdiction the defendant's case is heard in.

Triable-either-way offences are:

• Prescribed by statute, such as section 1 *Criminal Damage Act 1971* 'criminal damage'; section 3 *Theft Act 1978* 'making off without payment'; section 47 OAPA 'assault occasioning actual bodily harm' (ABH)
• Tried either at the magistrates' or the crown court

Research has shown that the defendant stands a higher chance of acquittal at the crown court. The disadvantages of crown court trial are that the process takes longer, it is more expensive and carries the risk that the accused will end up receiving a much higher sentence if found guilty by the jury (see Zander, 2000).

A 'mode of trial' hearing concerns 'either-way' offences, where magistrates decide whether a case should be tried 'summarily' or on 'indictment' at the crown court by judge and jury. When deciding on whether the case should be tried at the magistrates' or the crown court, magistrates consider the following criteria:

- What is the nature and seriousness of the offence?
- Is the punishment and sentencing power of the magistrates adequate enough?
- Is there any other circumstantial evidence why the case is more suitable for crown court?
- What are the representations by the prosecution?

If the defendant decides to have his case tried at the magistrates' court, the magistrates must still decide whether the case is suitable for their punishment powers (presently six months' imprisonment or a maximum fine up to £5,000). The justices may well decide that their sentencing powers are not enough, in which case they commit the case to the crown court. Magistrates then consider the following:

- The seriousness of the offence, for example, was the burglary in an occupied dwelling or an unoccupied warehouse?
- Are the magistrates' sentencing powers sufficient in this case? or
- Is the offence so serious that only custody will suffice?
- Is a discharge, fine or community sentence appropriate?
- What are the aggravating and mitigating factors? For example, in burglary, was there a forcible entry? Was there large damage?
- What are the public interest factors? For example, was the victim injured or vulnerable or a child?

## Bail

During a bail decision hearing, the prosecution will provide the justices with details of the alleged offence/s and any previous convictions (antecedents). The CPS advise the magistrates as to whether they should or should not grant bail. The defence then makes their representations by way of a bail application by giving details of the defendant's version of the allegations and his personal circumstances. The court listens to representations from both parties and can ask questions at this point.

On granting bail with or without conditions, magistrates must explain the purpose of imposing conditions and give specific reasons for applying these conditions. Here are types of bail:

- **The right to bail**: The defendant usually has the right to unconditional bail (except in 'trigger offences')
- **Unconditional bail** means that the defendant has a prima facie right to be 'free' whilst investigations into his case are ongoing
- **Conditional bail** means that the court will allow the defendant to be 'free' with conditions, but the court will impose certain conditions, such as that of residence; not to interfere with witnesses; reporting to the local police station; door-step curfew; electronic tagging on Home Detention Curfew (HDC) etc.

When is bail refused? For example in cases where the defendant is charged with murder or rape or has previously offended whilst on bail. Here are some reasons why magistrates may remand a defendant in custody:

- Abscond ('surrender to custody')
- Commit further offences whilst on bail
- Interfere with witnesses
- Obstruct the course of justice
- Pose a significant risk to public security (s. 14 CJA 2003, amending Sch. 1 of *Bail Act 1976*)
- For the defendant's own protection (police informer or suicide risk)

_____ *Criminal Justice and Immigration Act 2008* _____

The 2008 Act sets out new powers to deal with anti-social and violent behaviour, makes sentencing decisions clearer and introduces a new community sentence for young offenders. In its White Paper 2006, 'Rebalancing the criminal justice system in favour of the law-abiding majority', the Government set out its commitment to delivering an effective criminal justice system: how to cut crime, reduce reoffending and protect the public. The 2008 Act amends some schedules of the *Criminal Justice Act 2003*, such as the allocation of either-way offences. Committal proceedings for such offences will be abolished. Either-way offences are replaced by 'sending for trial' procedures, previously only used for indictable offences, such as rape and murder. The key areas of the 2008 Act are:

- **Trial in absence** of an adult defendant, including sentencing. The aim is to toughen up the trial processes when an offender fails to appear without good reason
- **Designated case workers** (DCW) for the CPS can prosecute in contested trials
- **Conditional cautions** are available for offenders under 18
- **Youth Rehabilitation Order** – this introduces a generic community sentence for young offenders, including reparation, curfew, unpaid work and supervision
- **Abolition of Suspended Sentences** for summary offences (e.g. criminal damage or harassment)
- **'Possession of extreme pornographic images'** – the creation of a new either-way offence to deal with violent pornography
- **Sexual offences committed abroad** are treated the same as if committed in the UK

- **Violent offender order** – this is a preventative order available to police and magistrates where the offender has been convicted of specified offences of violence, including manslaughter, soliciting, attempted murder, conspiracy to murder, wounding with intent to do GBH, malicious wounding (or equivalent foreign jurisdiction); the order is made with specified requirements to protect the public from further serious harm.

## 6.8 ___ Trial on indictment in the crown court ___

The crown court is part of the Supreme Court of Judicature and deals primarily with indictable-only offences. There are 78 crown court centres across England and Wales administered by Her Majesty's Court Service (HMCS), an executive agency of the Ministry of Justice. The most famous is the Central Criminal Court in London, also known as the 'The Old Bailey'. From June 2005 work sent to the Old Bailey was class 1 only: effectively homicide and terrorism.

Trials are heard by a judge and a 12-person jury, aged between 18 and 70, selected for jury service via the electoral roll and everyone has to attend jury service when called (CJA 2003). If the case is serious, the judge is likely to be a High Court judge, normally attached to the Queen's Bench Division. Otherwise the judge will be a circuit judge or recorder. The judge's role is limited to deciding matters of law and summing up for the jury. What goes on in the jury room is secret and cannot be publicly disclosed or researched (s. 8 *Contempt of Court Act 1981*). The jury decides whether the accused is guilty or not, by looking at the facts and the evidence presented at trial.

### ___ Evidence ___

What is the purpose of the law of evidence? It is commonly described as a body of 'exclusionary rules', which exists to protect the defendant in criminal proceedings and the parties in civil actions against injustice.

Parliament introduced important changes with the *Criminal Justice Act 2003* in relation to bad character and hearsay evidence admissible in criminal proceedings.

*Bad character (Part 11 CJA 2003)* Previously, the court was not permitted to hear of a defendant's previous convictions ('bad character') in a criminal trial. Part *11 CJA* 2003 abolished the common law of 'previous misconduct'. Now, the prosecution can apply under the 'enhanced relevance' test to have 'bad character' adduce at the trial, providing the previous convictions (antecedents) are related to the present offence the accused is charged with. The decision lies with the magistrates, who have to consider the following:

- Is bad character evidence relevant?
- Is the evidence supplied correcting a false impression given by the defendant?
- Has the defendant made an attack on another person's character?

If bad character evidence is permitted, police and the prosecution are entitled to know the antecedents at the earliest opportunity (*Bradley* [2005]).

*Propensity to commit crimes*    Under *section 103 (1) (a)* CJA 2003, evidence of bad character is admissible to show that a defendant has a propensity to commit offences 'of the kind with which he is charged'.

Practically, this means that a defendant's bad character is admissible in at least two situations. The first being that he may have a propensity to commit a particular crime, such as paedophilia (child sex abuse). 'Bad character' then includes not only previous convictions but also previous cautions or similar incidents.

The second situation is where a person has a habit of committing certain types of crime, describing the habitual criminal. For example, if the suspect is arrested for shoplifting and his defence is that he forgot to pay, evidence should be admissible of the numerous convictions for shoplifting. Similarly, if a defendant is charged with burglary, having been found in the front garden of a private dwelling, claiming that he went there to urinate, evidence should be admissible of his track record as a burglar.

There is a safeguard under *section 103 (3)* where bad character evidence of propensity should *not* be admitted if conviction was a long time ago. For example, the defendant now aged 55 is charged with burglary; it would be very unlikely that the court would admit evidence of his *only* previous conviction of burglary which happened 30 years previously.

*Hearsay*    Section 1 of the *Civil Evidence Act 1995* had already abolished the hearsay rule in civil proceedings. But, before the CJA 2003 came into force, *Kearley* [1992] had been the leading authority on hearsay. The case concerned telephone conversations and personal requests for drugs by the callers. The House of Lords had ruled that this amounted to inadmissible hearsay in criminal proceedings.

The final decision as to whether to allow hearsay now rests with the court, known as the 'safety valve' (s. 114 (1) (d) CJA 2003). The justices must consider:

- How valuable is the hearsay evidence in the case?
- Will other evidence suffice?
- What were the circumstances in which the statement was made?
- How reliable is the maker of the statement? (*Singh* [2006])
- Whether oral evidence of the matter stated can be given and, if not, why it cannot?
- What are the difficulties involved in challenging the statement?

The hearsay provisions apply equally to the defence and to the prosecution with the added safeguard for the defendant that any matters requiring proof must be proved to the heightened criminal standard by the prosecution ('beyond reasonable doubt') and on a balance of probabilities by the defence.

## 6.9 _____ Prosecutions in Scotland _____

The Lord Advocate, the Crown Office and Procurator Fiscal Service provide the public prosecution service in Scotland. The Lord Advocate is the Government Minister responsible for prosecutions in Scotland. Though a member of the Scottish Executive, the Lord Advocate is the head of the prosecution system in Scotland and is therefore independent of other Ministers.

### _____ The Procurator Fiscal _____

Very similar to the English Crown Prosecution Service (CPS), the Procurator Fiscal's office (the 'Fiscal') considers the evidence 'in the public interest' and decides whether criminal proceedings should take place. If there is enough evidence, the Fiscal then decides whether to lay charges or not.

In cases that will be heard by a jury in the High Court, the 'Fiscal' will interview witnesses, gather and review forensic and other evidence before a decision to prosecute is taken. The Fiscal's office will then make a report to Crown Counsel to take a decision on whether to prosecute. Like in England and Wales, the prosecution must prove these matters beyond reasonable doubt.

**The Scottish Prosecution Code** includes:

- The seriousness of the offence
- The length of time since the offence took place
- Interests of the victim and other witnesses
- The age of the offender, any previous convictions and other relevant factors
- Local community interests and 'general public concern'
- Any other factors according to the facts and circumstances of the case

## 6.10 _____ The Serious Organised Crime Agency (SOCA) _____

The Serious Organised Crime Agency ('SOCA') began its functions on 1 April 2006 with the primary aim to reduce serious organised crime *(Serious Organised Crime and Police Act 2005)*. SOCA's main functions are:

- **Asset freezing** – to undermine the profit motive of serious organised criminals locally and internationally
- **Intelligence gathering** – investigating serious organised crime

SOCA is an intelligence-led agency with seemingly unlimited law enforcement powers, working with Europol and Interpol (see Chapter 4.4).

Under Part 7 of the *Proceeds of Crime Act 2002*, SOCA can apply freeze orders to seize property in order to preserve assets that may subsequently be the subject of a confiscation order. These forfeiture orders last up to two years in order to investigate assets of suspected criminals and whether moneys were obtained through unlawful conduct.

## 6.11 ___ Case study _____

_____ R (Gibson) v Winchester Crown Court [2004] EWHC (Admin) 361 ___

The judicial review case (High Court) of *Gibson* concerns the issue of custody time limits, questioning the legality of keeping someone on remand for a very lengthy period, thereby contravening human rights legislation, namely Art. 5 ECHR 'Right to liberty and security' and Art. 6 ECHR 'Right to a fair trial'.

### Facts of the case

Leslie Gordon Gibson and his son David were charged with the murder of David's wife, Belinda, in February 2002. No body or trace had ever been found. Both were first arrested on 9 May 2002 and were still on remand in custody at their plea and directions hearing on 14 July 2003. Custody time limits periodically expired, yet the prosecution was granted repeated extensions for remand to continue, on 5 and 11 Nov 2003 by Judge Broderick at Winchester Crown Court under s. 22(3) *Prosecution of Offences Act 1985* until 10 June 2004, amounting eventually to a total of 211 days.

When challenged, Broderick J gave the following reasons for granting the extension: (1) Number 1 court at Winchester Crown Court had been occupied for a year with a complex fraud case which had been transferred there from Bournemouth; (2) That there were some 30 outstanding murders and 40 outstanding rape or child sex cases at the court which needed to be tried first.

### Judicial Review

Lord Bingham CJ referred to European Court of Human Rights (ECHR) legislation which had dealt with similar cases: *Wemhoff v Germany* [1968], *Stögmüller v Austria* [1969] and *Zimmermann v Switzerland* [1984], summarising that the Swiss Federal Court took three years to make an administrative law decision in *Zimmermann v Switzerland* and the Strasbourg human rights court (ECHR) ruled that the Swiss court had no right to use its excessive workload and its chronic backlog as an excuse; if anything, there was perhaps a partial excuse for such a delay. Lord Bingham referred to *W v Switzerland* [1994] concerning a defendant held in custody for just over four years between the date of his arrest and that of his conviction. Yet, in each of these cases, the Strasbourg court ruled that there had been *no* violation of Art. 5 ECHR, because of the complexity in each case, the wide scope of the investigation and the conduct of the defendant.

Bearing these Strasbourg rulings in mind, Lord Bingham reasoned in *Gibson* that these decisions could appropriately be applied in the present case and UK domestic legislation. He also referred to *R v Leeds crown court, ex p Briggs* (No 1)

*(Continued)*

[1998] where it was ruled that if an extension to a custody time limit is granted, the court must give reasons for reaching that decision.

For these reasons, the applicants' Leslie and David Gibson's requests were dismissed, stating that statutory custody time limits (including remand in custody) should be adhered to 'wherever possible', but could be extended where necessary. Permission to appeal to the House of Lords was refused.

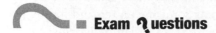

# Exam Questions

1 Compare and contrast the operational policies of the English and Welsh, Scottish and Northern Irish police forces.
2 What is meant by a 'mode of trial' hearing in court? Discuss.
3 Describe changes in hearsay and bad character evidence brought about by the *Criminal Justice Act 2003* by giving practical examples.
4 What were the main issues regarding bail procedures and custody time limits in the judicial review case of *Gibson*? Discuss with reference to human rights legislation and criminal procedure.

## Further Resources

Eugene McLaughlin's *New Policing* (2007) provides a comprehensive critique of issues confronting policing today.

Crawford, Lister and Blackburn's *Plural Policing* (2005) offers a valuable insight in to today's 'visible policing' in England and Wales.

Tim Newburn's *Handbook of Policing* (2003) looks at policing in its historical context, examining how policing has developed from its origins to present day community policing.

The fourth revised edition of the *Oxford Handbook of Criminology* (2007), edited by Maguire, Morgan and Reiner remains the most comprehensive and authoritative single volume text on the subject of criminology and criminal justice and combines key topics with extensive references, covering topics such as policing, race and gender, crime statistics and fear of crime.

*Blackstone's Police Manual: Evidence and Procedure* by Glenn Hutton and David Johnston (2007) covers all aspects of policing legislation.

## Notes

1 Communitarianism or 'collectivism' refers to any political or socio-economic theory or practice that encourages state ownership and control of the means of production and distribution. Examples of collectivist farmers' organisations were in the former Soviet Union or German Democratic Republic with fixed rates of remuneration.
2 *R v Hoey (Sean)* [2007] Omagh Judgement of 20 December 2007.

# 7

# PUNISHMENT AND SENTENCING

---

### Overview

Chapter 7 examines:

- The main theories of punishment, their aims and purposes linked to sentencing provisions in the criminal courts
- The role and functions of the correctional services of England and Wales
- Offender management in Scotland
- The Northern Ireland Prison Service
- Alternative forms of punishment in the form of non-custodial measures and generic community sentences
- Restorative justice and victim–offender mediation

---

You will by now have realised that criminal justice involves complex issues. Crime is invariably linked to punishment. Even though the levels of most crimes have fallen significantly since about 1999, the vast majority of the British public thinks that crime has gone up. This can be attributed in part to a lack of confidence in the criminal justice system and partly to media hype of crime which increased the public fear of crime, resulting in public pressure and demand for more severe sentences. This, in turn, has led to an increase in the prison population and prison overcrowding.

First, we will look at traditional punishment theories and how these link to practical sentencing in the courts. Then, we'll take a look at 'end-to-end' offender management by the 'National Offender Management Service' (NOMS), comprising prison and probation services.

This chapter will also look at reoffending rates, linked to Home Office research, which might explain some of the prison overcrowding. There is no doubt that sentences have increased in severity for serious and violent crimes, but have they reduced crime and reoffending?

## 7.1 ___ Punishment theories and sentencing

Traditional punishment theories usually include:

- Retribution
- Deterrence
- Rehabilitation
- Incapacitation

The origins of these punishment theories are largely based on either Christian morals or philosophical ideas. The German philosopher Immanuel Kant (1724–1804) defined the meaning of 'punishment' as:

- It must involve unpleasantness
- It must be for an offence
- It must be imposed by an authority

*Retribution*   Retributive justice believes that the guilty should be punished simply because they have done wrong, best known as the 'just deserts' theory of punishment (see McConville, 2003). Retributivism involves a fair and just allocation of punishment where the punishment should fit the crime.

How is retribution translated into sentencing practice by the courts? Sentencing should be proportionate to the seriousness of the offence, whereby justices tend to consider the defendant's past offending behaviour patterns or antecedents (see von Hirsch and Ashworth, 2005).

The *Criminal Justice Act 1991* is regarded as one of the most positive legislative frameworks in the retributive justice field. The underlying aim was to ensure that criminals are sentenced proportionate to the seriousness of their offence.

*Deterrence*   Although simple in its conception, deterrence theory can be extremely complicated in practical sentencing. Deterrence often reflects a penal policy, where the government attempts to control or 'deter' the behaviour of others by the use of threats. The 'deterrer' (the state) then tries to convince the 'deterree' (the criminal) that the costs of crime reduction, which is the ultimate goal of the deterrer, are substantially higher than any gain that the deterree might anticipate making from the action. Simply put, in an ideal world, the offender should 'stop and think' about the consequences of his actions before he commits the crime. This latter scenario is, as we know, only a perfect model (see Nagin, 1998).

Von Hirsch (1999) summarises deterrence as:

- Punishment aimed at deterring the criminal from repeat or future offending
- The anticipation of a penalty
- An 'unpleasant' sentence
- Encouraging the individual to be a law abiding citizen

- Harsher punishment for the repeat offender
- Deterring others from committing similar acts

In practice, deterrence should reflect a 'short, sharp, shock' sentence, best evidenced by the *Criminal Justice Acts* of 1982 and 1988. Bottoms et al. (2004) argued that this type of sentence was reasonably successful to deter first-time offenders.

*Rehabilitation*   This punishment paradigm focuses on the rehabilitation of the offender (*Rehabilitation of Offenders Act 1974*). Rehabilitative theorists believe that the offender needs professional support, usually by way of a community sentence, to achieve this aim. The probation service plays an important part in this process (see Brownlee, 1998).

In a rehabilitative sentencing scenario, justices will make every effort to change the offender's future behaviour, so that he can lead a 'useful and crime free life' after being released from custody or having served a community sentence.

*Incapacitation*   The concept of incapacitation identifies and targets particular groups of offenders, such as burglars, who do serious harm to society. Incapacitation theorists believe that certain criminals need to be removed from society for a long time, by way of imprisonment (Zimring and Hawkins, 1995).

In criminal justice policy terms, incapacitation means longer and harsher sentences, for example, for repeat burglars. The *Crime (Sentences) Act 1997* set a mandatory life term for a second serious offence, known as 'two-strikes' legislation, specifically for rape, robbery, 'clandestine injury to women', aggravated assault, possession and carrying of firearms, 'lewd, libidinous or indecent behaviour or practices' and drug trafficking. The *Criminal Justice Act 2003* introduced similar measures for serious young offenders (see Chapter 9).

## Sentencing

Let us turn to practical sentencing by the courts today where there are usually two main considerations: to protect the public and reduce offending. A prison sentence is generally automatic if the offender has been found guilty of a serious (indictable) crime. First, sentencing justices will consider an appropriate level of sentence, where the punishment must fit the crime (retribution). Second, they will decide on the level of punishment, based on the seriousness of the offence.

The *Criminal Justice Act 2003* made major changes to the sentencing framework, including:

- Various community sentences for adults were replaced by a single 'Community Order' with a range of possible requirements

- Serious violent and sexual offenders were given new sentences (Indeterminate or Extended Public Protection sentences), ensuring that they are kept in prison or under supervision for longer periods than previously
- Suspended Sentence Orders were increased

When sentencing, justices are usually faced with a number of considerations. Would a fine be appropriate? And if so what type and amount of fine? Would a Community sentence be appropriate? And if so, how many hours of unpaid work should the offender be ordered? Will only custody suffice? If so, what length of prison sentence? Or should the offender be given a 'warning'-type conditional discharge or a suspended prison sentence? By and large sentencing principles by the courts follow these steps:

1 Public protection
2 Punishment of the offender
3 Crime reduction
4 The seriousness of the offence
5 The defendant's antecedents (previous criminal record)
6 The defendant's personal circumstances and history
7 Did the defendant show remorse?
8 The rehabilitation of the offender
9 Restorative justice (victim–offender mediation and compensation)

There are four sentencing options available to the courts:

- Discharges (absolute and conditional)
- Fines
- Community sentences
- Prison

## 7.2 ___ Community justice in England and Wales ___

For a long time, criminological research literature has been preoccupied with establishing credible alternatives to prison sentences. Until the late 1960s the main alternative to a custodial sentence was the 'Probation Order' which introduced a glut of community-based penalties between 1967–1972. A generic community sentence was introduced with the *Criminal Justice Act 2003*.

Emeritus Professor Sir Anthony Bottoms devoted a life time of research to the 'penal crisis', warning us as far back as the mid-1970s that, apart from diverting convicted offenders from custody, the community sentence would draw in those who would otherwise have been discharged or fined, which he called 'widening the net':

> In attempting to rectify the perceived deficiencies of the current arrangements for custodial sentences, the new provisions... seem likely to blur the boundaries between custody and community penalties. Fine judgements will be required as to when to select an

intensive community sentence, when to give an offender a short taste of custody combined with or followed by community requirements and when to use the threat of custody to reinforce community requirements. (Bottoms et al., 2004)

## The work of the National Probation Service

The probation service goes back to circa 1907, when probation officers, originally linked to the church and temperance societies, were empowered by statute to work with offenders and to 'advise, assist and befriend offenders' placed under their supervision by the courts. In the 1970s and 1980s probation partnerships with other agencies resulted in cautioning schemes, alternatives to custody and crime reduction while changes in sentencing resulted in attendance centres for football hooligans on a Saturday, the probation order and unpaid work (see Brownlee, 1998).

The work of the probation service has long been linked to 'decarceration' and 'rehabilitation' theories, with a deliberate aim to divert people from prison (also known as 'diversion theory'). Decarcerationists like Cohen (1972) advocated that prison walls should be 'torn down' and alternative forms of punishment in and by the community should be found.

Since 2001, the National Probation Service (NPS) has undergone significant changes (*Criminal Justice and Court Services Act 2000*). Whilst the traditional role of the probation officer offered rehabilitative support to offenders in the community his new role is that of risk assessment officer to address and assess the offender's future dangerousness. Today, probation tasks can be onerous, from providing Pre-sentence Reports (PSR) for the courts to managing the plethora of community sentences and their programmed activities (see Whitfield, 2001).

In 2004, the National Probation Service became part of the correctional service of England and Wales known as the 'National Offender Management Service' (NOMS) and came under the auspices of the Ministry of Justice in May 2007. In line with the 42 CPS and police force areas, the Probation Service works with a wide range of independent and voluntary providers to secure the government's aim of 'end-to-end' offender management. A Probation Officer's tasks typically involve:

- Providing pre-sentence reports to assist the courts to decide on what sentence should be passed
- Managing and enforcing community orders made by the courts
- Ensuring offenders attend supervision with a probation officer
- Conducting offender risk assessments in order to protect the public
- Working with prisoners, helping them to re-integrate into the community
- Liaising with victims of serious crime to keep them informed about a prisoner's progress in prison
- Working with other agencies, such as police, local authorities, courts, health services, substance/misuse/drug services
- Prosecuting bail breaches and failed court orders

Multi Agency Public Protection Arrangements (MAPPA) were created by the Home Office in 2001 in order to identify and manage violent and sexual offenders within the criminal justice system (see Worrall and Hoy, 2005). Core functions of the 42 MAPPA areas are:

- The management of dangerous and sexual offenders
- Information sharing among criminal justice agencies involved in risk assessment
- The risk assessment of serious harm to the public
- The management of that risk

Similar public protection arrangements also exist in Scotland (ss. 10 and 11 *Management of Offenders (Scotland) Act 2005*).

_____ ASBOs _____

Section 1 of the *Crime and Disorder Act 1998* (CDA) introduced 'Anti-social Behaviour Orders' (ASBOs). These civil orders were initially meant for children over the age of ten to exclude young deviants from certain areas where they were known to terrorise their neighbourhoods (see *R (on the application of A) v Leeds Magistrates' Court and Leeds City Council* [2004]). The *Anti-social Behaviour Act 2003* extended ASBOs to adults – and these powers are now widely used by local authorities and the courts to combat crime and tackle anti-social behaviour by restricting deviants' movements in a particular area.

ASBOs can now be made alongside a prison sentence, as a form of post-release control order (*R v Vittles* [2004]). In *Parkinson* [2004], the ASBO was held as 'necessary' by the Court of Appeal, which imposed the banning order on the offender alongside his two-year prison sentence for robbery. There was sufficient evidence that Parkinson had harassed several housing estates in Preston.

_____ Community Warden Schemes _____

Community Wardens are an additional local resource to police constables, though they have no powers under PACE (see Chapter 6.2). They assist with quick responses to anti-social problems and provide a visible policing presence in neighbourhoods. Warden schemes have played a key role in 'joining up' communities and criminal justice services.

_____ Acceptable Behaviour Contracts (ABCs) _____

Acceptable behaviour contracts (ABCs) are written contracts between the local authority, police, youth offending teams and the individual deviant. ABCs have been introduced into a number of socially problematical areas where anti-social behaviour occurs. ABCs are not statutory tools; they are voluntary arrangements (compacts) between the deviant and the services.

## 7.3 ____ Imprisonment in England and Wales ____

It is fundamental in a free democratic society that loss of liberty should not be inflicted beyond what is necessary ('*just deserts theory*'). A custodial sentence should therefore only be given for the most serious crimes and where offenders pose a serious danger to the public (*incapacitation*).

The prison population of England and Wales has soared since 1993. In January of that year, the prison population stood at 41,561 and by the time the Ministry of Justice took over the management of the 141 prisons on 9 May 2007, the prison population stood at a record high of 80,658 in the 141 prisons and young offender institutions. The Ministry announced that an additional 8,000 prison places would be built by 2012 to cope with additional capacity (Ministry of Justice 'Penal Policy: a background paper', 2 May 2007).

Why the continuing increase in the prison population? This can be partly attributed to the increase in the lengths of sentences for serious offences, such as drug trafficking, partly to the increased use of remand imprisonment and bail breaches.

Despite the stable crime levels, one other contributing factor has been the change in the pattern of offending, particularly where drugs are involved. Another factor has been the 250 per cent rise in the number of people recalled to prison for breaching either bail conditions or community orders since the introduction of the *Criminal Justice Act 2003* in April 2005.

_____ Population in custody (at 31 December 2007) _____

The population in custody stood at 80,067 (75,275 males and 4,330 females) and the remand prison population decreased by 6 per cent to 12,236 (compared to 2006). The number of young adults (aged 18–21) in custody saw an increase of four per cent to 9,333 and the 15 to 17 year olds saw a decrease of 6 per cent to 2,191.

The largest percentage decreases on remand were in theft and motoring offences, down by 22 and 10 per cent respectively. Increases were seen in fraud and drug offences, up by 7 and 3 per cent respectively.

The largest proportionate increase in the sentenced population was for those serving indeterminate sentences (life sentences and indeterminate Sentences for Public Protection [IPP]), which increased by 24 per cent.

The largest percentage increases among the sentenced prison population were in violence against the person and sexual offences, up by 9 and 6 per cent

**Table 7.1**  Projected prison populations (England & Wales)

| YEAR | High | Medium | Low |
|---|---|---|---|
| 2007 | 80,420 | 79,380 | 78,380 |
| 2008 | 84,670 | 82,730 | 80,730 |
| 2009 | 89,410 | 86,290 | 83,320 |
| 2010 | 94,020 | 89,810 | 85,700 |
| 2011 | 98,310 | 92,970 | 87,590 |
| 2012 | 102,280 | 95,630 | 88,980 |
| 2013 | 106,550 | 98,190 | 90,250 |

*Source*: Home Office, 2006b

respectively. Motoring offences saw the largest percentage decrease, down by 15 per cent.

There were 11,310 foreign nationals in prison and Immigration Removal Centres (Dover, Haslar and Lindholme), held under the *Immigration Act 1971*. The largest foreign national population comprised Jamaican nationals, with a population of 1,278, followed by Nigeria (1,146), Republic of Ireland (639), Vietnam (460) and Pakistan (406).

Table 7.1 shows the future prison population trends

_____ Reoffending rates (recidivism) _____

'Reoffending' usually means that the offender committed an offence within the two-year follow-up period and was subsequently convicted in court. Results from the Home Office reconviction study from the 2003 cohort showed that 57.6 per cent of adult offenders were reconvicted within two years (Home Office, 2006a).

The *Offender Management Act 2007* created new statutory arrangements for the prison and probation services under NOMS, following the Carter Report 'Managing Offenders, Reducing Crime' 2003. Carter recommended a unified 'correctional service' to provide 'end-to-end management'. This led to the creation of the National Offender Management Service (NOMS) in 2004, though by 2008, it became clear the Ministry of Justice had other plans for the continued existence of NOMS. By July 2008, the prisons were run by the HM Prison Service agency, as part of the Ministry of Justice once again.

On 5 December 2007, the Secretary of State for Justice, Jack Straw, announced the building of 'Titan' prison, providing some 10,500 additional prison places by 2014, a response to Lord Carter's review *Securing the Future*. The three large Titan prisons will house around 2,500 prisoners each and old and inefficient prisons would be closed. The Titans will be built on brownfield sites located in the most populated areas in the South East, West Midlands and the North West of England.

Criminologists have already criticized the Titans as 'warehouses' where purposeful activities, such as employment and training, may not be a priority, thereby not addressing reoffending rates.

## Prison governance

The role of prison governors has changed. Bryans (2007) writes:

> Governors moved from being amateur and capricious gaolers, to military men, administering their institutions according to laid-down rules, to charismatic feudal barons exercising patriarchal authority over their prisons, to being general managers bound by bureaucracy and legal rules. (2007: 64)

The governor still remains the key player in the prison, and adds to the success or failure of that prison.

There are a number of ways in which prisons are regulated to ensure that each of the 141 public and private prison establishments are run safely, bearing staff and prisoner welfare firmly in mind.

## The Independent Monitoring Boards (IMBs)

By law every prison and immigration removal centre must have an Independent Monitoring Board (IMB). IMBs in prisons derive their responsibilities from section 6 of the *Prison Act 1952*, formerly known as 'Boards of Visitors' (BOV). IMBs in immigration removal centres, such as Harmondsworth Detention Centre, derive their responsibilities from the *Immigration and Asylum Act 1999* (formerly known as 'Visiting Committees'). IMBs are appointed by the Minister of Justice and all board members carry keys, thereby having unlimited access to the prison. They deal with the concept of a 'healthy prison' from prisoner and staff complaints to the investigation of serious incidents at the prison (riots or hostage situations). Typical concerns for IMBs are:

- visits
- kitchen cleanliness and food
- prison industries
- dedicated search teams
- sentence planning
- overcrowding

## HM Commissioner for Offender Management and Prisons

The office of the Prisons and Probation Ombudsman was subject to a heated debate in Parliament when the *Criminal Justice and Immigration Bill* reached its final committee stage in the House of Lords on 9 January 2008 (Hansard, HL Bill 16). For decades, the Ombudsman's role, as the independent prison watchdog, had never been put on a statutory footing, commented on by the Joint Committee on Human Rights in its December 2004 report:

> As a matter of priority parliamentary time should be set aside to bring in legislation giving a statutory basis to the Prisons and Probation Ombudsman, and providing him with investigatory powers equivalent to those of the Independent Police Complaints Commission. Until such a statutory basis is provided, investigations by the Ombudsman are unlikely to meet the obligation to investigate under Article 2 ECHR (at para 332).

Part 4 of the *Criminal Justice and Immigration Act 2008* established the HM Commissioner for Offender Management and Prisons, a statutory office holder legally independent of the Secretary of State and equipped with statutory powers of investigation. The Commissioner's role includes:

- The independent adjudication of complaints from prisoners and immigration detainees
- The investigation of deaths in custody, including YOIs, Secure Training Centres and Approved Premises (former Bail Hostels).

## The HM Chief Inspectorate of Prisons

The Inspectorate is independent of the prison service and reports directly to the Secretary of State for Justice on the treatment of prisoners and on the conditions of prisons in England and Wales. The independent prisons inspectorate was established in 1980 in line with a recommendation of the 'May Committee of Enquiry into the United Kingdom Prison Services' (s. 5A *Prison Act 1952*, as amended by s. 57 *Criminal Justice Act 1982*).

Prison establishments are inspected at least once every five years and inspections are split into full announced, unannounced or follow-up inspections.

## The Parole Board

The Parole Board was established under the *Criminal Justice Act 1967*. The main duty today is to decide whether a 'lifer' prisoner should be allowed to be released from prison 'on licence'. Some radical changes were made under the *Criminal Justice Act 2003* where, at the half way point of a sentence, there exists an automatic release for all but the most dangerous offenders (*The Criminal Justice (Sentencing) (Licence Conditions) Order 2005*). The Parole Board consists of highly qualified people, usually justices, psychiatrists or criminologists. Board members decide on the suitability of a life sentence prisoner for release and his risk assessment in order to return to society.

Does prison work? Statistics tell us that about two-thirds of released prisoners will reoffend within two years of release from prison. This means that prison does not work for repeat offenders and should be used only for serious and dangerous offenders in order to protect the public. Arguably, the rest of convicted offenders should be given community sentences so that offenders can make amends to their victims and society for the harm done by their crimes.

What is prison for? It should be for punishment, but the prison system is very costly. Each 'normal' male adult offender costs the state about £37,000 per year, with women and young offenders being much more expensive, since they need greater medical care, education or counselling. Meanwhile, prison figures, released by NOMS in February 2007, showed that prison violence had increased by some 600 per cent over the past decade. Violent incidents had reached nearly 14,000 that year, a rise of about 541 per cent in prisoner-on-prisoner violence (compared with 2,342 in 1996).[1] Some prisoner-on-prisoner violence is linked to drugs, which in itself remains a crisis within prisons. Bullying in prisons has created an unsafe environment for both staff and prisoners, particularly in Young Offender Institutions (see Smartt and Kury, 2002).

_____ Private Prisons _____

By May 2007, 11 prisons were contracted out and managed privately, accounting for 10 per cent of total capacity. This makes the UK, the most privatised prison system in Europe, with long established public–private partnerships, so-called 'Private Finance Initiatives' or PFIs.

Private sector prisons are subject to the same scrutiny inspections by the HM Chief Inspector of Prisons and have to comply with the *Prison Rules 1999* (as amended in 2005) and Prison Service Orders and Instructions.

James et al. (1997) compared penal practice and prison privatisation through the 1990s in the UK, North America, Europe and Australia. In particular, the authors and researchers from Hull University looked at the first UK private prison, HMP Wolds, from 1992 onwards and the way in which prisoners were treated in the private sector compared with the public sector HMP Hull 'next door'. The evidence suggests that some types of public service projects may be more suited to the PFI than others, such as prison projects which apparently have achieved reasonable efficiency gains with relatively minimal effects on the treatment of prisoners and the running of prisons. The main reason for this is that for PFI prison projects, there is no partition of core and ancillary services, enabling the private sector contractor to design, build and manage. Private prisons are intended by governments to help deal with a rising prison population. Generally speaking, private prisons have lower staff–prisoner ratios and inferior pay and conditions for staff compared with public prisons (see Allen, 2001).

## 7.4 ___ Offender management in Scotland _____

In the late 1960s and early 1970s the implementation of the Kilbrandon Report in Scotland led to a major reorganisation of social services (*Social Work (Scotland) Act 1968*) (see also Chapter 9.5). Unlike in England and Wales, the Scottish Probation Service was integrated with the social work departments and became the responsibility of local authorities, whereas the English Probation Service remained independent.

In 2004, Lord Coulsfield's Report on 'Crime, Courts and Confidence' compared the English and Scottish prison services and their effectiveness, with the outcome that short prison sentences do not work. The Report also confirmed criminological research that community sentences do not demonstrate reduced reconviction rates compared with prison. Lord Coulsfield advised the Scottish Executive that custody needs to be justified, particularly short custodial sentences and criticised NOMS which had turned the English Prison and Probation Services into a remote and bureaucratic organisation, hampered by Key Performance Indicators (KPIs) rather than focusing on their main aim to tackle recidivism.

*The Management of Offenders (Scotland) Act 2005* brought about the most radical reform in the Scottish criminal justice system for more than a generation.

### _____ Community justice in Scotland _____

Community Justice Authorities (CJAs) were established in each local authority, following the *Criminal Justice (Scotland) Act 2003*, bringing together all agencies, such as social work departments, police and the Scottish Prison Service, to create a more coherent and flexible system of offender management.

Warden schemes were introduced in the most problematic areas under the Scottish Executive's 'Partnership for a Better Scotland' initiative. Some warden schemes have been particularly effective in rural and island areas, such as Orkney, in order to assist widely dispersed populations. The warden scheme in Angus was introduced in 2004, where six wardens work in Arbroath and Forfar funded by the local council. They assist with police intelligence and have since substantially helped to reduce anti-social behaviour in some of the troubled areas. The aim with all warden schemes is high visibility within the neighbourhoods to enhance community safety. Community warden schemes are very diverse, but the main functions are:

- identifying and dealing with environmental problems including the removal of graffiti and abandoned vehicles

- helping to prevent crime and anti-social behaviour whilst also providing support for vulnerable members of the community
- assisting with housing management, tenant liaison and monitoring of empty properties
- fostering social cohesion, community engagement and development

The main difference between the Scottish and English community justice schemes is that the Scottish Executive chose a non-enforcement model. Scottish Community Wardens are seen more as civilian professional witnesses, the 'eyes and ears' of the local community (Scottish Parliament, 2003).

## Imprisonment in Scotland

For such a relatively small country, the prison population in Scotland is relatively high. In August 2003 there were 6,558 people imprisoned in Scottish prisons (130 per 100,000 inhabitants), rising to 7,273 in 2007. This represents one of the highest imprisonment rates in Western Europe.

Houchin (2005) linked the Scottish imprisonment rate to poverty and deprivation. He took the 'Scottish Index of Multiple Deprivation' (SIMD) of 2003 and examined the main criminogenic factors which had led to offending behaviour and imprisonment. These were:

- Low income
- Unemployment
- Poor health and disability
- Poor education, skills and training
- Poor geographical access to services

Houchin's research recognised the vital link between social exclusion and imprisonment, linked to poverty, chronic unemployment and generally poor life expectancy of prisoners in Scotland. Houchin's research team also found a high level of illiteracy amongst male prisoners; most of them had suffered chronic unemployment. Here are some of his main findings:

- Scottish men are 24 times more likely to be in prison than women
- 28 per cent of the prisoner population came from 'the poorest council estates' (compared with 10 per cent of the general population)
- 60 per cent of prisoners from Glasgow came from poor or social housing (Houchin, 2005)

## 7.5 —— The Northern Ireland Prison Service

With the *Northern Ireland (Sentences) Act 1998* – after the Belfast Agreement 1998 – the government permitted the early release of prisoners convicted of scheduled offences; most of them were IRA and terrorism-related (see McEvoy, 2001) (see Table 7.2).

- Acceptable Behaviour Contracts (ABCs)
- Post sentence requests by the victim (Probation Service)
- Community sentence with an 'activity' requirement, for instance, in domestic violence

There are a number of schemes operated by the various criminal justice agencies that incorporate restorative justice programmes which bring victims, offenders and communities together to decide on a response to a particular crime. Approaches can be used for a wide range of incidents, from minor anti-social behaviour like graffiti to serious crimes like assault and robbery. Victim participation is always voluntary and offenders need to have admitted some responsibility for the harm they have caused. Some restorative justice benefits include:

- **Victim–offender mediation** – where the offender is made to realise how the crime has affected the victim's or community's life
- **Forgiveness** – where the victim or community openly forgive the offender
- **Making amends** – where the offender makes good the harm caused directly to the people or organisations
- **Victim awareness** – victims are given a greater voice in the criminal justice system
- **Accountability** – offenders have to take responsibility for their actions
- **Community confidence** – that offenders are making amends for their wrong doing

Pilot studies have indicated that restorative justice approaches are not a soft option, as many offenders find it extremely difficult to face up to the impact of their crimes. Some have said that they'd rather do prison then face the uncomfortable truths of the restorative justice approach. Some practical examples can include:

- Repairing damaged property and graffiti removal
- Bringing shoplifters face to face with store managers to hear how shop theft affects others
- Writing a letter of apology to the victim
- Direct mediation, where victim, offender and the facilitator meet face to face
- Indirect mediation, where victim and offender communicate through letters passed on by a facilitator
- Conferencing – involving supporters for both parties
- Wider community mediation, involving the family or community as a support structure for the offender (particularly useful with young offenders)

## 7.7 ___ Case study

_____ R v Oliver and others [2003] 1 Cr LR 127 _____

*Oliver* deals with a number of offenders, all of whom were convicted of possession of indecent photographs of children on the Internet. In all cases, police forensic experts had impounded the defendants' personal computers, containing excessive numbers of downloads of pornographic images involving children, adults and animals. This type of netcrime is notoriously difficult to prove which in itself posed enormous technological challenges in court to prove 'possession' (see Home Office, 2004d).

The offence becomes more serious if the accused has not only downloaded the indecent child images from Internet sites, but has also created images himself by using modern technology (*Young* [2005]). The charge will then be 'making indecent photographs of a child' (s. 1(1)(a) and (b) of the *Protection of Children Act 1978* and the *Criminal Justice and Court Services Act 2000.*

---

### Facts of the case

Oliver had a habitual and compulsive habit to make or obtain indecent photographs or images of children on the Internet in vast quantities. The court had to prove 'possession' in this case, of 'indecent pseudo-photographs of a child', contrary to sections 160(1)(2)(a) and (3) of the *Criminal Justice Act 1988*, which states:

(1)   ...it is an offence for a person to have any indecent photograph [or pseudo-photograph] of a child ... in his possession.

(2)   Where a person is charged with an offence under subsection (1) above, it shall be a defence for him to prove

(a)   that he had a legitimate reason for having the photograph [or pseudo-photograph] in his possession; or

(b)   that he had not himself seen the photograph [or pseudo-photograph] and did not know, nor had any cause to suspect, it to be indecent; or

(c)   that the photograph [or pseudo-photograph] was sent to him without any prior request made by him or on his behalf and that he did not keep it for an unreasonable time

(2A)   A person shall be liable on conviction on indictment of an offence under this section to imprisonment for a term not exceeding five years or a fine, or both.

(3)   A person shall be liable on summary conviction of an offence under this section to [imprisonment for a term not exceeding six months or] a fine not exceeding level 5 on the standard scale [or both].

The offence becomes indictable dependent on the seriousness and gradients of the pictures. The '*Oliver*-guidelines', issued by the Court of Appeal, comprised a five-point scale which determines the mode of trial. These are:

Level 1:   images of children depicting erotic posing with no sexual activity
Level 2:   sexual activity between children, or solo masturbation by a child
Level 3:   non-penetrative sexual activity between adults and children
Level 4:   penetrative sexual activity between adults and children
Level 5:   sadism and bestiality involving children

---

The main problem for the Court of Appeal in *Oliver* was to address the level of crime involved and therefore the type and level of sentencing. Justices now have to take into account:

1   What types of images of children?
2   How young are the children?
3   What pose did the child feature in?
4   What type of sexual activity do the pictures feature and with whom?
5   Are the adults involved?
6   Are there scenes of rape, extreme fetish pseudo masochism or bestiality?

This question was particularly acute at Level 2. Once the mode of trial had been established – whether to try the defendant at the magistrates' or crown court – and the defendant had been found guilty – the next question arose as to *how* to sentence the defendant. The result could mean the difference between a six month suspended sentence at the magistrates' court or a 30 month custodial sentence at the crown court.

McVean and Spindler (2003) found that perpetrators involved in this type of Internet crime are only too keen to give evidence in court, once charged with possession of indecent images of children. They established that this type of offender usually possesses a high intelligence quotient, yet tends to be a socially and emotionally isolated middle-aged male.

 ■ Exam Questions ■

1   What does the presumption of innocence mean? Explain by reference to common law and punishment theories.
2   Discuss the significance of the concepts of culpability and commensurability for the theory of retribution.
3   Does restorative justice have an impact on the rehabilitation of offenders? Discuss.
4   Comment on the notion of 'risk' regarding the early release of prisoners in Northern Ireland following the Belfast Agreement in 1998.
5   Is community punishment a meaningful alternative to ease prison overcrowding?

■ ■ Further Resources ■

Ian Brownlee's *Community Punishment* (1998) provides a comprehensive account of non-custodial sentencing practices, including comparative data from the USA and Europe.

Martin Wright has devoted a lifetime to promoting restorative justice. In his *Restoring Respect for Justice* (1999) he presents us with a symposium and a survey on modern-day developments in the field, including victims, offenders, courts, mediators and restorative justice practitioners. Wright is a founder member of the Restorative Justice Consortium, and has spread the concept of Restorative Justice across Europe, including the training of senior judges.

Dennis Sullivan and Larry Tifft's *Handbook of Restorative Justice* (2006) gives a global perspective on the theme from eminent international scholars. The text gives some examples, such as the truth and reconciliation commissions in Northern Ireland, South Africa, Rwanda and the former Yugoslavia.

Anne Worrall and Claire Hoy's *Punishment in the Community* (2005) provides a critical analysis of professional and criminal justice developments relating to non-custodial penalties. The authors examine reasons why the public still sees community punishment as a 'soft option'.

## Notes

1  *Source*: Prison population figures and prisoner incidents, NOMS, April 2007.
2  House of Commons Northern Ireland Committee (2004) 'The separation of paramilitary prisoners at HMP Maghaberry', Second Report of Sessions 2003–04; 35ff. HC 302.
3  *Sources*: House of Commons (2003) The Steele Report on HMP Maghaberry in Northern Ireland. Submitted to the Secretary of State for Northern Ireland. EV 107; and joint statement by the POA and the Northern Ireland Office, 16 January 2004.

# 8

# HUMAN RIGHTS LEGISLATION

---

| **Overview** |

Chapter 8 examines:

- The practical application of human rights legislation in relation to criminology
- The meaning and functions of the European Convention on Human Rights and the *Human Rights Act 1998*
- The roles and functions of the European Court of Human Rights (Strasbourg) and the International Criminal Court (The Hague)
- The use of the death penalty in the world compared with countries that use life imprisonment

---

This chapter seeks to provide criminologists with an overview of human rights legislation, both in the European and the international arena. In Europe we have the *European Convention on Human Rights* of 1950, brought into UK law by way of the *Human Rights Act 1998* on 2 October 2000. The 1998 Act marked the biggest constitutional change in UK law for decades. You need to understand that the respect for fundamental human rights is an integral part of the general principles of law and that the 1998 Act affects all areas of law. Article 6 ECHR – 'right to a fair trial' – for instance, includes a suspect's right to silence at a police station (*Murray v UK* [1996]). But this is not absolute right and a judge may instruct a jury that inferences may be drawn from the accused's silence during a police interview (*Condron v UK* [2001]).

Amongst the many human rights topics and violations, this chapter will discuss the use of the death penalty. We will examine the interdisciplinary nature of international human rights law and will ask the overarching question: are human rights really universal?

## 8.1 ___ Historical background

The concept of human rights can possibly be traced back to the Ten Commandments or to early communitarianist ancient Greek philosophers' beliefs, such as Sophocles' (495–406 BC) theories on the individual's right to fight state repression or Plato (427–348 BC), who developed early ethical standards. Or to Aristotle's (384–322 BC) concept of distributive justice and his fight for the individual's right and justice in the community.

The Swiss philosopher Rousseau (1712–1778) talked about the 'social contract' between the individual and society. His French counterpart Montesquieu (1684–1755) stressed the importance of a state's separation of powers: the executive, the legislature and the judiciary and that they must be independent from each other. Some of these ancient concepts later shaped the principles of the United Nations (UN), whose remit is based on universal social justice in a democratic society.

As we already saw in Chapter 4, diplomatic efforts of some six states had succeeded in creating economic interdependence amongst its member states with the first trade-free customs union of the EEC based on the *Treaty of Rome* of 1957. But the EEC Treaty did not consider a global social order for Europe, nor did it address human rights of its community, because this had been left to the Universal Declaration of Human Rights, signed on 10 December 1948 by 48 members of the United Nations (UN).

## The Council of Europe (Strasbourg)

The Council of Europe was founded on 5 May 1949, when five EU governments signed the Brussels Treaty: Belgium, France, Luxembourg, the Netherlands and the United Kingdom. Denmark, Ireland, Italy, Norway and Sweden signed the statute in London. Presently, some 47 member states of the Council of Europe act through a Committee of Ministers, usually foreign secretaries. The Council of Europe's main objectives are security and greater human rights understanding and cooperation between member states with the Parliamentary Assembly situated in Strasbourg.

Since terrorism is a key challenge for Europe's open societies, the Assembly's 'Committee on Legal Affairs and Human Rights' urged all member states in 2007 to ensure that the fight against terrorism would not serve as a pretext to undermine or reduce the scope of fundamental human rights embodied in the European Convention.

## The European Convention on Human Rights

On 4 November 1950 the *European Convention for the Protection of Human Rights and Fundamental Freedoms 1950* – known either as 'the European Convention' or 'the Convention' (ECHR) – was signed by the member states of the Council of Europe. The Convention came into force on 3 September 1953 and various protocols were added in 1954, 1968, 1970, 1971, 1988 and

1990. Its primary objective was to avoid the atrocities and abuses of human rights witnessed in Europe during the First and Second World Wars.

You need to know that some of the Convention rights are only 'substantive'. This means they are not necessarily 'absolute' in domestic law and in certain situations, like in times of emergency or national security, national courts may derogate (deviate or even abolish) from the Convention under Art. 15 ECHR. Substantive human rights include:

- Art. 1: Obligation to respect human rights
- Art. 2: Guarantees the 'right to life'
- Art. 3: 'Freedom from torture, inhuman and degrading treatment'
- Art. 4: 'Freedom from slavery, forced or compulsory labour'
- Art. 5: 'Right to liberty and security of person'
- Art. 6: 'Right to a fair trial' (or right to a fair hearing)
- Art. 7: 'No punishment without law' (non-retrospectivity, i.e. prohibition from retrospective penal legislation)
- Art. 8: 'Right to privacy' (the right to respect for private and family life)
- Art. 9: 'Freedom of thought, conscience and religion'
- Art. 10: 'Freedom of expression'
- Art. 11: 'Freedom of peaceful assembly and association'
- Art. 12: 'Right to marry' (men and women of marriageable age have the right to marry and to found a family, according to the national laws)
- Art. 13: Remedies – it is the duty of a member state to provide effective remedies for any violation of the substantive rights protected by the Convention
- Art. 14: 'Non-discrimination'

In addition to the substantive articles of the Convention, there exist a series of Protocols on matters ranging from the 'right to peaceful enjoyment of possessions' (First Protocol, Art. 1), education (First Protocol, Art. 2), the holding of regular free elections (First Protocol, Art. 3), freedom of movement (Fourth Protocol), abolition of the death penalty (Sixth Protocol), appeals in criminal cases and sexual equality (Seventh Protocol), procedural matters under the Convention (Ninth Protocol) and minority right (Tenth Protocol). The UK is not a party to the Fourth, Sixth or Seventh Protocols.

It was only in 1998 that the British Government incorporated the European Convention into UK law by way of the *Human Rights Act 1998*. The 1998 Act came into force on 2 October 2000 and marked a significant change in British constitutional life. The Convention requires British courts not only to protect substantive Convention rights, but also to make 'declarations of incompatibility' where domestic law is concerned.

Since the Convention's incorporation into UK legislation, the judiciary is expected to be 'bold' in applying the Convention strictly. Individuals have to exhaust all domestic remedies, before they turn to the European Court of Human Rights in Strasbourg. This means, only where there is no remedy in domestic law, an individual can petition the human rights court. Lord Hope stated in the judicial review cases of *Sofiane Kebeline, Ferine Boukemiche* and

*Sofiane Souidi* [1999]:

> In this area, difficult choices may have to be made by the executive or the legislature between the rights of the individual and the needs of society. In some circumstances it will be appropriate for the courts to recognise that there is an area of judgement within which the judiciary will defer, on democratic grounds, to the considered opinion of the elected body or person whose act or decision is said to be incompatible with the Convention.

This means that the *Human Rights Act 1998* created new challenges to existing UK legislation, with new lines of defence in criminal trials. For example, the statute introduced the right governing the treatment of suspects, affecting the use of evidence in criminal trials.

What does the Convention prohibit? Here follows a brief summary:

- Torture and inhuman or degrading treatment or punishment
- Arbitrary and unlawful detention
- Discrimination in the enjoyment of the rights and freedoms set out in the Convention
- The expulsion by a state of its own nationals or its refusing them entry
- The death penalty
- The collective expulsion of aliens

Take a look at the judicial review case of Girling who, as a life sentence prisoner, applied for early release on licence due to being terminally ill:

---

### *R (on the application of Girling) v Parole Board* [2007] 2 All ER 688

Norman Girling (born 27 July 1943) applied for parole on the grounds of ill health; he had been diagnosed with acute myeloid leukaemia in June 2000. Girling had been convicted of a considerable number of criminal offences between 1956 and 1983 and on 25 September 1984, was convicted of murdering his partner, Edith Gorton. He was sentenced to life.

He had asked the local Parole Board for early release on licence (6 July 2001 and 8 October 2004) and on both occasions, the Board decided not to release him. He applied for judicial review on the grounds that the board had acted unreasonably and that the procedure contravened human rights.

His judicial review was granted on 7 January 2005. Girling argued that s. 32(6) *Criminal Justice Act 1991* contravened Art. 5 (1) ECHR *'right to liberty and security of person'*. Because Girling died on 9 August 2005, his appeal was reverted to the Home Secretary.

The Court of Appeal held that s. 32(6) CJA 1991 should be construed as giving the Home Secretary power to give directions to the Parole Board in each case where a prisoner challenges his human rights when licence on parole issues are addressed.

---

The decision in *Girling* cannot be seen as fully satisfactory and the government still has to address this situation.

In *Hirst v UK* (No 2) [2006] prisoners' voting rights were challenged in the European Human Rights court, since UK legislation bars people detained in prisons or mental hospitals from voting in parliamentary or local elections (s. 3 *Representation of the People Act 1985*). The Strasbourg court considered whether the UK was in breach of Art. 3 ECHR – 'freedom from torture' – by not allowing convicted prisoners to vote.

John Hirst, a life sentence prisoner at HMP Rye Hill in Warwickshire, challenged the voting ban, and on 6 October 2005, the European Court of Human Rights confirmed that the UK had breached Art. 3 ECHR, stating that voting was a right not a privilege and that free elections were part of the tolerance and broadmindedness of a democratic society. By taking this right away from prisoners, the UK had not offered him public opinion. In spite of the ECHR ruling, the UK Parliament has not changed its legislation at the time of going to print.

## 8.2 ___ The European Court of Human Rights ___

The European Court of Human Rights (ECHR) is an international court based in Strasbourg, France, set up by the Council of Europe in 1959. Since its inception, the court has made a considerable contribution to improving the standards of protection of human rights, based on the constitutional traditions common to the founder member states of the EU (see Chapter 4.1) and to international treaties on the protection of human rights, such as the Geneva Convention (see Chapter 8.3 below).

It is the Court's duty to examine complaints ('applications'), lodged either by individuals or by member states to the Council of Europe. Where the court finds that a member state has violated one or more of the Convention rights, the Strasbourg court delivers a judgement which binds the relevant state under an obligation to comply with the ruling – though as we have seen in *Hirst* above this is not always the case.

The Strasbourg court is presently composed of 47 judges, commensurate to the contracting member states and judges are elected by the Parliamentary Assembly of the Council of Europe, with a term of six years in office. Human rights court judges sit in their individual capacity and should not represent the interests of their state. Article 46 (1) ECHR ensures that the contracting states respect the judgements of the court. Most judgements are given by chambers, comprising seven judges each. Where a judgement has been delivered, either party may, within a period of three months, request referral of the case to the Grand Chamber. If this request is granted, the whole case is reheard. The Grand Chamber of the European Court of Human Rights is composed of 17 judges, including ex officio members, the President, Vice-Presidents and Section Presidents.

How can an individual lodge an application to the Strasbourg court? He must show that he has been a victim of a particular human rights violation, citing the article/s of the Convention (ECHR), rather than making a general complaint about a law in his country. Most importantly, the individual must have exhausted all legal remedies in his own state, which in the UK means the House of Lords. He also needs to show that the violation/s he is complaining of must have been committed by the state within its jurisdiction and territory (see *R v Secretary of State for the Home Department ex parte Duggan* [1994]). The time period for lodging an application at the Strasbourg court is six months, following the final judgement at his final or constitutional court (see *Cyprus v Turkey* [2001]).

Article 8 ECHR – 'right to respect for private and family life' – and Article 12 ECHR – 'right to marry and found a family' – were tested in prisoners' cases of *GS and RS v UK* [1991], where the delicate issue of conjugal visits in prison were at issue, together with artificial insemination facilities for long-term and lifer prisoners, where the wife in each case was considered too old to conceive by the time the prisoner husband was released from prison (see Chapter 8.7 case study *Mellor*).

## 8.3 ___ The Geneva Convention

International norms and standards have various legal effects depending on their sources. The basic source for international human rights standards can be found in the Geneva Convention, consisting of four treaties (agreements in international law). The main concern of the Geneva Convention of 1863 was the treatment of non-combatants and prisoners of war. The Geneva Convention was brought about in the Swiss city by the social activist Henri Dunant (1828–1910) who, motivated by the atrocities and horrors of war he witnessed at the Battle of Solferino in 1859, drew up the first human rights standards which became the basis for the first Resolution of the Geneva International Conference on 26–29 October 1863.

All four conventions were last revised and ratified in 1949, based on previous revisions and partly on some of the 1907 Hague Conventions. The whole set is referred to as the 'Geneva Conventions of 1949'. Some 200 countries are presently signatory nations. The Geneva Convention comprises:

- **The First Geneva Convention of 1863** – '*for the Amelioration of the Condition of the Wounded and Sick in Armed Forces in the Field*'
- **The Second Geneva Convention of 1949** – '*for the Amelioration of the Condition of Wounded, Sick and Shipwrecked Members of Armed Forces at Sea*'
- **The Third Geneva Convention 1929**, revised 1949 – '*relative to the Treatment of Prisoners of War*'
- **The Fourth Geneva Convention 1949** – '*relative to the Protection of Civilian Persons in Time of War*' (based on parts of The Hague Convention of 1907)

Three additional amendment protocols were added to the Geneva Convention:

- **Protocol I (1977)** – relating to the 'Protection of Victims of International Armed Conflicts', ratified by 167 countries
- **Protocol II (1977)** – relating to the 'Protection of Victims of Non-International Armed Conflicts', ratified by 163 countries
- **Protocol III (2005)** – relating to the 'Adoption of an Additional Distinctive Emblem', ratified by 17 countries and signed but not yet ratified by an additional 68 countries (as at June 2007)

It has been argued that the detention of some 770 captives from 26 countries to Camp X-Ray at Guantánamo Bay in Cuba has contravened the Geneva Convention. A further 194 captives were held at other US camps in Afghanistan. The detention facilities were set up by the USA in January 2002 to detain foreign prisoners suspected of links with Al Qaida or the Taliban. Guantánamo was not subject to normal US court rules and human rights watch groups found that prisoners were held under inhuman and degrading conditions (see Stafford Smith, 2007). The legality of the Guantánamo prison camp was challenged by Yemeni prisoner Salim Ahmed Hamdan, held at Guantánamo since November 2001. His appeal was granted in February 2007 by the US District Court of Columbia ruling that the United States had seriously violated all the detainees' human rights. Following this momentous decision, the US Supreme Court declared in June 2007 that the first military commissions authorised by President George Bush had been 'unlawful' and most prisoners were released and returned to their country of citizenship.

## 8.4 ___ The International Criminal Court in The Hague

The International Criminal Court (ICC) was established by the 'Rome Statute of the International Criminal Court' on 17 July 1998 by the 'United Nations Diplomatic Conference of Plenipotentiaries on the Establishment of the International Criminal Court' in Rome. The ICC in The Hague is an independent, permanent court 'of last resort'. This means the ICC tries persons accused of the most serious international crimes, such as genocide, crimes against humanity and war crimes. There are presently 104 'parties' (countries) to the ICC Treaty comprising 29 African states, 12 Asian states, 16 Eastern European, 22 Latin American and the Caribbean and 25 Western European and other states.

The International Criminal Court has its own procedural rules and legislation regarding laws on evidence, compelling a witness or disclosure. The ICC's 'Rules of Procedure and Evidence' grant a series of rights to victims, where they have an opportunity to present their views and observations before the court. Trials involve victims who have been damaged in the most severe manner. In the event of a violation finding, the ICC victims' trust fund provides victims with compensation to enable them to rebuild their lives which have often been destroyed by war or rape, for example after the atrocities in the Democratic Republic of Congo concering the recruitment and deployment of child soldiers (*ICC Prosecutor v Thomas Lubanga Dyilo* [2006]). The ICC will not act if a case is investigated or prosecuted by a national court, unless the national proceedings are not genuine. This is known as the 'principle of complementarity'.

One famous trial was that of Slobodan Milosevic which began on 11 February 2002. The ICC Prosecutor claimed that Milosevic was responsible for ordering the deaths of nearly a quarter of a million people in former Yugoslavia. He was charged with 66 crimes against humanity, genocide and 'ethnic cleansing' of Albanians to make room for the Serbs between 1992 and 1995. But before the trial could be concluded, Milosevic died in his cell at the Dutch Scheveningen Prison in mysterious circumstances on 11 March 2006. There were claims that he had been poisoned, though suicide was never ruled out.

## 8.5 ___ Control orders

In July 2000 Parliament enacted the *Terrorism Act 2000*, a substantial measure, with 131 sections and 16 Schedules, intended to overhaul, modernise and strengthen the law relating to the growing problem of terrorism. Following on from the 9/11 atrocities the British government reacted by quickly introducing the *Anti-terrorism, Crime and Security Act 2001* and by making the *Human Rights Act 1998 (Designated Derogation) Order 2001*. This legislation came in addition to existing arrest and deportation already in force where the Secretary of State wished to arrest or exclude non-British nationals from the UK if they were a threat to national security. No warrant was needed for the long-term detention of such suspects (paras 2(2) and 2(3) of Schedule 3 *Immigration Act 1971*).

In the House of Lords' 'Belmarsh Ruling' of 16 December 2004,[1] Lord Hoffmann delivered the 8:1 majority judgement (Lord Walker dissenting), stating that Britain's anti-terror laws were 'unlawful' and contravened human rights, namely that the detention of 16 men for an indefinite period was unlawful and contravened Art. 3 of the European Convention on Human Rights (ECHR), amounting to 'inhuman or degrading treatment or punishment'. Lord Nicholls of Birkenhead stated:

> Indefinite imprisonment without charge or trial is anathema in any country which observes the rule of law. It deprives the detained person of the protection a criminal trial is intended to afford. Wholly exceptional circumstances must exist before this extreme step can be justified. (Belmarsh ruling at para 74)

All men were Muslim asylum seekers, from countries like Algeria, Morocco, Egypt and Tunisia, accused of having links to Al Qaida and detained under the

*Anti-terrorism, Crime and Security Act 2001*, certified by the Home Office as 'suspected international terrorists'. Ten of the men were detained at the high security units of Belmarsh and Woodhill prisons for over 16 months. One man was held at Broadmoor high security mental hospital, named only in a judicial review case as 'M'. None of the detainees were charged with any offence since it emerged that the Home Office had no sufficient or admissible evidence against them, for example tapped phone evidence or taped conversations.

The appeals by the detainees were allowed and their Lordships declared that the government's derogation order and the provisions under the 2001 Act were contravening Arts. 3 and 5 of the European Convention on Human Rights. The men were released. This momentous judgement called into question the very existence of freedom from arbitrary arrest and detention and the House of Lords' judgement meant that they had ruled against the government. Their Lordships mentioned *inter alia* that the UK had been the only EU country that had contravened the European Convention post 9/11, considering France, Italy and Germany had been under similar terrorism threats.

After their release most of the 'Belmarsh' detainees were rearrested and put on control orders, introduced under the *Prevention from Terrorism Act 2005*, granting ministers the power to put individuals suspected of involvement in terrorism under close supervision or house arrest.

What are control orders? Issued by the Home Secretary the orders can apply to both British citizens and foreign nationals. The first type of control order lasts for twelve months and gives the Home Secretary the power to impose strict conditions on a subject's activities, including a ban on using the internet or mobile phones, coupled with curfew or travel restrictions. A detainee must report regularly to a designated police station. The second order is called a 'derogating control order' because it involves a special opt-out clause from the human rights convention which covers rights to liberty. The derogating control order last six months and is not renewable. These orders severely restrict the movements of an individual and must be served by a Home Office minister before both houses of Parliament at least 40 days before being served. Control orders can include the following restrictions:

- Electronic tagging
- No passport
- Live at one address
- Home detention curfew
- Restrictions on visitors
- No internet access
- Attend only one mosque
- Daily reporting to the police
- Daily monitoring by phone

Civil liberty groups have fiercely criticised control orders, saying that they are a 'draconian tool' and contravene human rights legislation. Shami Chakrabarti,

Director of 'Liberty', told the BBC on 24 May 2007, that 'innocent people are punished without trial and the potentially less innocent easily escape.' The Court of Appeal ruling in *MB* means that the validity of any control order must be reconsidered carefully by any Home Secretary or Minister of Justice.[2]

By 21 May 2007, some 17 control orders were in force and six detainees had absconded. One of the escapees, a 25-year-old British national, only named as AD, had escaped in September 2006 from a mental health unit. A month earlier, in August 2006, an Iraqi known as LL disappeared even before police officers could serve the control order and in January 2007, a third individual absconded soon after being served with the order.

On 13 February 2008, the government suffered a blow to its terrorism legislation. In *Zafar* [2008], the Court of Appeal ruled that section 57 of the *Terrorism Act 2000* was unsound, and that the legislation should be completely overhauled.[3] Five young British Muslim appellants were acquitted, having been previously found guilty of offences of possessing articles for a purpose connected with the commission, preparation or instigation of an act of terrorism, contrary to section 57 of the 2000 Act. The appellants had been arrested by the police for being in possession of radical Islamic material and internet chatroom discussions between all Bradford-four students and a cousin in Pakistan. The prosecution had alleged some of them had plans to go to train with militants in Pakistan.

The appellants won on the grounds that the prosecution should have proved that the material was directly connected to something that was clearly about to happen, rather than something that could possibly happen in the future. The Court of Appeal agreed that in counter-terrorism operations it was difficult for the police to decide when to make an arrest since it is their job to prevent a terrorist plot before it comes close to fruition, which is the key justification for section 57 – it is a law that helps the police stop dangerous people before they come up with a viable plot. In their ruling, the three appeal lords said the jury should have been told to decide whether there was a connection between the extremist literature and a clear terrorist plan.

The appeal judges did not just rule the convictions unsafe, they ruled that the law needed to be curtailed.

## 8.6 ___ The death penalty or life imprisonment? _____

Capital punishment has been regarded by many societies as the ultimate form of punishment. The death penalty is seen by some countries as the necessary deterrence, justified by governments of 67 countries in the world for crime committed within their legal systems in 2007.

The USA still actively supports and practices capital punishment as well as nations in Africa and the Middle East. It has been known that capital punishment, say in Texas, by lethal injections or electrocution have not always been smooth and painless. They can cause painful deaths and are actually a form of torture. Keeping prisoners on death row in the Californian state prison of St Quentin for many years is in itself cruel, degrading and a form of torture, by allowing repeated appeals to condemned prisoners on death row. The world leader in the death penalty is China, which applies capital punishment to about 68 crimes, including non-violent offences, such as tax fraud by 'embezzling state property' and accepting bribes. According to Amnesty International, over 1,770 people were executed and 3,900 sentenced to death in 2005; but true figures are believed to be much higher.

One argument against the death penalty is that miscarriages of justice do happen. Since 1945, three people have received posthumous pardons in the UK, the first being Timothy Evans in 1966. Evans was sentenced to death for the murder of his child and was hanged on 9 March 1950 at Pentonville Prison. Then there was 28 year-old Somali-born merchant seaman Mahmood Hussein Mattan who was found guilty of the murder of Lily Volpert at the Glamorganshire Assizes in September 1952 and subsequently hanged. Probably the most famous case that people in the UK will remember is that of 19-year old educationally backward Derek Bentley who was found guilty of the murder of PC Miles and hanged at Wandsworth Prison on 28 January 1953. Bentley was pardoned in 1998 (you may wish to see the film *Let Him Have It*, 1991).

There are clearly abolitionist countries and retentionist countries. Two-thirds of the countries in the world, about 133, had abolished the death penalty in law or practice by 2008, and in December 2007, New Jersey became the first of the US states to abolish capital punishment in 40 years. In 2006, 91 per cent of all known executions took place in six countries: China, Iran, Pakistan, Iraq, Sudan and the USA. International law prohibits the use of the death penalty for crimes committed by juveniles, yet the execution of child offenders continues in a few countries, particularly Iran (Amnesty International, 2007). Once abolished, the death penalty is seldom reintroduced but four abolitionist countries reintroduced the death penalty and two of them – Nepal and Philippines – have since abolished capital punishment again. There have been no executions in the other two – Gambia and Papua New Guinea (see Hood, 2002).

At the 62nd Assembly, the United Nations called on 27 countries to abolish capital punishment (Statement on World Day Against the Death Penalty by Benita Ferrero-Waldner, 10 October 2007). Methods of execution in these countries include:

- Beheading (Saudi Arabia)
- Electrocution (USA)
- Hanging (Egypt, Iran, Japan, Jordan, Pakistan, Singapore)
- Lethal injection (China, Guatemala, Thailand, USA)
- Shooting (Belarus, China, Somalia, Taiwan, Uzbekistan, Vietnam)
- Stoning (Afghanistan, Iran)

Emeritus Professor of Criminology, Roger Hood, has campaigned tirelessly to abolish the death penalty (see also Hood and Seemungal, 2006). He argues that one of the most important developments in recent years has been the adoption of international treaties whereby states commit themselves to abolish the death penalty. These are:

- **Protocol No. 6 to the European Convention** – this is an agreement to abolish the death penalty in peacetime
- **Protocol No. 13 to the European Convention** – this provides for the total abolition of the death penalty in all circumstances
- **The Second Optional Protocol to the International Covenant on Civil and Political Rights** – this provides for the total abolition of the death penalty but allows states wishing to do so to retain the death penalty in wartime as an exception
- **The Protocol to the American Convention on Human Rights**

What then are the common myths and arguments about the death penalty?

### The death penalty is a deterrent?

It has never been statistically proven that capital punishment deters future crime more effectively than other punishments. Numerous studies have failed to establish that execution deters better than a life sentence. The USA, for example, has the highest murder rate in the industrialised world, with the highest rates occurring in Southern states, where the most executions occur (Hood, 2002: 230).

### Sweet revenge: murderers deserve no mercy!

The logical argument usually put forward by supporters of capital punishment is, if someone has committed murder, he must be punished in the same way, as stated in the Bible, Matthew 5.38, 'An eye for an eye and a tooth for a tooth'; or the Holy Qur'an verses 5.32 and 5.33.

Arguably, everyone is entitled to full protection before the law and full observance of their human rights, including the right to a fair trial (Art. 3 ECHR) and therein to seek pardon. Then there is the finality of capital punishment in that it does not allow the convicted criminal the opportunity to repent. Miscarriages of justice have occurred when the death penalty was inflicted on the innocent: 95 people have been released from death row in the USA since 1973, when condemned prisoners were wrongly convicted. Retribution and revenge then become the weakest arguments for the law makers to justify capital punishment, even for the most heinous killings.

### Most countries have the death penalty

This is not the case. You have seen with the above statistics that show that about 133 countries have ended capital punishment in law or practice, leaving about 63 retentionist states.

Not true. Van Kesteren et al. (2000) found that recent International Crime Victim Surveys have increasingly found that more and more people support the abolition of the death penalty, even in former communist Eastern European states, where the death penalty was commonplace and public attitudes to punishment were harsh (see Kury et al., 2002: 93–115).

Many countries, even some of the US states, are now moving towards the abolition of capital punishment and trends indicate an increase in the number of offences that carry the sanction of life imprisonment, though many without the possibility of parole.

## _____ Life imprisonment _____

Art. 2 of the European Convention, 'right to life', has long been at the forefront of abolitionists' thinking. Countries that have life imprisonment instead of the death penalty have legislated for various sentence lengths. Some European countries have a mandatory life sentence only for specific categories of murder, such as Germany where a conviction for '*Mord*' (murder) has to prove a specific motive (§ 211 *Strafgesetzbuch* – Penal Code). There are present concerns regarding the release of some of the most notorious German terrorists, the Red Army Faction or RAF ('*Rote Armee Faktion*') on licence, many of whom have served more than 20 years of a life sentence in German high security prisons.

In August 2007, the Higher Regional Court in Frankfurt ordered the release on parole of Eva Haule, convicted and sentenced to life for participating in the bombing of the US Rhine-Main Airbase and the murder of US soldier Edward Pimental. Brigitte Mohnhaupt, an RAF leader, was released on parole after serving 24 years in prison in March 2007. However, the German President, Horst Koehler, refused the parole application by Christian Klar in May 2007; Klar is serving a life sentence for the murders of the Dresdner Bank Chief Executive Jürgen Ponto and the kidnapping and killing of the industrialist Hanns Martin Schleyer in 1977.

In the USA, life sentences are imposed for drug crimes and non-violent offences resulting from the 'three strikes' legislation in some states, resulting in an immense increase of 'lifers', by 83 per cent between 1992 and 2003. In Michigan, 200 people were serving life terms for drug offences under the '650 lifer' law in 2003; this legislation refers to the selling of 650 grams of illegal drugs (e.g. cocaine or heroin) which imposes a mandatory life sentence (Maurer et al., 2004).

Van Zyl Smit (2005) stated that the lifer population in South Africa increased from 443 to 5,745 between 1995 and 2005 – an increase of over 1,000 per cent. Unlike in Britain where life sentence prisoner conditions are generally satisfactory, prisoners in South Africa are said to suffer worse conditions compared with those endured by 'ordinary' categories of prisoner.

Since the abolition of the death penalty in Britain, the Prison Reform Trust has highlighted the plight of some 5,268 life sentence prisoners (see Prison Reform Trust, 2004) whereby England and Wales have the highest lifer population out of all the 47 member states of the Council of Europe. Between 1994 and 2004, Britain's 'lifer' prisoner population increased by 75 per cent. The *Criminal Justice Act 2003* introduced the 'Sentence of Imprisonment for Public Protection' (IPP) in April 2005. There were 1,570 IPP receptions and 590 receptions for all other indeterminate sentenced prisoners in 2006. This further increased the lifer population with a result that British prisons are faced with an increasingly ageing population.

Receptions of prisoners with indeterminate sentence – either a life sentence[4] or an IPP – increased from 1,050 in 2005 to 2,160 in 2006, up 106 per cent. Of these, 390 were mandatory lifers (see Ministry of Justice, 2007b; see also Creighton et al., 2004). This poses significant challenges for the care and treatment of life sentence and long-term prisoners, particularly for those who require specialist medical treatment on a long-term basis (see Coyle, 2005).

## 8.7 ____ Case study

### R (Mellor) v Secretary of State for the ————— Home Department [2001] QB 13 —————

Life sentence prisoner Mellor's judicial review case relates to his application regarding his right – under Art. 8 ECHR – to artificial insemination on the grounds that his wife would be too old to conceive by the time he might be granted parole.

---

### Facts of the case

In February 1995, Gavin Mellor was given a mandatory 12-year life sentence for murdering 71-year-old grandfather and war veteran George Sims, as he walked home from a working men's club in Crewe, Cheshire. Mellor's life sentence tariff was due to expire in 2006, when he would be 35 and his wife would be 31. The earliest parole application would be in 2004.

Mellor had met his wife Tracey McColl in 1997 while she was working as an administrative officer in Gartree prison where Mellor was serving part of his life sentence. They married in July 1997, after Tracey resigned from the Prison Service and Mellor sought permission to provide semen to allow his wife to be artificially inseminated because they 'desperately wanted to start a family'.

*(Continued)*

---

The Home Secretary, Jack Straw, refused the applicant's request on the ground that there was no medical need for artificial insemination and expressed his concern about the long-term stability of the marriage. Mellor applied for judicial review in October 2000, claiming that artificial insemination was his 'human right', under Art. 12 ECHR 'right to marry and found a family' and that the Prison Service had also contravened Art. 8.

On 18 June 2001, Mr Justice Forbes at the High Court refused Mellor's application for judicial review, giving reason that one of the purposes of imprisonment was to punish the criminal by depriving him of certain rights and pleasures which he could only enjoy when at liberty, including the enjoyment of family life, the exercise of conjugal rights and the right to found a family. He summarised that fundamental human rights did not include the right of a prisoner to inseminate his wife by artificial means; therefore the Prison Service had not infringed Arts. 8 or 12 ECHR. Mellor was refused permission to appeal to the Court of Appeal.

The case of *Mellor* shows that human rights legislation is not absolute and has to be seen proportionately within the criminal justice system. The High Court Judge Mr Justice Forbes also referred to public perception in relation to legitimate penal policy, in that it was the duty of the courts to maintain public confidence in the criminal justice system. What would the public, and indeed the media, have made of the fact that the prison authorities had granted a prisoner the right to beget children by artificial insemination? By granting Mellor this right, this case would set a precedent for all prisoners.

On 4 December 2007, the European Court of Human Rights ruled that the UK had contravened Art. 12 ECHR on the application of life sentence prisoner Kirk Dickson, convicted of murder in 1994, to artificially inseminate his wife Lorraine (born 1958) in 2001, given Dickson's earliest release date of 2009. The Grand Chamber of the Strasbourg court ruled that Britain's decision had violated the European Convention of Human Rights' article on the 'right to respect for private and family life', awarding the applicants 5,000 euros in damages and 21,000 euros for expenses (*Dickinson v UK* [2007]).

## ■ Exam Questions

1  Are human rights absolute? Discuss with reference to legislation.
2  Discuss the arguments for and against capital punishment.
3  What is the main purpose of the International Criminal Court? Discuss.
4  Should artificial insemination and conjugal visits for prisoners be left to the courts to decide? Discuss with reference to common law.

## ■ ■ Further Resources ■

Steve Uglow, Deborah Cheney, Lisa Dickson and John Fitzpatrick's excellent Chapter 6 'Prisoner's Rights' in the rather volumous *Criminal Justice and the Human Rights Act* (1999) provides detailed analysis of the far-reaching implications of the *Human Rights Act 1998* in relation to prisoners' rights.

Stephen Shute et al.'s *A Fair Hearing? Ethnic Minorities in the Criminal Courts* (2005) examines the extent to which ethnic minority defendants and witnesses are perceived to be discriminated against in the criminal courts.

## ___ Notes

1 *A (FC) and others (FC) v Secretary of State for the Home Department; X (FC) and another v Secretary of State for the Home Department (FC)* [2004] UKHL 56 (sub nom 'Belmarsh Ruling'] of 16 December 2004, House of Lords.
2 *Secretary of State for the Home Department v MB* [2006] EWCA Civ 1140.
3 *Zafar and others v R* [2008] EWCA Crim 184, CA.
4 A life sentence is wholly indeterminate. There is no entitlement to release at any stage but offenders may be considered for release on licence by the Parole Board once the minimum period imposed to meet the requirements of retribution and deterrence has been served. The main criterion governing the Parole Board's consideration is the level of risk of serious harm that the lifer may pose to others. If released, life sentence prisoners are on licence for the rest of their lives and liable to recall at any time. Sentence prisoners are released under the terms of the *Crime (Sentences) Act 1997*.

# 9

# YOUNG PEOPLE AND THE LAW

<table>
<tr><td>

**Overview**

Chapter 9 examines:

- Youth justice legislation in England and Wales, Northern Ireland and Scotland
- The criminal process which treats children and young persons differently to adults in each jurisdiction
- Young offending teams and restorative justice programmes in all three jurisdictions
- Custodial punishments for young offenders and extended custody provisions for dangerous offenders
- Community justice and youth conferencing

</td></tr>
</table>

This final chapter gives you an overview of youth justice procedures related to all three jurisdictions, England and Wales, Scotland and Northern Ireland. The age of criminal responsibility in England, Wales and Northern Ireland is ten years old, with Scotland imposing an even lower age of criminal responsibility, at eight years old, though the chapter will stress that youth justice in Scotland is mostly diverted to the Children's Hearings system rather than for prosecution in the courts.

The criminological literature will tell you, however, that not all deprived youngsters or those from one parent families turn to crime. This means their environment has toughened their resilient identities and many young people have become mentors with intelligence and smartness in their school or higher educational environment (see Smartt, 2006a: 33–44).

Restorative justice plays a major part in the youth justice process, the idea being to make young deviants aware of their victims and instruct them how to take account of the harm caused to society by their anti-social and criminal behaviour.

## 9.1 ____ Youth crime

You learnt at the start of this book that certain criminogenic factors can bring about deviant and criminal behaviour in young people, including:

- A troubled home life
- Poor attainment at school + truancy + school exclusion
- Drug or alcohol misuse + mental illness
- Deprivation, such as poor housing or homelessness
- Peer group pressure

According to the Home Office (2007b) youth crime has not actually increased substantially since 2001 and the number of known young offenders fell by 14 per cent between 1995 and 2001. The British Crime Survey 2006 established that violent crime had fallen by 41 per cent since it peaked in 1995. The risk of being a victim of violent crime was 3.6 per cent and young men, aged 16 to 24, remain most at risk, with 13.8 per cent experiencing a violent crime of some sort in 2006 (Home Office, 2007c).

The survey also showed that 10- to 15-year-olds were more likely than 16- to 25-year-olds to have been victims of personal crime. The majority of incidents against 10- to 15-year-olds happened at school. Young males were also significantly more likely than females to have carried a knife (5 per cent versus 2 per cent) (Home Office, 2006c).

## Gun violence, illegal and offensive weapons

What do we know about gun crime in the UK? According to Home Office figures, there were 58 firearms-related homicides in 2006–07, compared with 49 in the previous year, an increase of 18 per cent in one year. There were 413 firearms incidents that resulted in serious injury – more than one a day. But at the same time, the trend in gun crime overall has decreased since UK gun laws changed after the Hungerford (1987) and Dunblane (1996) massacres and is mostly related to adult offending. Overall, firearms offences fell by 13 per cent in 2006–07 to 9,608 incidents – the lowest number in seven years, though handgun and stabbing offences amongst young people have risen sharply.

The terrible killing of 11-year-old Rhys Jones, shot dead by a youth on a BMX bicycle at a pub car park in Croxteth, Liverpool, on 22 August 2007 brought the number of gun-related killings to eight young people in 2007: six in London, one in Manchester and Rhys Jones in Liverpool. Another example was the killing of 12-year-old Kamilah Peniston in Manchester in 2003. She was accidentally shot by her 16-year-old brother, a gang member.

It would be wrong to draw simple nationwide conclusions about gun crime, particularly in relation to young people. What we can say with some certainty, is that gun crime and stabbings are a problem amongst the young, particularly in some metropolitan areas of the UK, resulting in some terrible deaths.

The most common weapon used in violent youth crime is the knife. Of the 24 violent teenager deaths nationwide since the beginning of 2007, 16 had been stabbings (Centre for Crime and Justice Studies, 2006). Brookman and

Maguire (Home Office, 2003b) found that young people over 16 are generally at greater risk of becoming a victim than children or older adults, with the peak ages among adults tending to be aged between 21 and 25. Offenders tend to be young, with most aged between 18 and 35. Young males are more likely than females to be offenders and victims of homicides; this means that males comprise 80–90 per cent of offenders and 60 per cent of victims. Around half of all homicides involve a male offender and male victim. The study further established that both offenders and victims tend to come from lower socio-economic groups (Home Office, 2003b).

The Metropolitan Police Authority stated in 2004 that younger children were increasingly involved in gangs, with at least 171 gangs in London, three of which were girl gangs. The police authority recommended early intervention by families, youth workers and schools to protect young children from joining gangs. 39,000 offences were committed by young men and 15,000 by young women in 2006. Only 1,500 resulted in some form of detention – nine involved a life detention order.[1]

Muncie (2004) strongly believes that there needs to be a radical overhaul of the way society tackles the growing problem of teenage violence that has spread from the inner cities to rural towns and villages. He also sees peer and sibling pressure as one of the key drivers for gang recruitment, as young children are drawn into criminal activity. He argues that policing alone will not make a lasting impact on the threat of gang violence which is as serious as that of terrorism in terms of the deaths and injuries caused.

## 9.2 ____ Youth courts in England and Wales _____

There is one case which changed the way young offenders are tried in criminal courts in England and Wales – the heinous killing of 18-month-old toddler James Bulger in February 1993 by two 10-year-old boys, Robert Thompson and Jon Venables. Following this singular incident, Parliament lowered the age of criminal responsibility from 13 down to 10 years old under section 34 of the *Crime and Disorder Act 1998*. Before, there existed the doctrine of *doli incapax*, the presumption that a child was incapable of committing an offence, unless he knew that what he was doing was seriously wrong.

Today, Youth Courts (part of a magistrates' court) normally try young persons aged between 10 and 18 and they operate *in camera*, that is with the exclusion of the public. Any serious crimes will go to the adult crown court. Appearance in court is usually informal and the young defendant will not stand outside the dock, accompanied by either a parent, guardian or youth offending team worker or youth service worker. The Youth bench must contain at least one woman.

The Youth Justice Board (YJB) was put on a statutory footing with the *Crime and Disorder Act 1998*; its remit was broadened in 2001, introducing more restorative justice practices under the *Youth Justice and Criminal Evidence Act 1999*. The main aim of the YJB is to prevent offending by children and in doing so, it delivers a range of services, often in partnership with others, to help children and young offenders address their offending behaviour, divert them from crime, assist their integration into the community, and to meet the needs of victims of crime. The Youth Justice Board's Restorative Justice (RJ) programmes include:

- **Neighbourhood and community policing teams** Police Community Support Officers (PCSOs) deal with low-level incidents, providing effective diversion from court. The idea is to ease the pressure on the youth justice system and support simple and speedy summary justice.
- **Secure estate support** YOTs deliver intensive conflict resolutions and behaviour management courses at young offender institutions (YOIs) and secure units
- **Children's homes and schools** YOTs deliver anti-bullying programmes and manage conflict between young people; the idea is to reduce the risk that young people may become involved in crime and anti-social behaviour
- **Parenting Academies** Where parents and their children learn to live together through RJ.

## Youth Offending Teams

Youth Offending Teams (YOT) are a part of the Youth Justice Board; their multidisciplinary nature means that they offer young deviants a range of services to meet their wider needs, such as health, education, training and employment, substance misuse and homelessness. The ultimate aim is to stop reoffending and to bring some support and stability into certain young people's chaotic lifestyles. By far the most common used by the courts for a first court appearance for a young offender who pleads guilty is the Referral Order – even for a very serious offence such as arson or ABH. The order usually follows a reprimand and Final Warning.

## The Youth Offender Panel (Community Panels)

Similar to the Scottish Children's Hearing System, some English and Welsh counties have introduced Youth Offender Panels, also known as 'Community Panels'. Such panels comprise local volunteers and the emphasis lies on the young person (YP) taking responsibility for his own (criminal) actions. Failure to comply with the conditions agreed in a contract between the panel and the

YP becomes the responsibility of the parent or guardian. If there is a repeated failure to attend appointments, the Youth Justice Officer informs the panel and 'breach' proceedings before the Youth Court will begin. A 17-year-old may choose not to have a supporter with him at court or at the panel hearing.

Victim presence has been introduced at panel hearings. This is seen as a very powerful tool though many victims tend not to appear at panel hearings. The panel can request a review at the three months stage of a nine to twelve month Referral Order to assess the YP's progress. The results tend to be positive, particularly where the YP has been assessed as 'high-risk' or even 'dangerous'.

## 9.3 ___ Dangerousness and bad character _____

The *Criminal Justice Act 2003* introduced the notion of 'dangerousness' into criminal proceedings for youths (Chapter 5, ss. 224–236 CJA 2003). This means, when a young person has been convicted of a 'specified offence' (see below), the court must assess them for dangerousness. A member of the YOT-team has to prepare a pre-sentence report that should indicate the key risk factors identified through *'Asset'* database assessment on risk and the likelihood any behaviour could have on harming other people. The question should be asked: does the young offender pose a *significant risk* of serious harm to members of the public through the commission of further specified offences? The following sentencing guidelines may assist you regarding youth justice proceedings:

- **Dangerousness**   A category of specific sexual and violent offences
- **Detention for Public Protection (DPP)**   An indeterminate sentence
- **Extended Sentence for Public Protection**
- **Youth Community Order**   For 16–17 year olds, includes all youth community sentences
- **Bad Character**   Now admissible, same as in the adult court
- **Parenting Order Residential Requirements**
- **Individual Support Orders (ISOs)**   For young people on Anti-Social Behaviour Orders (ASBOs)
- **Automatic conditional release**   At mid-point of sentence for offenders serving determinate sentences (under Her Majesty's Pleasure)

_____ Bad character _____

Similar to what you already learnt in Chapter 6.8 for adults, the *Criminal Justice Act 2003* introduced bad character evidence to be adduced in youth court proceedings. What is important here is the reference to 'future behaviour' when such evidence is adduced during trial proceedings concerning a young person which possibly goes against the spirit of the *Children and Young Persons Act of 1933* which had an essentially rehabilitative aim. YOTs and youth justices now have to critically assess the likelihood of future behaviour and dangerousness (*R v D* [2005]). The Youth Justice Board has laid down the following guidelines for youth magistrates when bad character evidence may be permitted:

- What is the nature of the behaviour causing concern?
- What is its impact?
- Who is likely to be the victim?
- What would be the impact on the victim or victims?
- What is the likelihood of the behaviour occurring?
- In what circumstances is the behaviour likely to happen?
- How likely is it that the young person will find himself in these circumstances?
- What are the protective factors that would reduce the likelihood of this behaviour occurring?

## Specified offences (Schedule 15, CJA 2003)

Specified – or 'Schedule 15' – offences are grave crimes and if they were committed by an adult, they would attract a maximum sentence of at least 14 years' imprisonment. In total there are 153, some of which are listed below:

- Wounding with intent to cause grievous bodily harm (GBH) (s. 18 OAPA)
- Malicious wounding (s. 20 OAPA)
- Carrying a firearm with criminal intent (s. 18 *Criminal Justice Act 2003*)
- Robbery (s. 8 *Theft Act 1968*)
- Arson (s. 1 *Criminal Damage Act 1971*)
- Causing death by dangerous driving (s. 1 *Road Traffic Act 1988*)
- Putting people in fear of violence (s. 4 *Protection from Harassment Act 1997*)
- Racially or religiously aggravated assault (s. 29 *Crime and Disorder Act 1998*)
- Rape (s. 1 *Sexual Offences Act 1956*; s. 1 *Sexual Offences Act 2003* [SOA])
- Intercourse with a girl under 13 (s. 5 SOA 2003)
- Intercourse with a girl under 16 (s. 6 SOA 2003)
- Indecent assault on a woman (s. 14 SOA 2003)
- Soliciting by men (s. 32 SOA 2003)
- Inciting girl under 16 to have incestuous sexual intercourse (s. 54 *Criminal Law Act 1977*)
- Sexual assault (s. 3 SOA 2003)

## Significant risk

Apart from being assessed as 'dangerous', young offenders are also assessed as to whether they pose a *significant risk* to the public. This is not defined in statute and we have to rely on common law definitions, such as the Court of Appeal's ruling in *Lang and Ors* [2005]:

The risk identified must be significant. This is a higher threshold than mere possibility of occurrence and in our view can be taken to mean noteworthy, of considerable amount or importance.

## 9.4 —— Sentencing young offenders

The general sentencing options for young offenders include:

- **Referral Order** – the young person has to agree to a behaviour contract with their parents/guardians and the victim (where appropriate), to repair the harm caused by the offence and address the causes of the offending behaviour
- **Action Plan Order** – three-month, intensively supervised community service programme, focusing on education and involving the young person's parents/guardians
- **Reparation Order** – a court order requiring a young person to repair the harm caused to an individual or the community, for example, through mediation or community service work
- **Parenting Order** – a requirement for parents to attend counselling and guidance sessions where they receive help in dealing with their children
- **Drug Treatment and Testing Requirements** attached to Supervision Orders and Action Plan Orders
- **Electronic tagging** as part of an **Intensive Supervision and Surveillance Programme (ISSP)** – for the most persistent offenders aged 12–16, on bail or on remand in local authority accommodation

—————— Detention and custody of young offenders ——————

*The Powers of Criminal Courts (Sentencing) Act 2000* imposed certain restrictions on young persons under 18, extended to 'young adults', aged 18–21, who have committed serious and 'dangerous' offences.

Young offenders who commit murder when under 18 continue to be detained at Her Majesty's Pleasure (HMP) (*Children and Young Persons Act 1933*). Section 91 of the 2000 Act gives the courts for offenders under 18 specified powers where the offence is so serious that the young person – assessed as 'dangerous' – can receive an 'Extended Sentence'. Offences include:

a   Sentencing to at least 14 years' imprisonment
b   An indecent assault on a woman (s. 14 *Sexual Offences Act 1956*)
c   An indecent assault on a man (s. 15 *Sexual Offences Act 1956* post 30 september 1997)
d   Causing death by dangerous driving (s. 1 *Road Traffic Act 1988*)

The following 'life' sentencing options are available to the courts:

1   **Detention for Life**: the offence is so serious the young person must receive a 'life' sentence at Her Majesty's Pleasure.
2   **Extended Sentence**: if the offence is not serious enough to justify a 'Detention for Life' sentence, the court can impose an 'Extended Sentence'.
3   **Detention for Public Protection**: if it is felt that an Extended Sentence would not be adequate for the purpose of protecting the public from *serious harm*.

Young offenders on determinate sentences no longer get automatic conditional release at the mid-point of their sentence. If they are released on licence, granted by the Parole Board, the licence period in the community will last until the full sentence expiry date, irrespective of sentence length.

## 9.5 ___ Youth justice in Scotland

The age of criminal responsibility starts early in Scotland, at the age of eight. In 1961, a senior judge, Lord Kilbrandon, was appointed by the Secretary of State for Scotland, 'to consider the provisions of the law of Scotland relating to the treatment of juvenile delinquents and juveniles in need of care or protection or beyond parental control' (Kilbrandon Report 1964). This means that young offenders between the ages of eight and fifteen are seldom subjected to the adult criminal court system in Scotland (see Burman et al., 2006: 439–472).

### ___ The Children's Hearing system ___

Section 41(1) *Criminal Procedure (Scotland) Act 1995* reads:

> No child under the age of 16 years shall be prosecuted for any offence except on the instructions of the Lord Advocate, or at his instance; and no court other than the High Court and the sheriff court shall have jurisdiction over a child under the age of 16 for an offence.

This means that most children under 16 are dealt with by the Children's Hearing system in Scotland. For more serious offences the case may be heard in the Sheriff or even High Court.

Each local authority area has a Children's Panel, part of the Children's Hearing system in Scotland, made up of volunteers appointed by the First Minister on the advice of the area's Children's Panel Advisory Committee (*Children (Scotland) Act 1995*).

The grounds for bringing a young person before a Children's Hearing Panel include that the youngster is:

- beyond the control of parents or carers
- likely to suffer serious harm to health or development through lack of care
- misusing drugs, alcohol or solvents
- accused of an offence
- truanting from school
- subject to an ASBO (*Antisocial Behaviour (Scotland) Act 2004*)

What then happens at a Children's Hearing? The tribunal is held in the young person's home area and the young person must attend, accompanied by a relevant adult.

In serious cases, the Procurator Fiscal refers the young person first to the Children's Reporter for a decision on whether referral to a Children's Hearing is more appropriate.

One such case was that of Luke Mitchell, who at age 16 was found guilty of stabbing his 14-year-old girlfriend Jodi Jones to death in Dalkeith, Midlothian. He was convicted by a majority jury verdict at the Edinburgh High Court on 21 January 2005 and sentenced to life imprisonment by presiding judge, Lord Nimmo Smith.

The Children's Reporter acts as 'gatekeeper' to the Children's Hearing System and all young people who may need compulsory measures of supervision must be referred first to the Reporter. In practice, referrals come mainly from the police, social workers, health or education officials.

Recently, the Children's Hearing system has encountered some criticism whereby questions have been asked about their ability to deal effectively with dangerous and very violent young offenders. Some critics argue that that Children's Hearing Panels are perhaps too lenient and outdated.

## Youth warden community schemes

The City of Edinburgh Council operates a youth justice programme, funded by the Scottish Executive, linking community wardens and specialist youth workers. Each warden scheme includes a restorative justice element. Youth warden schemes can include:

- Cooperation with local schools to build up relationships of trust and respect
- Youth clubs
- Reduce bullying at school
- Improve school attendance
- Encourage healthier lifestyles
- Drugs outreach teams

## 9.6 — Youth justice in Northern Ireland

Under section 53(6) of the *Justice (Northern Ireland) Act 2002*, a 'youth' is a child under the age of 17 (also Criminal Justice (Children)(Northern Ireland) Order 1998 for youth criminal proceedings). On 1 April 2003, the Northern Ireland Youth Justice Agency was launched as an Executive Agency and part of the Northern Ireland Office, replacing the Juvenile Justice Board.

The principal aim of the Youth Justice Agency is to reduce youth crime and to build confidence in the youth justice system. Unlike in England and Wales, the juvenile custody population has fallen dramatically in Northern Ireland. During the late 1980s to the mid-1990s, there were some 200 juveniles held in custody – known as 'training schools' – across the province. Custody lengths for juveniles were generally longer than for adults convicted for similar offences.

Similar to statistics from England and Wales, the reconviction data shows that the majority of juveniles released from custody re-offend within three years, that is 97 per cent of boys released from training schools reconvicted within three years (O'Mahony and Deazley, 2000). The *Justice (Northern Ireland) Act 2002* introduced new measures with the aim to prevent re-offending by children. The 2002 Act introduced 'community based' sanctions, intended at low level disposals for minor offences. The main aim of the legislation was to attend to the welfare of children without prejudice by everyone in the community. This had the effect that – from 2002 onwards – the juvenile population in custody began to decrease to an average of only about 30 to 35 youngsters per year, which equates to about 20 per 100,000 of the relevant population; about half were held on remand and the rest were sentenced. Prison for young offenders really has become the last resort in Northern Ireland.

Youth Courts are specially constituted courts of summary jurisdiction composed of a Resident Magistrate and two Lay Magistrates – one must be a woman. Since the abolition of the lay magistracy in 2005, most of the lay magistrates were re-trained as youth magistrates.

Reparation Orders are part of the restorative justice principle in Northern Ireland, introduced via section 36(a) of the *Justice (Northern Ireland) Act 2002*, whereby the offender has to 'make such reparation for the offence, otherwise than by the payment of compensation'. The young offender must be found guilty of an offence and consent to being subject to the order and a written report must be presented to court, compiled by either a probation officer or social worker (similar to Pre-Sentence Reports (PSR) in England).

If the offender is under 14, only two hours a day of reparation are permitted. A reparation order must be sensitive to the religious beliefs of the youngster, in order to avoid any sectarian conflict. Community responsibility orders focus particularly on community and victim awareness. The order is made by a court as the sole disposal for an offence and must be completed within six months. An order can only be made with the consent of the young person and the young deviant is required to undertake 'instruction in citizenship' as part of the order. He will be given practical activities in the community and may have to make some form of reparation to the victim.

## 9.7 ___ Youth custody

Receiving a custodial sentence can have a major impact not only on the young individual who has received the sentence, but also on family members and close supportive friends. Families have to deal with worries and fears about how they can cope with the situation and they are sometimes left in the dark about what happens in prison. Most Young Offender Institutions (YOI) now involve families in order to address young deviants' needs.

Powell et al. in their research for the Welsh Assembly (2006) established that many young people in custody felt let down by public services such as care proceedings and the appropriateness of the education in and out of prison. There was a strong feeling that vocational training inside the secure estate was inadequate and insufficient. The research clearly showed that the young people's lifestyles or the nature of opportunities in their home communities had affected the extent to which they had been able to access their entitlements outside the secure estate. The researchers recommended that the resettlement process for young offenders should be improved.

## England and Wales

Punishments available to courts in criminal proceedings dealing with those under 18 are different from those imposed on adults. Criminal procedure is partly covered by the *Children and Young Persons Act 1933*, the *Crime and Disorder Act 1998* and the *Criminal Justice Act 2003* (Chapter 5). The minimum age for sentence to imprisonment is 21 by a youth court. Those 'young adults' aged between 18 and 20 go to a Young Offender Institution (YOI).

## Custodial sentences for dangerous young offenders (Chapter 5, ss. 226–228 CJA 2003)

The following types of sentences can only be passed in the crown court. If a young person is both convicted of a specified offence and assessed by the court as 'dangerous', a public protection custodial sentence is the only possible outcome. As we already mentioned in Chapter 9.4 above, there are special measures and custodial provision for dangerous young offenders, including:

*   The Extended Sentence for Public Protection (determinate)
*   The Detention for Public Protection (indeterminate)

The Extended Sentence is determinate and the custody length is set by the judge. This sentence comprises two parts, which the court must specify as:

1   A custodial period that must be at least 12 months
2   An extended licence period – this may be quite long.

Youth Offending Team (YOT) officers usually continue a rigorous risk assessment throughout the custody period and make arrangements with the probation service once the offender reaches the age of 18. The recall of Extended Sentence cases is managed by the National Offender Management Service (NOMS) 'Release and Recall Section'. All recall decisions are reviewed by the Parole Board within 14 days of recall.[2]

## Detention for Public Protection

This is an indeterminate prison sentence and sets the minimum term for the young offender. The Detention for Public Protection (DPP) sentence must be served in full before the Parole Board considers release on licence. The Parole Board will not recommend release until a full risk assessment has indicated that the offender no longer poses a *significant* risk to the public. Home Detention Curfew is not available in these circumstances. The DPP is like a life sentence. Once released, the young person may remain on licence indefinitely but, in contrast to adult life licensees, he can apply to have the licence reviewed at the ten-year point by the Parole Board and yearly thereafter. The licence depends on the Parole Board's consideration whether it is safe to release the offender on the grounds of public protection.

## Scotland

The Scottish Office recognised that young offenders commit a disproportionate percentage of recorded crime (about 40 per cent) and influence significantly the continuing high levels of fear of crime. HM YOI Polmont, Falkirk, in central Scotland has become the largest centre for holding young prisoners. Polmont accommodates young men, between the ages of 16 and 21, who have been given a prison sentence, or who are on remand, awaiting trial. The total number varies between 600 and 700. The numbers of those convicted, as well as those placed on remand continued to rise in 2008. The youth custody facility works with a wide range of agencies, including parents, drug workers and healthcare teams, who offer a wide range of interventions in order to tackle the problem of youth crime and persistent young offending. Activities and vocational training include plumbing, plastering, roofing and forklift driving. 'Slopping out' was only abolished in 2007.

McAra (2006) warns that, despite the inclusion of restorative justice practices in Scotland's juvenile justice system, the Scottish system is losing its distinct identity of protection of children, historically based on Kilbrandon philosophy that the problems of children who offend stemmed from the same source: failures in the upbringing and familial process and society. The author contends that a moral panic concerning persistent young offenders and anti-social behaviour among youth has brought in a complex set of penal rationales towards the end of the 1990s, focusing on increased police powers and locking children away. This has had a 'net-widening' effect in terms of increasing juvenile contact with the formal justice system (2006: 127–145).

Section 56 of *The Justice (Northern Ireland) Act 2002* restricts the use of custody for 10 to 13 year olds in that they must not be held with older children in a juvenile justice centre; they should rather be accommodated in the child care system. This effectively means that it is unlawful to detain children under 14 years of age in a juvenile justice centre – other than those convicted of a most serious offence, as directed by the Secretary of State. It was clearly recognised over 30 years ago in Northern Ireland that children in need of care requiring placement away from their homes should not be held in the same institution as children who had offended (see O'Mahony and Deazley, 2000).

The Woodlands Juvenile Justice Centre for Northern Ireland opened in May 2007 and provides youth custody for the whole of the province where a dedicated team of professionals aims to reduce offending behaviour by involving the whole community in life skills and educational programmes.

## 9.8 ___ Non-custodial sanctions

### ___ Youth community orders in England and Wales (s. 147 CJA 2003) ___

Similar to adult community sentences, the *Criminal Justice Act 2003* introduced a generic youth community sentence, known as a 'Youth Community Order'; this includes young offenders aged 10 to 17 years old, comprising:

- Curfew Order
- Exclusion Order
- Attendance Centre Order
- Action Plan Order
- Community Rehabilitation Orders
- Community Punishment and Rehabilitation Orders
- Supervision Order
- Drug Treatment and Testing Orders (DTTO)

The idea behind this form of sentencing was to ensure that children and young offenders would not be drawn into the new adult sentencing framework.

### ___ ASBOs and parental compensation orders ___

Anti-social Behaviour Orders (ASBOs) were introduced for children over the age of ten under section 1 *Crime and Disorder Act 1998*. Since children under the age of ten cannot be prosecuted in England and Wales, sections 13A–13E of the 1998 Act deal with 'Parental Compensation Orders'; these require parents to pay compensation in respect of the anti-social behaviour of their children (see also s. 144 *Serious Organised Crime and Police Act 2005*). Parental Compensation Orders usually comprise specific financial payments to a person whose property was taken or damaged (not exceeding £5,000). The order is treated like a fine imposed on the parent in criminal proceedings and requires immediate payment. The ASBO can be made jointly with an 'Individual Support Order' (ISO) to address the underlying causes of the young person's deviant or offending behaviour that led to the original ASBO being made (Part 13, s. 322 CJA 2003). An ISO is a civil court order and imposes certain conditions on the young offender.

## Youth Offender Panels and Referral Orders

Similar to Youth Conferencing in Northern Ireland (see below), a court may refer a deviant youth to a Youth Offender Panel (YOP). This is done via a Referral Order which requires the parent or guardian to attend the meetings with the panel. The Referral Order is a court order, given to 10 to 17-year-olds pleading guilty on a first time conviction; unless the charge is serious enough to warrant custody. After appearing in court, the young offender is referred to a Youth Offender Panel who considers the best course of action. The idea behind these panels is a form of community or communal justice, giving community a say in creating effective punishment orders for young offenders and to make sure that the young person repairs the harm done to individual victims of crime or the local community. It is hoped that this will prevent future offending, combining restorative justice and retributive punishment theories (see Chapter 7.6).

A Youth Offender Panel consists of two volunteers recruited directly from the local community, alongside one member of the Youth Offending Team (YOT). They talk to the youngster, the parents and possibly the victim, to agree a tailor-made contract aimed at putting things right. The contract might include a letter of apology to the victim, removing graffiti or cleaning up estates and communities. It will also include activities to prevent further offending, such as getting young people back into school and help with alcohol or drug misuse. The Panel meets with the young person and their parents or appropriate adult to discuss reasons for the offending behaviour and suggest ways forward. The victim is encouraged to attend the meeting to tell the young person how the crime affected them. If the parent fails to comply with this order, the panel may send the case back to the youth court, so allowing a further opportunity to make a Parenting Order.

A Home Office study conducted by Jolliffe and Farrington (2007) measured youth reoffending by looking a young offender mentoring schemes in England and Wales. The researchers found that mentoring significantly reduced subsequent offending by 4–11 per cent. The idea behind the offender mentoring programme is that an 'appropriate adult' from the community takes charge of a young offender or delinquent once a week. The study found that successful programmes were those where the mentor and mentee met at least once a week, for example to do homework together or spend time at a museum. Mentoring was found to be most effective when it was applied to those apprehended by the police and 'diverted' to Youth Offending Teams (YOT).

_____ Youth conferencing in Northern Ireland _____

Youth conferencing, also known as 'Diversionary Conferences' (DC), is available to young offenders aged 10 to 16 (*The Justice (Northern Ireland) Act 2002*). DCs are restorative justice based, balancing the needs of the victim and the young offender by agreeing plans of action which satisfy the victim and create opportunities for the young person to make amends and stop committing crime.

A Diversionary Conference can only take place if the offender admits to the offence and agrees to meet the victim. Most importantly, the prosecutor must agree and consider a conference appropriate. It is the Public Prosecution Service or the court that affirm the 'Public Prosecution Plan' which is like a contract. If the youngster does not comply with the plan, breach proceedings will ensue. A Public Prosecution Plan is citable on a criminal record but is not classed as a conviction unlike the Youth Conference Court Order. A Public Prosecution Plan may include:

- A verbal or written apology to the victim
- Participation on a drugs or alcohol prevention course
- An awareness course on non-racist behaviour to ethnic minorities
- An intergenerational course with older people as mentors
- A citizenship course, including voluntary work for disadvantaged groups or public services
- Conditions for school attendance or restricting offenders' whereabouts or activities
- Reparation to the victim or restitution to the victim (RJ)

What happens at a diversionary youth conference? This usually involves the young offender, the victim, the young person's family, the police, the community and any other relevant supporters – all are there to help the offender put right the harm caused. The theme usually includes a discussion regarding the ways in which the young offender can make good the harm caused to the victim and how he can stop future offending. A conference usually lasts about an hour and takes the following format:

- The facts are presented: what happened? The consequences? How has the crime affected the victim? What can the young person do to make amends?
- Everyone will be asked to sign a statement of confidentiality
- Everyone speaks in turn
- No names or details are made public

If the prosecutor considers it appropriate to make a prosecution, instead of granting a DC, the case will be referred to the youth court. In all instances, an action plan will be drawn up by the court to prevent further offending and make amends to the victim.

## 9.9 ____ Case study _____

_____ *R v H (a minor)* [2007] EWCA Crim 53; Attorney General's Reference (No 126 of 2006) _____

The case concerns the cruel and sadistic murder of 11 year old Joe Geeling, a cystic fibrosis sufferer in Bury, Greater Manchester on 1 March 2006, by 14-year-old Michael Hamer. In Re. H, the appellant challenged his extended life sentencing tariff at Her Majesty's Pleasure where the Court of Appeal considered the meaning of 'dangerousness'.

---

### Facts of the case

Joe Geeling, born in June 1994, suffered from cystic fibrosis. Though his condition affected his weight and his growth, his parents had sent him to a normal school in the area. Joe remained a lonely, isolated boy, suffering significant bullying at school.

The offender, Michael Hamer, aged 15 at the time of the murder trial, was of low intelligence and emotionally damaged and suffering from an adjustment disorder. He had spent some weeks planning a way to bring little Joe to his home, which culminated in a falsified letter to Joe. When the police searched Hamer's home, they found draft letters in the offender's bedroom, indicating some sexual motivation. Hamer's letter to Joe pretended to come from the Deputy Headmistress of Bury School, telling Joe that Michael Hamer had been appointed as his mentor and that Joe should go to Hamer's home during the morning break, 'to go to a year 10's house to have bum sex'. Joe did go to Hamer's home on 1 March 2006.

There, Joe was physically assaulted by his assailant with a frying pan and stabbed numerous times, inflicting serious injuries across his body. The next day, when Joe's disappearance became known, police attended Hamer's home, where he immediately admitted his responsibility for Joe's death. In his defence, Hamer told the court that his sexual advances to Joe had been rejected and that he had attacked and killed Joe in order to silence him. He pleaded guilty to murder at the first opportunity.

In his mitigation, the court heard that Michael Hamer had no history of violence. It was commonly known that he was suffering from an adjustment disorder, had been bullied by his peers at school and was emotionally immature and vulnerable. At Manchester Crown Court, Mr Justice McCombe imposed a sentence of detention during Her Majesty's Pleasure with a minimum term of 12 years (Schedule 21, para. 7 CJA 2003).

But the Attorney General, being troubled by this violent and fraught case and the relatively lenient sentence, appealed to the Court of Appeal (s. 36 *Criminal Justice Act 1988*).

*(Continued)*

---

## The Court of Appeal

The Court of Appeal concluded that the aggravating and mitigating features of the case balanced each other out, commenting that Hamer's culpability and the consequential seriousness of the offence were reduced by his age and mental illness. But some striking features included the deliberate selection of the victim for the purpose of exposing him to bullying and some form of sexual abuse; the elements of planning, which survived the intervention of school staff on the day of the killing itself, the sustained violence with more than one weapon and the murderous nature of the attack, and finally the calm efforts at concealing Joe's body, were all significant in themselves, but even for an offender of this age, with this offender's disadvantages. Taken together they represented a formidable level of culpability and seriousness.

Finally, the CA allowed the AG's Reference and appeal to succeed and extended the 12 year minimum term to a minimum of 15 years in prison.

 ## Exam Questions

1  Explain the sentencing guidelines in England and Wales for serious young offenders who kill with reference to common law (*Re. H*) and statutory provision.
2  How are young offenders dealt with in the Scottish and Northern Irish criminal justice systems?
3  Children and young people aged between 10 and 17 years in England, Wales and Northern Ireland (from age 8 in Scotland) who break the law are considered 'young offenders'. What are the reasons for this and how might society assist to prevent youthful offending? Discuss.

## Further Resources

John Muncie's second edition of *Youth and Crime* (2004) is a very readable text comprising critical analysis on wide ranging topics surrounding young people, disorder and crime. He asks: Why are certain aspects of young people's behaviour perceived as 'anti-social? What makes a young criminal? Are young people now more of a threat than ever before? Is penal policy soft on young criminals? – and draws on traditional criminological concepts, such as cultural studies, gender studies, social policy and political science. The text can be complemented by Muncie et al.'s *Critical Readings* (2002) where the authors expand on the punishment of young people.

Martin Stephenson (2007) examines the theoretical and practical functions of school and family and links these to why young people commit crime. He links criminological theories, with a useful literature review, to possible familial and societal failures, arriving at educational facilities in our youth prisons of today. The book is useful for those working in youth courts, as YOTs, teachers or criminologists interested in youth crime.

## Notes

1 MPA Chair calls for change in gun culture and engagement with gunmen', Metropolitan Police Authority, Press Release No. 08/04, 9 February 2004.
2 Source: Home Office (2005). Probation Circular 91/2005: Case Transfer Protocol between Youth Offending Teams (YOTs) and Probation Areas sets out the relevant procedures for transferring cases.

# APPENDIX 1 TABLE OF STATUTES

## ___ Legislation _____

Unless otherwise stated, the following statutes cover the jurisdiction of Great Britain; there are also separate enactments concerning Scotland and Northern Ireland, as well as secondary legislation, and EU primary and secondary different legislation.

| | |
|---|---|
| 1688 | Bill of Rights 1688 (c. 2) |
| 1824 | Vagrancy Act 1824 (c. 83) |
| 1861 | Offences Against the Person Act 1861 (c. 100) |
| 1868 | Capital Punishment (Amendment) Act 1868 (c. 24) |
| 1876 | Customs Consolidation Act 1876 (c. 36) |
| 1883 | Explosive Substances Act 1883 (c. 3) |
| 1908 | Punishment of Incest Act 1908 (c. 45) |
| 1911 | Official Secrets Act 1911 (c. 28) |
| 1925 | Criminal Justice Act 1925 (c. 86) |
| 1929 | Infant Life (Preservation) Act 1929 (c. 34) |
| 1933 | Children and Young Persons Act 1933 (c. 12) |
| 1952 | Customs and Excise Act 1952 (c. 44) |
| | Prison Act 1952 (c. 52) |
| 1953 | Prevention of Crime Act 1953 (c. 14) |
| | Births and Deaths Registration Act 1953 (c. 20) |
| | Post Office Act 1953 (c. 36) |
| 1956 | Sexual Offences Act 1956 (c. 69) |
| 1957 | Homicide Act 1957 (c. 11) |
| 1959 | Restriction of Offensive Weapons Act 1959 (c. 37) |
| 1960 | Indecency with Children Act 1960 (c. 33) |
| | Administration of Justice Act 1960 (c. 65) |
| 1963 | Children and Young Persons Act 1963 (c. 37) |
| 1964 | Police Act 1964 (c. 48) |
| | Criminal Procedure (Insanity) Act 1964 (c. 84) |
| 1965 | Murder (Abolition of Death Penalty) Act 1965 (c. 71) |
| 1967 | Sexual Offences Act 1967 (c. 60) |

| | |
|---|---|
| | Fugitive Offenders Act 1967 (c. 68) |
| | Criminal Justice Act 1967 (c. 80) |
| 1968 | Criminal Appeal Act 1968 (c. 19) |
| | Theft Act 1968 (c. 60) |
| 1971 | Town and Country Planning Act 1971 (c. 8) |
| | Attachment of Earnings Act 1971 (c. 32) |
| | Misuse of Drugs Act 1971 (c. 38) |
| | Criminal Damage Act 1971 (c. 48) |
| | Immigration Act 1971 (c. 77) |
| 1972 | Road Traffic Act 1972 (c. 20) |
| | European Communities Act 1972 (c. 68) |
| | Criminal Justice Act 1972 (c. 71) |
| 1974 | The Juries Act 1974 (c. 23) |
| | Health and Safety at Work Act 1974 (c. 37) |
| | Rehabilitation of Offenders Act 1974 (c. 53) |
| 1975 | Sex Discrimination Act 1975 (c. 65) |
| 1976 | Bail Act 1976 (c. 63) |
| | Race Relations Act 1976 (c. 74) |
| | Sexual Offences (Amendment) Act 1976 (c. 82) |
| 1977 | Criminal Law Act 1977 (c. 45) |
| 1978 | Theft Act 1978 (c. 31) |
| | Protection of Children Act 1978 (c. 37) |
| | Employment Protection (Consolidation) Act 1978 (c. 44) |
| 1979 | Customs and Excise Management Act 1979 (c. 2) |
| | Sale of Goods Act 1979 (c. 54) |
| 1980 | Magistrates' Courts Act 1980 (c. 43) |
| 1981 | Criminal Attempts Act 1981 (c. 47) |
| | Contempt of Court Act 1981 (c. 49) |
| | Supreme Court Act 1981 (c. 54) |
| 1982 | Planning Inquiries (Attendance of the Public) Act 1982 (c. 21) |
| | Taking of Hostages Act 1982 (c. 28) |
| | Aviation Security Act 1982 (c. 36) |
| | Criminal Justice Act 1982 (c. 48) |
| 1983 | Mental Health Act 1983 (c. 20) |
| 1984 | County Courts Act 1984 (c. 28) |
| | Matrimonial and Family Proceedings Act 1984 (c. 42) |
| | Police and Criminal Evidence Act 1984 (c. 60) |
| 1985 | Representation of the People Act 1985 (c. 2) |
| | Prosecution of Offences Act 1985 (c. 23) |
| | Interception of Communications Act 1985 (c. 56) |
| | The Child Abduction and Custody Act 1985 (c. 60) |
| 1986 | The Family Law Act 1986 (c. 9) |
| | Public Order Act 1986 (c. 64) |

| 1987 | Criminal Justice Act 1987 (c. 38) |
|------|-----------------------------------|
| 1988 | Merchant Shipping Act 1988 (c. 12) |
|      | Coroners Act 1988 (c. 13) |
|      | Criminal Justice Act 1988 (c. 33) |
|      | Legal Aid Act 1988 (c. 34) |
|      | Road Traffic Act 1988 (c. 52) |
|      | Road Traffic (Consequential Provisions) 1988 (c. 54) |
| 1989 | Prevention of Terrorism (Temporary Provisions) Act 1989 (c. 4) |
|      | Extradition Act 1989 (c. 33) |
|      | Children Act 1989 (c. 41) |
| 1990 | Law Reform (Miscellaneous Provisions) Act 1990 (c. 40) |
|      | Courts and Legal Services Act 1990 (c. 41) |
| 1991 | Criminal Justice Act 1991 (c. 53) |
| 1992 | Aggravated Vehicle-Taking Act 1992 (c. 11) |
|      | Further and Higher Education Act 1992 (c. 13) |
|      | Sexual Offences (Amendment) Act 1992 (c. 34) |
|      | Transport and Works Act 1992 (c. 42) |
| 1993 | Trade Union Reform and Employment Rights Act 1993 (c. 19) |
| 1994 | Intelligence Services Act 1994 (c. 13) |
|      | Criminal Justice and Public Order Act 1994 (c. 33) |
| 1995 | Civil Evidence Act 1995 (c. 38) |
| 1996 | Criminal Procedures and Investigations Act 1996 (c. 25) |
|      | Offensive Weapons Act 1996 (c. 26) |
|      | Theft (Amendment) Act 1996 (c. 62) |
| 1997 | Knives Act 1997 (c. 21) |
|      | Protection from Harassment Act 1997 (c. 40) |
|      | Crime (Sentences) Act 1997 (c. 43) |
|      | Sex Offenders Act 1997 (c. 51) |
| 1998 | Public Interest Disclosure Act 1998 (c. 23) |
|      | Data Protection Act 1998 (c. 29) |
|      | Crime and Disorder Act 1998 (c. 37) |
|      | Human Rights Act 1998 (c. 42) |
| 1999 | Access to Justice Act 1999 (c. 22) |
|      | Youth Justice and Criminal Evidence Act 1999 (c. 23) |
|      | Immigration and Asylum Act 1999 (c. 33) |
| 2000 | Powers of Criminal Courts (Sentencing) Act 2000 (c. 4) |
|      | Financial Services and Markets Act 2000 (c. 8) |
|      | Terrorism Act 2000 (c. 11) |
|      | Regulation of Investigatory Powers Act 2000 (c. 23) |
|      | Postal Services Act 2000 (c. 26) |
|      | Freedom of Information Act 2000 (c. 36) |
|      | Criminal Justice and Court Services Act 2000 (c. 43) |
|      | Sexual Offences (Amendment Act) 2000 (c. 44) |

| 2001 | International Criminal Court Act 2001 (c. 17) |
|---|---|
| | Anti-terrorism, Crime and Security Act 2001 (c. 24) |
| 2002 | Proceeds of Crime Act 2002 (c. 29) |
| 2003 | Licensing Act 2003 (c. 17) |
| | Anti-social Behaviour Act 2003 (c. 38) |
| | Country Courts Act 2003 (c. 39) |
| | Extradition Act 2003 (c. 41) |
| | Sexual Offences Act 2003 (c. 42) |
| | Criminal Justice Act 2003 (c. 44) |
| 2004 | Domestic Violence, Crime and Victims Act 2004 (c. 28) |
| 2005 | Prevention from Terrorism Act 2005 (c. 2) |
| | Constitutional Reform Act 2005 (c. 4) |
| | Serious Organised Crime and Police Act 2005 (c. 15) |
| | Drugs Act 2005 (c. 17) |
| 2006 | European Union (Accessions) Act 2006 (c. 2) |
| | Criminal Defence Service Act 2006 (c. 9) |
| | Terrorism Act 2006 (c. 11) |
| | Police and Justice Act 2006 (c. 48) |
| 2007 | Tribunals, Courts and Enforcement Act 2007 (c. 15) |
| | Corporate Manslaughter and Corporate Homicide Act 2007 (c. 19) |
| | Forced Marriages (Civil Protection) Act 2007 (c. 20) |
| | Offender Management Act 2007 (c. 21) |
| | UK Borders Act 2007 (c. 30) |
| 2008 | Criminal Justice and Immigration Act 2008 |

## Wales

| 2006 | Government of Wales Act 2006 (c. 32) |
|---|---|
| | Parliamentary Constituencies and Assembly Electoral Regions (Wales) Order 2006 (S.I. 2006/1041) |

## Scotland

| 1707 | Acts of Union (c. 7) |
|---|---|
| 1800 | Glasgow Police Act 1800 |
| 1815 | Jury Trials (Scotland) Act 1815 (55 & 56 Geo. 3, c. 42) |
| 1833 | Burgh Police (Scotland) Act 1833 |
| 1933 | Administration of Justice (Scotland) Act 1933 (23 & 24 Geo. 5, c. 41) |
| 1937 | Children and Young Persons (Scotland) Act 1937 (1 Edw. 8 & 1 Geo. 6, c. 37) |

| | |
|---|---|
| 1967 | Police (Scotland) Act 1967 (c. 77) |
| 1968 | Social Work (Scotland) Act 1968 (c. 49) |
| 1971 | Sheriff Courts (Scotland) Act 1971 (c. 58) |
| 1973 | Local Government (Scotland) Act 1973 (c. 65) |
| 1974 | Criminal Procedure (Scotland) Act 1974 (c. 21) |
| 1976 | Fatal Accidents and Sudden Deaths Inquiry (Scotland) Act 1976 (c. 14) |
| 1977 | Presumption of Death (Scotland) Act 1977 (c. 27) |
| 1978 | Adoption (Scotland) Act 1978 (c. 28) |
| 1980 | Bail (Scotland) Act 1980 (c. 4) |
| | Law Reform (Miscellaneous Provisions) (Scotland) Act 1980 (c. 55) |
| | Solicitors (Scotland) Act 1980 (c. 42) |
| | Criminal Justice (Scotland) Act 1980 (c. 62) |
| 1982 | Civic Government (Scotland) Act 1982 (c. 45) |
| 1984 | Mental Health (Scotland) Act 1984 (c. 36) |
| 1986 | Legal Aid (Scotland) Act 1986 (c. 47) |
| 1993 | Damages (Scotland) Act 1993 (c. 5) |
| | Carrying of Knives (Scotland) Act 1993 (c. 13) |
| 1995 | Children (Scotland) Act 1995 (s. 36) |
| | Criminal Procedure (Scotland) Act 1995 (c. 46) |
| | Criminal Procedure (Consequential Provisions) (Scotland) Act 1995 (c. 40) |
| 1997 | Crime and Punishment (Scotland) Act 1997 (c. 48) |
| 1998 | Human Rights Act (Scotland Act) 1998 (c. 46) |
| 2000 | Judicial Appointments (Scotland) Act 2000 (asp 9) |
| | Regulation of Investigatory Powers (Scotland) Act 2000 (asp 11) |
| 2002 | Freedom of Information (Scotland) Act 2002 (asp 13) |
| 2003 | Criminal Justice (Scotland) Act 2003 (asp 7) |
| 2004 | Vulnerable Witnesses (Scotland) Act 2004 (asp 3) |
| | Criminal Procedure (Amendment) (Scotland) Act 2004 (asp 5) |
| | Antisocial Behaviour (Scotland) Act 2004 (asp 8) |
| 2005 | Protection of Children and Prevention of Sexual Offences (Scotland Act) 2005 (asp 9) |
| | Management of Offenders (Scotland) Act 2005 (asp 14) |
| 2007 | The Criminal Proceedings etc. (Reform) (Scotland) Act 2007 (c. 40) |

_____ Northern Ireland _____

| | |
|---|---|
| 1908 | Punishment of Incest Act 1908 (c. 45) |
| 1939 | Infanticide Act (Northern Ireland) 1939 (c. 5) |

| 1967 | Criminal Laws (Northern Ireland) Act 1967 |
|------|-------------------------------------------|
| 1968 | Children and Young Persons Act (Northern Ireland) 1968 (c. 34) |
| 1969 | Theft (Northern Ireland) Act 1969 (c.16) |
| 1970 | Police (Northern Ireland) Act 1970 (c. 9) |
| 1973 | Northern Ireland (Emergency Provisions) Act 1973 Criminal Laws (Northern Ireland) Act 1977 The Judicature (Northern Ireland) Act 1978 (c. 23) |
| 1977 | Criminal Laws (Northern Ireland) Act 1977 |
| 1978 | The Judicature (Northern Ireland) Act 1978 (c. 23) |
| 1980 | Criminal Appeal (Northern Ireland) Act 1980 (c. 47) |
| 1995 | Northern Ireland (Remission of Sentences) Act 1995 (c. 47) |
| 1998 | Northern Ireland (Elections) Act 1998 (c. 12) Police (Northern Ireland) Act 1998 (c.32) Northern Ireland (Sentences) Act 1998 (c. 35) |
| 2000 | Police (Northern Ireland) Act 2000 (c. 32) |
| 2002 | Justice (Northern Ireland) Act 2002 (c. 26) |
| 2007 | Northern Ireland (St Andrew's Agreement) Act 2007 (c. 4) Justice and Security (Northern Ireland) Act 2007 (c. 6) |

## Statutory Instruments (S.I.)

| 1964 | Prison Rules 1964 (S.I. 1964/388) |
|------|-----------------------------------|
| 1974 | The Juries (Northern Ireland) Order 1974 (S.I. 1974/2143 (N.I. 6)) |
| 1977 | The Family Law Reform (Northern Ireland) Order 1977 |
| 1978 | European Communities (Services of Lawyers) Order 1978 Health and Safety at Work (Northern Ireland) Order 1978 (S.I. 1978/1039 (N.I. 9)) |
| 1979 | The Crown Court Rules (Northern Ireland) 1979 [SR 1979 No. 90] |
| 1980 | Rules of the Supreme Court (Northern Ireland) 1980 [SR No. 346] Criminal Justice (Northern Ireland) Order 1980 (N.I. 6) |
| 1981 | Magistrates' Courts Rules 1981 (S.I. 1981/552; amending instruments relevant to this Part are S.I. 1983/523, 1986/1332, 2001/610 and 2003/1236) The Magistrates' Courts (Northern Ireland) Order 1981 (No 1675 (N.I. 26)) |
| 1982 | Crown Court Rules (S.I. 1982/1109) Homosexual Offences (Northern Ireland) Order 1982 (N.I. 19) |
| 1984 | Coroners Rules 1984 (S.1 1984 No 552) |
| 1985 | Child Abduction (Northern Ireland) Order 1985 (N.I. 17) |

| | |
|---|---|
| 1986 | Mental Health (Northern Ireland) Order 1986 (N.I. 4) |
| 1987 | The Adoption (Northern Ireland) Order 1987 |
| 1988 | The Family Homes and Domestic Violence (Northern Ireland) Order 1988 |
| | The Family Law Act 1986 (Commencement No.1) Order 1988 (c. 9) |
| 1989 | The Police and Criminal Evidence (Northern Ireland) Order 1989 (S.I. 1989/1341 (N.I. 12)) |
| | Family Proceedings Courts (Children Act 1989) Rules r16 |
| 1995 | The Children (Northern Ireland) Order 1995 |
| | Northern Ireland Prison and Young Offenders Rules 1995 |
| | Prison (Amendment) Rules 1995 (S.I. 1995/983) |
| 1996 | Copyright and Related Rights Regulations (S.I. 1996/2967) |
| | Juries (Northern Ireland) Order 1996 |
| | Criminal Justice (Northern Ireland) Order 1996 (S.I. 1996/3160/N.I. 24) |
| 1997 | Copyright and Rights in Databases Regulations (S.I. 1997/3032) |
| 1998 | Civil Procedures Rules (S.I. 1998/3132) |
| | Criminal Justice (Children) (Northern Ireland) Order 1998 |
| 1999 | Prison Rules 1999 (S.I. 1999/728) |
| 2000 | Data Protection (Processing of Sensitive Personal Data) Order (S.I. 2000/417) |
| 2001 | Human Rights Act 1998 (Designated Derogation) Order 2001 (S.I. 2001/3644) |
| | The Police and Criminal Evidence Act 1984 (Drug Testing Persons in Police Detention) (Prescribed Persons) Regulation S.I. 2001 No. 2645 |
| 2002 | The Allowances to Members of the Assembly (Winding up Allowance) (Amendment) Order (Northern Ireland) 2002 (Statutory Rule 2002 No. 230) |
| 2003 | The Protection of Children and Vulnerable Adults (Northern Ireland) Order 2003 |
| | The Extradition Act 2003 (Designation of Part 1 Territories) (S.I. 2003 No. 3333) Order 2003 |
| | The Sex Discrimination Act 1975 (Amendment) Regulations 2003 (S.I. No. 1657) |
| | Money Laundering Regulations (MLRs) of 2003 (S.I. No. 3075) |
| 2004 | Crown Court (Amendment) Rules 2004 |
| | The Civil Procedure (Modification of Supreme Court Act 1981) Order 2004 (S.I. 2004/1033) |
| 2005 | The Misuse of Drugs Act 1971 (Amendment) Order 2005 (S.I. No. 2005) |

The Prison (Amendment) Rules 2005 (S.I. 2005/869)
The Criminal Justice (Sentencing) (Licence Conditions)
Order 2005 (S.I. 648)
The Licensing Act 2003 (Transitional provisions) Order 2005

2007     The Criminal Proceedings etc. (Reform) (Scotland) Act 2007
(Commencement No. 2 and Transitional Provisions and Savings)
Order 2007 (S.I. 479)

## European Union Law

| | |
|---|---|
| 1950 | European Convention for the Protection of Human Rights and Fundamental Freedoms (The Convention) |
| 1957 | Treaty of Rome |
| 1972 | European Communities Act 1972 (c. 68) |
| 1986 | Single European Act |
| 1992 | Treaty on European Union ('Maastricht Treaty') (c. 191) |
| 1997 | Treaty of Amsterdam (amending the Treaty on European Union, the Treaties establishing the European Communities and certain related Acts) (c. 340/03) |
| 2001 | Treaty of Nice (amending the Treaty on European Union, the Treaties establishing the European Communities and certain related Acts) (c. 80) |
| 2002 | Treaty Establishing the European Community (c. 325/33) Sale and Supply of Goods to Consumers Regulations 2002 |
| 2003 | Treaty of Athens 2003 |
| 2004 | Treaty establishing a Constitution for Europe, Rome (c. 310) |
| 2005 | Council of Europe Convention on the Prevention of Terrorism, Warsaw, 16.V.2005 (CETS No. 196). |
| 2007 | Lisbon Treaty (not yet ratified) |

## EC/EU Directives

| | |
|---|---|
| 1976 | Directive on Equal Treatment (Council Directive 76/207/EEC) |
| 1995 | Directive on the protection of individuals with regards to the processing of personal data and on the free movement of such data (95/46/EC) which gave effect to the Data Protection Act 1998 |
| 2002 | Directive on Electronic Commerce (see S.I. 2002/2013) |
| 2003 | Directive on Privacy and Electronic Communications (see S.I. 2003/2426) Directive on the Implementation of the European Arrest Warrant to designated MS (15585/03) |

Directive on Sex Discrimination (76/207/EEC) as amended by Council Directive 2002/73/EC

## EU Council Decisions

2002        Council Framework Decision 2002/584/JHA of 13 June 2002 on the European Arrest Warrant and the surrender procedure between Member States

## Other foreign legislation

Geneva Convention 1863 (w 196)
Geneva Convention 1923 (TS 1 (1926); Cmd 2575)
Universal Postal Convention 1974 (renewed at
Lausanne; Cmnd 6538); came into force on
1 January 1976 (TS 56 (1976))
Nordic Extradition Act No 27 of 3 February 1960 (Denmark)
Nordic Extradition Act No 270 of 3 February 1960 (Finland)
Sweden Act 1959:254, concerning extradition to Denmark,
Finland, Iceland and Norway for criminal offences

# APPENDIX 2    TABLE OF CASES

A (FC) and others (FC) v Secretary of State for the Home Department; X (FC) and another v Secretary of State for the Home Department (FC) [2004] UKHL 56 (sub nom 'Belmarsh Ruling'], HL.

A v United Kingdom [1997] (Application No 35373/97), 17 December 2002.

Airedale NHS Trust v Bland [1993] AC 789; [1993] 2 WLR 316; [1993] 1 All ER 821.

AJ (Cameroon) v Secretary of State for the Home Department [2007] EWCA Civ 373.

Aksoy v Turkey [1997] 23 EHRR 553.

Attorney General's Reference (No. 126 of 2006) R v H [2007] EWCA Crim 53; [2007] All ER 282.

Attorney General's Reference (No. 4 of 2004) [2005] 1 AC 264.

Attorney General's Reference (No. 2 of 1992) QB 91; [1994] 1 WLR 409.

Attorney-General's Reference (No. 2 of 1992) [1994] QB 91; [1993] 3 WLR 982; [1993] 4 ALL ER 683.

Attorney General for Northern Ireland's Reference (No. 1 of 1975) [1977] AC 105.

Attorney General v Guardian Newspapers Ltd. [1987] (sub nom Spycatcher case) 3 ALL ER 316.

Attorney General v Guardian Newspapers Ltd. (No. 2) ('Spycatcher') [1990] 1 AC 109.

Attorney General v Guardian Newspapers Ltd. ('Spycatcher') (No. 3) [1992] 1 WLR 874.

BvDPP [2000] 1 All ER 833.

Beckford v R (The Queen) [1988] AC 130, HL.

British Airways plc v Commission [2007] ECJ (2/93).

Condron v United Kingdom Appl 35718/97 [2001] 31 EHRR 1.

Council of Civil Service Unions v Minister for the Civil Service (sub nom GCHQ case) [1985] AC 374.

Cork v McVicar, *The Times*, 31 October 1995.

Cyprus v Turkey (application no. 25781/94) ECHR, 10 May 2001.

Demicoli v Malta, Comm Rep [1992] Series A/210, 14 EHRR 47.

Dickinson v UK [2007] (application no. 44362/04) ECHR, 4 December 2007.

Diennet v France [1996] 21 EHRR 554.

Director of Public Prosecutions (DPP) v Camplin [1978] AC 705.

Donoghue v Stevenson [1932] AC 562.

DPP v Majewski (Robert Stefan); R v Majewski [1977] AC 443

DPP v Lynch [1975] AC 653.

DPP v Morgan (William Anthony) (sub nom R v Morgan (William Anthony) [1976] AC 182.

DPP v Smith [1961] HL.

Douglas v Hello! Ltd. [2001] 2 WLR 992; [2001] UKHRR 223.

Douglas v Hello! Ltd [2007] see OBg v Allan.

Draper v United Kingdom [1980] 24 DR 72.

Elliott v C (a minor) 1 WLR 939; [1983] 2 All ER 1005.

Fagan v Metropolitan Police Commissioner [1969] 1 QB 439.

Findlay v United Kingdom (case no. 22107/93) 24 EHRR 221, Judgement of 25 February 1997.

Golder v United Kingdom [1975] Series A/18, 1 EHRR 524.

GS and RS v United Kingdom [1991] ECHR application no. 17142/90.

Hennessy (Andrew Michael) [1989] 1 WLR 287; [1989] 2 All ER 9.

Hill v Baxter [1958] 1 QB 277; [1958] 2 WLR 76.

Hill v Chief Constable of West Yorkshire [1989] AC 53; [1988] 2 WLR 1049.

Hirst v United Kingdom (No 2) (application no. 74025/01) [2006] EHRR 42.

ICC Prosecutor v Thomas Lubanga Dyilo (Case ICC-01/04-01/06) Recruitment of child soldiers in the Democratic Republic of the Congo.

Re J (a minor) (wardship: medical treatment) [1990] 3 All ER 930.

Jaggard v Dickinson [2004] 72 Cr App R 33.

Keating (a minor) v Knowsley Metropolitan Borough Council [2004] EWHC 1933.

Kraus [1993] (Case C-19/92) ECR I-1663.

L and others v Kennedy (Reporter to Children's Panel, Strathclyde Region) [1993] SLT 1310; [1993] SCLR 693.

Re. Lawrence (1999) *Times*, 13 July 1999.

Lee Chun-Chuen v R [1963] AC 220.

Leech v Deputy Governor of Parkhurst Prison [1988] 1 All ER 485.

Lynch v DPP [2002] 1 Crim App R 420.

MacDougall v Knight [1889] AC 194.

Mahon v Air New Zealand [1984] AC 808.

Malone v Metropolitan Police Commissioner [1979] 1 Ch 344.

Malone v United Kingdom [1984] 7 EHRR 14.

McArdle v Orr (Procurator Fiscal, Inverness) [1994] SLT 463; [1993] SCCR 437.

McCormick v Lord Advocate [1953] SC 396.

Mr and Mrs F v Belgian State [1975] (Case 7/75) ECR 679; [1975] 2 CMLR 293–4.

Murray (John) v United Kingdom [1996] 22 EHRR 29.

Re. Officer L (Respondent) (Northern Ireland) [2007] UKHL 36; [2006] NI QB 75.

OBG Ltd. and others v Allan and others; Douglas and another and others v Hello! Ltd and others; Mainstream Properties Limited v Young and others and another [2007] UKHL 21 (sub nom Douglas v Hello! [2007]).

Osman v United Kingdom (Case 87/1997/871/ 1-83) [1998] 29 EHRR 245.

Parker v R [1964] 2 All ER 641, [1964] AC 1369.

Parkes v Prescott [1869] LR4 EX 169.

Pretty v UK [2002] FCR 97.

Raymond v Honey [1983] 1 AC 1.

Real Estates Opportunities Ltd v Aberdeen Asset Managers Jersey Ltd and others [2006] EWHC 3249 (Ch) [2006] All ER 237.

R v A [2002] 1 AC 45; [2001] UKHL 25.

R (on the application of A) v Leeds Magistrates' Court and Leeds City Council [2004] EWHC 554.

R v Abdul-Hussain [1999] Crim LR 570.

R v Acott [1997] 1 All ER 706.

R v Adomako (John Asare) [1995] 1 AC 171; [1994] 3 All ER 79.

R v Ahluwalia [1992] 4 All ER 889; [1993] Crim LR 63.

R v Alden and Jones [2001] 5 Archbold News 3.

R (on the application of Al-Fawwaz) v Governor of Brixton Prison [2001] UKHL 69; [2002] 1 AC 666.

R (on the application of Begum) v Headteacher and Governors of Denbigh High School [2006] UKHL 15.

R v Allen (Kevin) [1988] Crim LR 698.

R v Andrews v DPP [1937] 2 All ER 552.

R v Bailey [2004] 77 Cr App R 76.

R v Belfon [1976] 1 WLR 741.

R v Berry [1996] 66 Cr App R 156.

R v Bradley [2005] EWCA Crim 20.

R v Bree [2007] EWCA Crim 256.

R v Briggs [1977] 1 WLR 605.

R v Brown (Anthony); Lucas; Jaggard; Laskey; Carter [1994] 1 AC 212; [1993] 2 All ER 75.

R v Bryson [1985] CrimLR 669.

R v Bruzas [1972] Crim LR 367.

R v Burgess [1991] 2 WLR 1206.

R v Caldwell (James) (sub nom Commissioner of Police of the Metropolis v Caldwell) [1982] AC 341; [1981] 2 WLR 509.

R v Camberwell Green Youth Court, ex parte D & others. Unreported, QBD Administrative Court, 3 February 2003.

R v Camplin [1978] QB 254.

R v Cato and others [1976] 1 All ER 260.

R v Cawthorne [1996] 2 Cr App R 445.

R v Chan Fook (Mike) [1994] 1 WLR 689; [1994] 99 Cr App R 147.

R v Cheshire (David William) [1991] 1 WLR 844; [1991] 3 All ER 670.

R v Clarence (Charles James) [1888] 22 QBD 23.

R v Clegg (Lee William) [1995] 1 AC 482; [1995] 2 WLR 80.

R v Cocker [1989] Crim LR 740.

R v Cole [1994] Crim LR 582.

R v Conway (Francis Gerald) [1989] QB 290; [1988] 3 WLR 1238.

R v Cox [1995] Crim LR 741.

R v Cunningham (Anthony Barry) [1982] AC 566.

R v Cunningham (Roy) [1957] 2 QB 396; [1957] 2 All ER 412.

R v D [2005] EWCA Crim 2292.

R v Dalby (Derek Shaun) [1982] 1 WLR 621; [1982] 1 All ER 916.

R v Dica (Mohammed) [2004] EWCA Crim 1103; [2004] QB 1257.

R v Dica (Nr 2) [2005] All ER 405.

R v Director of Public Prosecutions, ex parte (1) Sofiane Kebeline (2) Ferine Boukemiche (3) Sofiane Souidi [1999] 3 WLR 175.

R v Doughty [1986] 83 Cr App R 319.

R v DPP, ex parte C [1995] 1 Cr App R 136.

R (on the application of Pretty) v DPP (Secretary of State for the Home Department intervening) [2001] UKHL 61.

R v Dudley and Stephens (1884–5) 14 QBD 273, [1881–5] All ER Rep 61.

R v Duffy [1949] 1 All ER 932.

R v Egan [1992] 4 All ER 470.

R v Evesham Justices ex parte McDonagh and Another [1988] QB 553.

R v G [2004] (Re. G)

R v G and R [2004] 1 AC 1034; [2003] UKHL 50; [2003] 3 WLR 1060.

R v Gibbins & Proctor [1918] 13 Cr App R 134.

R (on the application of Gibson) v Winchester Crown Court [2004] EWHC 361.

R (on the application of Girling) v Parole Board and another [2007] 2 All ER 688.

R v Governor of HMP Swaleside ex parte Wynter (case No. CO/845/98, 11 May 1998) ECHR judgement of 13 May 1998.

R v Governor of Pentonville Prison ex parte Azam [1974] AC 18.

R v Great Western Trains Co, Central Criminal Court, 30 June 1999, unreported.

R v H [2007] EWCA Crim 53 (see Attorney General's Reference (No. 126 of 2006)).

R v Hall (1928) 21 Cr App R 48.

R v Hancock (Reginal Dean); R v Shankland (Russell) [1986] AC 455.

R v Hardie [2004] 80 Cr App R 157.

R v Hatton (Jonathan) [2005] EWCA 2951.

R v Hayward [1833] 172 ER 1188.

R v Henn; R v Derby (Case 34/79) [1979] ECR 3795; [1980] 1 CMLR 246; [1981] AC 850; [1980] 2 WLR 597.

R v Hobson (Kathleen) [1998] 1 Cr App R 31.

R v Hoey (Sean) [2007] Omagh Judgement by the Crown Court Sitting in Northern Ireland at Belfast, No. [2007] NICC 49. Ref: WEI7021 of 20 December 2007. Bill No: 341/05.

R v Howe [1987] 1 AC 417; [1987] 1 All ER 771.

R v Humphreys [1995] unreported, *The Times*, 7 July 1995.

R v Hurst [1995] 1 Cr App R 82.

R v Ireland (Robert Matthew); R v Burstow (Anthony Christopher) [1998] AC 147; [1997] 3 WLR 534.

R v Jackson [1891] 1 QB 671.

R v Jenkins and others [2002] 3 Archbold News 3.

R v Jordan (James Clinton) [1956] 40 Cr App R 152.

R v K (age of consent: reasonable belief) [2001] UKHL 41; [2002] 1 AC 462.

R v Kearley [1992] 2 All ER 345.

R v Kennedy (Simon) (Nr 1) [1999] Cr LR 65.

R v Kennedy (Simon) (Nr 2) [2005] EWCA Crim 685.

R v Kennedy (Simon) [2007] UKHL 38, HL; [2007] 4 All ER 1083.

R v Kingston (Barry) [1995] 2 AC 355; [1994] 3 WLR 519.

R v Kirk [2006] EWCA Crim 725.

R v Konzani [2005] EWCA Crim 706; [2005] All ER 292.

R v Krause [1902] 18 LTR 238.

R v Kray [1969] 53 Cr. App. Rep 412.

R v Lamb (Terence Walter) [1967] 2 QB 981.

R v Lambert (Steven) [2002]; R v Ali (Mudassir Mohammed); R v Jordan (Shirley) [2001] UKHL 37; [2002] AC 545.

R v Lang & Ors [2005] EWCA Crim 2864.

R v Lawrence (Stephen Richard) [1982] AC 510; [1981] 2 WLR 524; [1981] 1 All ER 974, HL.

R v Lawrence [1981] 1 All ER 974.

R v Lee (a minor) [1993] 2 All ER 170; [1993] 1 WLR 103.

R v Leeds Crown Court, ex p Briggs (No 1) [1998] 2 Cr App R 413.

R v Lewis [2004], *The Times*, 22 May 2004.

R v Lipman (Robert) [1970] 1 QB 152.

R v Lynsey (Jonathan Simon) [1995] 3 ALL ER 654.

R v Malcherek (Richard Tadeusz), R v Steel (Anthony) [1981] 1 WLR 690; [1981] 2 All ER 422.

R v Martin (Anthony Edward) [2003] QB 1; [2002] 2 WLR 1.

R v McGregor [1962] NZLR 1069.

R v McKnight and Groark [1999] Crim LR 669.

R v McNaghten [1843] UKHL J16.

R (Mellor) v Secretary of State for the Home Department [2001] QB 13; [2001] EWCA Civ 472, 20 March 2001.

R v Miller (James) [1983] 2 AC 161.

R v Mitchell (Luke) [2004–05] Unreported.

R v M'Loughlin [1838] 173 ER 651.

R v Moloney (Alistair Baden) [1985] AC 905.

R v Morrissey and R v Staines [1997] TLR 231.

R v Nedrick (Ransford Delroy) [1986] 1 WLR 1025.

R v Newcastle upon Tyne Coroner ex parte A [1998], *The Times*, 19 January 1998.

R v Newell (1980) 71 Cr App R 331.

R v Newtownabbey Magistrates' Court ex parte Belfast Telegraph Newspapers Ltd [1997], August 27, QBD.

R v O'Connor [1991] Crim LR 135.

R v O'Donnell [1996] 1 Cr App R 286.

R v O'Grady [1987] 3 WLR 321·

R v Oliver; R v Hartrey; R v Baldwin [2003] 1 Cr LR 127; [2002] All ER 320 (Nov).

R v Parkinson [2004] EWCA Crim 2757.

R v Pommell [1995] 2 Cr App R 607.

R v Pritchard [1836] 7 C & P 303.

R v Purcell [2006] EWCA Crim 1264.

R v R (rape: marital exemption) [1992] 1 AC 599, [1991] 3 WLR 767.

R v Richardson and Irwin [1999] 1 Cr App R 392.

R v Roberts (Kenneth Joseph) [1972] 56 Cr App R 95; [1972] Crim LR 27.

R v Robertson [1968] 52 Cr App R 690.

R v Sanderson [1994] 98 Cr App R 325.

R v Savage; R v Parmenter [1992] 1 AC 699, HL; [1991] 3 WLR 914.

R v Secretary of State for the Home Department ex parte Duggan [1994] 3 All ER 277.

R v Secretary of State for the Home Department, ex parte Venables; R v Secretary of State for the Home Department, ex parte Thompson [1998] AC 407; [1997] 3 WLR 23.

R v Secretary of State for the Home Department, ex p Simms [2000] 2 AC 115; [1999] 3 WLR 328.

R (on the application of Lin and others) v Secretary of State for Transport [2006] EWHC 2575.

R v Seymour [1983] 2 All ER 1058.

R v Sheehan (Michael); R v Moore (George Alan) [1975] 2 All ER 960.

R v Singh [2006] EWCA Crim 660, [2006] 1 WLR 1564.

R v Smith (Sandie) [1982] Crim LR 531.

R v Smith (Thomas Joseph) [1959] 2 QB 35.

R v Stephens [2002], *The Times*, 27 June 2002.

R v Stephenson (Brian Keith) [1979] QB 695.

R v Sullivan (Patrick Joseph) [1984] AC 156; [1983] 3 WLR 123.

R v Sutcliffe [1982] (unreported)

R v Thornton (Sara Elizabeth) [1992] 1 All ER 306.

R v Thornton (Sara Elizabeth) (No. 2) [1996] 1 WLR 1174; [1996] 2 ALL ER 1023.

R v Vittles [2004] EWCA Crim 1089.

R v Wacker (Perry) [2002] EWCA Crim 1944; [2003] QB 1207; [2003] 2 WLR 274.

R v Weller [2003] 3 Archbold News 2.

R v West [1996] 2 Cr. App 374.

R v Willer [1987] 83 Cr App R 225.

R v Wilson (Clarence George) [1984] AC 242; [1983] 3 WLR 686.

R v Woollin (Stephen Leslie) [1999] AC 82, HL; [1998] 4 All ER 103.

R v Wright [2000] Crim LR 510.

R v Young [2005] All ER 329.

Secretary of State for the Home Department v MB [2006] EWCA Civ 1140; [2006] 3 WLR 839.

Sheldrake v DPP [2005] 1 AC 264.

Silver v United Kingdom [1983] Series A/61, 5 EHRR 347.

Soering v United Kingdom [1989] 11 EHRR 439.

Stögmüller v Austria [1969] 1 EHRR 155.

Tomasi v France [1992] 15 EHRR 1.

Unterpertinger v Austria [1991] 13 EHRR 175.

V v UK; T v UK (sub nom, Venables and Thompson) [1999] 30 EHRR 121.

Venables and another v News Group Newspapers Ltd. [2001] Fam. 430; [2001] 2 WLR 1038.

W v Switzerland [1994] 17 EHRR 60.

Wemhoff v Germany [1968] 1 EHRR 55.

Woolmington v DPP [1935] AC 462.

X v Denmark Yearbook [1965] Vol 8 p 370, ECHR.

X v United Kingdom [1975] 2 DR 105, ECHR.

Zafar and others v R [2008] EWCA Crim 184, CA (Crim Div): Aitzaz Zafar; Akbar Butt; Awaab Iqbal; Mohammed Raja and Usman Malik (Appellants) v R (Respondent) [2008] EWCA Crim 184, CA (Crim Div), 13 February 2008.

Zimmermann v Switzerland [1984] 6 EHRR 17.

# APPENDIX 3    GLOSSARY OF CRIMINOLOGICAL AND LEGAL TERMS

## A

ACCUSED

The person charged. The person who has allegedly committed the offence.

ACQUITTAL

Discharge of defendant following verdict or direction of not guilty.

ACT OF PARLIAMENT

Primary legislation; Statute. Usually the House of Commons and the House of Lords both debate proposals for new laws and at this stage they are called Bills.

ACTS OF UNION

The Acts of Union were a pair of parliamentary acts passed in 1706 and 1707 by the English and Scottish parliaments; they took effect from 1 May 1707 and dissolved both the parliaments of England and Scotland and replaced them with a new Parliament, the Parliament of Great Britain, based in Westminster.

ACTUS REUS

The 'external' element of a crime or 'guilty act'. The commission of a crime requires causation or 'conduct'; there can also be an act of omission or failure to act. In order for criminal conduct to be proved, both the *actus reus* and the *mens rea* elements of the offence must be present. See also: *mens rea*.

AN GARDA SÍOCHÁNA

Ireland's National Police Force.

ANTECEDENTS

Information about an offender's background received in court as part of the sentencing process.

APPEAL

Application to a higher Court or authority for review of a decision of a lower Court or authority.

| | |
|---|---|
| ANTI-SOCIAL BEHAVIOUR ORDER (ASBO) | A civil order made against a person who has been shown to have engaged in anti-social behaviour (*Crime and Disorder Act 1998*: 'conduct which caused or was likely to cause alarm, harassment, or distress to one or more persons not of the same household'). |

**B**

| | |
|---|---|
| BAIL | Release of a defendant from custody, until his/her next appearance in Court, subject sometimes to security being given and/or compliance with certain conditions. |
| BAR | The collective term for barristers. |
| BARRISTER | A member of the bar: the branch of the legal profession which has rights of audience before all courts. |
| BASIC INTENT CRIMES | An offence where recklessness will suffice. Offences of basic intent include:<br><br>• Involuntary manslaughter (*Lipman* 1970)<br>• Rape (s.1 *Sexual Offences Act 2003*)<br>• Malicious wounding [GBH] (s. 20 OAPA 1861; *Majewski)*<br>• Criminal damage (s. 1(1) *Criminal Damage Act 1971; R v G* 2003, HL)<br>• ABH (s. 47 OAPA 1861)<br>• Common assault and battery (s. 39 CJA 1988). |
| BATTERY | A person is guilty of battery if he intentionally or recklessly applies unlawful force to the body of another person (s. 39 CJA 1988) (see: *Fagan v Metropolitan Police Commissioner* [1969] 1 QB 439). |
| BILL | Proposal for a new law, which is debated by Parliament. A Bill becomes an Act when it has received Royal Assent. A Bill may be introduced into either House, with the exception of Money Bills which the Lords cannot initiate or amend (see *Act of Parliament*). |
| BURDEN OF PROOF | In general, the prosecution must prove the defendant's guilt beyond any reasonable |

doubt (see *Woolmington v DPP* 1935 HL) (see also *diminished responsibility*).

| | |
|---|---|
| BURGLARY | Trespassing into another's property and stealing or attempting to steal. |

## C

| | |
|---|---|
| CAUTION | (i) Warning given by a Police Officer to a person charged with an offence; (iii) Warning given by a Police Officer, instead of a charge. |
| CHILD SAFETY ORDER | An order made by a magistrates' court, placing a child under the supervision of a responsible officer where the child has committed acts which could constitute an offence had he been over 10 years old at the time; or which were likely to cause harassment, alarm or distress. |
| CIRCUIT JUDGE | A judge who sits in the County Court and/or Crown Court. |
| CIVIL | Matters concerning private rights and not offences against the state. |
| CJA | *Criminal Justice Act* e.g. CJA 2003. |
| COMMITTAL | (i) Committal for trial: following examination by the Magistrates of a case involving an indictable or either-way offence; the procedure of directing the case to the Crown Court to be dealt with there because of seriousness; |
| | (ii) Committal for Sentence: where Magistrates consider that the offence justifies a sentence greater than they are empowered to impose, they may commit the defendant to the Crown Court for sentence to be passed by a judge; |
| | (iii) Committal Order: An order of the Court committing someone to prison. |
| COMMON LAW | The law established, by precedent, from judicial decisions and established within a community (also known as 'case' or 'judge made' law). |

| | |
|---|---|
| COMMUNITY SENTENCE | Single 'community punishment' order under CJA 2003 with a number of options attached (e.g. unpaid work in the community) available to justices instead of a prison sentence. |
| COMPENSATION ORDER | Sum of money to make up for or make amends for loss, breakage, hardship, inconvenience or personal injury caused by another (*Crime and Disorder Act 1998*). |
| CONDITIONAL DISCHARGE (CD) | A form of sentence; convicted defendant is discharged on condition that he does not re-offend within a specified period of time. |
| CONTEMPT OF COURT | Disobedience or wilful disregard to the judicial process (*Contempt of Court Act 1981*). |
| COUNSEL | See *Barrister*. |
| COURT OF APPEAL (CA) | Divided into: (i) civil and, (ii) criminal divisions; Hears appeals: (i) from decision in the High Court and County Courts and, (ii) against convictions or sentences passed by the Crown Court. |
| CPS | Crown Prosecution Service. |
| CRIME | An activity that is classified within the criminal laws of a country. Specific form of deviance; breaking of legal state norms (rules). |
| CRIMINAL | Person who has been found guilty of a criminal offence. |

**D**

| | |
|---|---|
| DAMAGES | An amount of money claimed as compensation for physical/material loss, e.g. personal injury, breach of contract (ordered in a civil court). |
| DEFENDANT | A person standing trial (the accused). |
| DEVOLUTION | Decentralisation of governmental power, e.g. setting up of Scottish Parliament, National Assembly for Wales, Northern Ireland Assembly. |
| DIMINISHED RESPONSIBILITY | *The Homicide Act 1957* s. 2 (1) provides that: 'Where a person kills or is a party to the killing of another, he shall not be convicted of murder if he was suffering from such |

abnormality of mind (whether arising from a condition of arrested or retarded development of mind or any inherent causes or induced by disease or injury) as substantially impaired his mental responsibility for his acts and omissions in doing or being a party to the killing'. A successful plea of diminished responsibility reduces liability from murder to manslaughter (s. 2(3)).

DISMISSAL — Notice given to the court by the CPS that the case is dismissed.

DISTRICT JUDGE — A judicial officer of the court whose duties involve hearing applications made within proceedings and final hearings subject to any limit of jurisdiction (previously known as 'Stipendiary Magistrates').

DIVISIONAL COURT — As well as having an original jurisdiction of their own, all three divisions of the High Court have appellate jurisdiction to hear appeals from lower Courts and tribunals. The Divisional Court of the Chancery Division deals with appeals in bankruptcy matters from the County Court. The Divisional Court of the Queen's Bench Division deals largely with certain appeals on points of law from many Courts. The Divisional Court of the Family Division deals largely with appeals from Magistrates' Courts in matrimonial matters.

DOLI INCAPAX — The presumption that a child is incapable of committing an offence, unless he knew that what he was doing was seriously wrong.

E

ECHR — European Convention on Human Rights and Fundamental Freedoms (The Convention); also refers to the *European Court of Human Rights* in Strasbourg.

EITHER-WAY OFFENCE — An offence for which the accused may elect the case to be dealt with either summarily by the Magistrates' Court or by committal to the Crown Court to be tried by jury.

| | |
|---|---|
| EUROPEAN ARREST WARRANT (EAW) | Brought into UK law by way of the *Extradition Act 2003*. Facilitates legal and law enforcement cooperation in the procedure to extradite suspects from one EU country to another where they are wanted on criminal charges. |
| EUROPEAN CONVENTION | On 4 November 1950 the European Convention for the Protection of Human Rights and Fundamental Freedoms ('the European Convention') was signed by the then Council of Europe member states. |
| EUROPEAN COURT OF HUMAN RIGHTS (ECHR) | An international court based in Strasbourg. It consists of a number of judges equal to the number of member states of the Council of Europe that have ratified the Convention for the Protection of Human Rights and Fundamental Freedoms. |
| EUROPEAN COURT OF JUSTICE (ECJ) | An EU institution, located in Luxembourg. Cases brought by an EU member state, individual or community institution must be heard in a plenary session. |
| EUROPEAN PARLIAMENT (EP) | Directly elected democratic Parliament of the EU with presently 27 member states representatives democratically elected. |
| EUROPOL | European Police Office, the EU's law enforcement organisation that handles criminal intelligence, set up in 1995 by the *Europol Convention* ratified on the1 October 1998. |
| EUROJUST | EU agency that helps EU member states deal with the investigation and prosecution of serious cross-border and organised crime. It provides legal and practical information on mutual legal assistance to practitioners. |

**F**

| | |
|---|---|
| FRAUD | Obtaining property by deception. |

**G**

| | |
|---|---|
| GBH | Grievous bodily harm, defined in *DPP v Smith* as meaning 'really serious harm'. GBH also |

includes psychological harm (see *Burstow* 1998 HL).

| | |
|---|---|
| GOOD FRIDAY AGREEMENT | or 'Belfast agreement' of 10 April 1998 states that Northern Ireland should remain in the UK so long as the people wish it. It made provision for devolved government with the Assembly at Stormont. |

## H

| | |
|---|---|
| HATE CRIME | Group harms which are aimed at specific minority groups (e.g. homosexuals); hate crimes involve racial intimidation, ethnicity, religion, or other minority groups. Include assaults, graffiti, property attacks. |
| HEARSAY EVIDENCE | Oral or written statements made by someone who is not a witness in the case but which the court is asked to accept as proving what they say. |
| HIGH COURT | A civil court which consists of three divisions: (i) Queen's Bench (can be known as King's Bench Division if a King is assuming the throne) – civil disputes for recovery of money, including breach of contract, personal injuries, libel/slander;

(ii) Family – concerned with matrimonial matters and proceedings relating to children, e.g. wardship;

(iii) Chancery – property matters including fraud and bankruptcy. |
| HOME OFFICE | Its role changed from 9 May 2007, now with responsibility for public protection, the fight against terrorism, anti-social behaviour, border control and the police service (see also *Ministry of Justice*). |
| HOMICIDE | There are a number of offences involving homicide. The two most important are murder and manslaughter. They share a common *actus reus* – the killing of a human being. Involuntary manslaughter differs from murder in terms of the *mens rea* required, in that it is the availability of one of a |

number of specific defences that distinguishes voluntary manslaughter from murder (see *diminished responsibility; intention*).

| | |
|---|---|
| HOUSE OF COMMONS | Lower chamber of the UK Parliament where elected Members of Parliament (MPs) sit in debate. |
| HOUSE OF LORDS | Upper chamber of the UK Parliament. The Law Lords are part of the House of Lords and the Appellate Committee acts as the court of appeal (see *Supreme Court*). |
| HOSTILE WITNESS | A witness seemingly biased against the person calling them as a witness (e.g. domestic violence cases), evading what they said in a previous, out of court, statement. If the court agrees, they can be cross-examined by the person calling them. |
| HRA | Human Rights Act 1998. |
| HUMAN TRAFFICKING | or people-smuggling; a very serious crime against persons and an abuse of human rights. Traffickers target, deceive and exploit vulnerable individuals like women or children from underprivileged countries, with the promises of well-paid employment opportunities and improved social conditions. |

**I**

| | |
|---|---|
| INDICTABLE OFFENCE | A criminal offence triable only at the Crown Court with judge and jury. |
| INJUNCTION | A High Court order that either restrains a person from carrying out a course of action (e.g. in domestic violence) or directing a specific course of action be complied with. Once an injunction is breached it becomes a criminal action and may be punished by the courts. |
| INTENTION (*mens rea*) | The *mens rea* for a number of offences is defined in terms of 'intention' or 'with intent to …', or 'intentionally', indicating that recklessness will not suffice. Where it is not the defendant's aim or purpose, but he foresaw that it was a virtually certain result of |

| | his actions, the jury may infer that he intended it. (*Hancock & Shankland* [1986]; *Savage & Parmenter* [1991]). |
|---|---|
| INTERNATIONAL CRIMINAL COURT (ICC) | The ICC in The Hague was established by the Rome Statute of the International Criminal Court ('The Rome Statute') on 17 July 1998 by the United Nations Diplomatic Conference of Plenipotentiaries on the Establishment of the International Criminal Court. It punishes crimes against humanity and genocide. |
| INTOXICATION | Although a lack of *mens rea* caused by voluntary intoxication will 'excuse' a crime of 'specific intent' the defendant may be convicted of an offence of 'basic intent' despite his lack of *mens rea* (*Majewski* [1977]). |
| INQUISITORIAL | Refers to civil code justice systems (e.g. Germany, France, Spain, Greece) in which the 'inquisitorial' judge has primary responsibility to investigate the case. |

## J

| | |
|---|---|
| JUDGEMENT | Final decision of a court. |
| JUDICIARY | A judge or other officer empowered to act as a judge. |
| JUROR | A person who has been summoned by a court to be a member of the jury (see *jury*). |
| JURY (ENGLAND/ WALES) | Consists of a body of 12 jurors, sworn to reach a verdict according to the evidence in a Crown Court; there can be a jury in the High Court in defamation or libel actions and also in an inquest. |
| JURY (SCOTLAND) | In the Scottish High Court, a 15 member jury-hears all criminal trials with a simple majority verdict to establish guilt or innocence (such as 8:7). |
| JUSTICE OF THE PEACE (JP) | A lay magistrate and unpaid member of the public, appointed to administer judicial business in a magistrates' court in England and Wales. |

| | |
|---|---|
| JURISDICTION | The area and matters over which a court has legal authority. |
| **L** | |
| LAW | The system made up of rules established by an Act of Parliament, custom or practice enjoining or prohibiting certain actions (see also *common law*). |
| LAW LORDS | Or 'Lords of Appeal in Ordinary'; senior judges or holders of high judicial office, who are given life peerages in order to carry out the judicial work of the House of Lords (see *House of Lords*). |
| LAW REPORTS | Record of 'test' cases in common law that lay down important legal principles known as precedent, such as 'The Weekly Law Reports' (WLR). |
| LEGISLATION | An Act of Parliament or statute. |
| LITIGATION | Legal proceedings. |
| LORD CHIEF JUSTICE | Senior judge (law lord) of the Court of Appeal (Criminal Division) who heads the Queens Bench Division (QBD) of the High Court of Justice. |
| LORD JUSTICE OF APPEAL | Title given to certain judges sitting in the Court of Appeal (CA). |
| **M** | |
| MAGISTRATE | see *Justice of the Peace*. |
| MAGISTRATES' COURT | A court where criminal proceedings are commenced before Justices of the Peace (or magistrates), who examine the evidence/ statements and either deal with the case themselves or commit to the Crown Court for trial or sentence. Also has jurisdiction in civil matters, such as the family court. |
| MALICE AFORETHOUGHT | A misleading term, signifying the *mens rea* for murder, i.e. an intention to kill or cause grievous bodily harm (see *GBH*). |

| | |
|---|---|
| MALICIOUS WOUNDING | Inflicting *GBH*. Inflicting grievous bodily harm is an offence under s. 20 OAPA 1861, punishable with a term of imprisonment not exceeding five years. GBH can include very serious psychological harm. |
| MANSLAUGHTER | There are several modes of committing manslaughter: |

There are several modes of committing manslaughter:

(i) *Constructive manslaughter*. Also known as 'killing by an unlawful act', this offence is committed where the defendant *intentionally* commits an unlawful and dangerous act resulting in death.

(ii) *'Reckless' manslaughter* requires *Caldwell*-type recklessness with respect to some injury.

(iii) *Provocation manslaughter*. A person (the defendant) who killed with malice aforethought will, nevertheless, be acquitted of murder and convicted of manslaughter if at the time of the killing the defendant, as a result of *provocation*, suffered a sudden and temporary loss of self control and the jury are satisfied that the reasonable man would, in the circumstances, have done as the defendant did.

(iv) *Diminished responsibility manslaughter*. If the defendant killed with malice aforethought but was, at the relevant time, suffering from diminished responsibility, then s/he will be convicted of manslaughter (*Ahluwalia* [1993]).

MENS REA — Refers to the mental element of the offence accompanying the *actus reus*. Terminology can include, 'direct intention', where the accused has clear foresight of the consequences of his actions, or 'oblique intention', where the result is a virtually certain consequence of the defendant's actions (*R v Nedrick* [1986]); other terms are 'knowingly' or 'recklessly', where the accused foresees that particular consequences may occur and proceeds with his actions, not caring whether those

| | |
|---|---|
| | consequences actually occur or not (*R v Cunningham* [1957]; *R v G and R* [2004]. See also: *actus reus*. |
| MI5 | The British Intelligence and Security Service, responsible for protecting the UK against threats to national security. |
| MI6 | The international arm of the British Intelligence Service. |
| MINISTRY OF JUSTICE | Since 9 May 2007 responsible for: criminal law and sentencing, the reduction in reoffending, prisons and probation. |
| MITIGATION | Reasons submitted by the defence on behalf of the accused, to partly excuse (or mitigate) the offence committed in an attempt to minimise the sentence. |
| MURDER | Murder is committed where the defendant, *intending* to kill or cause grievous bodily harm (GBH), caused the death of a human being. The offence carries a mandatory penalty of imprisonment for life (life imprisonment – life sentence). |

**N**

| | |
|---|---|
| NOMS | National Offender Management Service, including the administration of prison and probation services. |
| NORTHERN IRELAND ASSEMBLY | Devolved government for Northern Ireland at Stormont, Belfast. Deals with Executive Bills and secondary legislation for Northern Ireland, such as 'Orders in Council', for example, agriculture, rural development, education and employment. |
| NPS | National Probation Service. |

**O**

| | |
|---|---|
| OPEN JUSTICE PRINCIPLE | The public has the statutory right to attend most court proceedings – unless held *in camera*. |

## P

**PARLIAMENT**

The UK Parliament at Westminster is made up of: the Crown, the House of Lords and the House of Commons. Parliament is where new laws are debated and agreed.

**PAROLE BOARD**

The Parole Board is a panel of experts who decide whether a life sentence prisoner should be allowed to be released from prison. The Parole Board makes judgement about the suitability of a prisoner and his risk assessment in order to return to society.

**PLEA**

A defendant's reply to a charge put to him by a court; i.e. guilty or not guilty.

**POWER OF ARREST**

An order attached to some injunctions to allow the police to arrest a person who has broken the terms of the order.

**PRECEDENT**

The decision of a case which established principles of law that act as an authority for future cases of a similar nature (see *common law*).

**PRIMARY LEGISLATION**

Acts of Parliament or statutes (or treaties in EU law).

**PROCURATOR FISCAL**

The Procurator Fiscal's office is responsible for all criminal prosecutions in Scotland, all investigations into sudden and suspicious deaths and complaints against the police.

**PROSECUTION**

The institution or conduct of criminal proceedings against a person (see also *CPS*).

## Q

**QUALIFIED RIGHT**

Right by virtue of the European Convention on Human Rights (ECHR) and the *Human Rights Act 1998*; so that in certain circumstances and under certain conditions, it can be interfered with by the national courts.

**QUASH**

To annul and declare a sentence no longer valid.

**QUEEN'S BENCH DIVISION (QBD)**

See *High Court*.

| | |
|---|---|
| QUEEN'S COUNSEL (QC) | Barristers of at least ten years' standing may apply to become Queen's Counsel. QCs traditionally undertake work for the Crown and have traditionally been recruited from the bar. They are also known as 'Silks'. |

**R**

| | |
|---|---|
| RECKLESSNESS | For most offences recklessness as to whether a particular consequence will result from the defendant's actions or as to whether a particular circumstance exists will suffice for liability. For certain crimes, recklessness bears a broader meaning. This used to be determined by the *Caldwell*-type (objective) recklessness and has now been superseded by the ruling in *R v G* [2003]. |
| REMAND | To order an accused person to be kept in custody or placed on bail pending further court appearance. |
| REPARATION ORDER | An object of sentencing (and a form of sentence operating only in the youth court) i.e. reparation to a victim. The term is also used more generally to mean 'making good' by an offender and may feature in mitigation. It is also a statutory basis for deferment of sentence (*Crime and Disorder Act 1998*). |
| RESTORATIVE JUSTICE | Form of criminal justice that seeks to 'repair' harm as between offenders and victims (see *Crime and Disorder Act 1998*). |
| ROBBERY | Theft, or threat of theft, by force or intimidation of another. |

**S**

| | |
|---|---|
| SEX OFFENDER REGISTER | Local record maintained by the police, social services and the local authority, for which convicted sex offenders are obliged to provide information about themselves and their whereabouts. Failure to report a change of address or regularly to the police can result in imprisonment. |

| | |
|---|---|
| SHERIFF COURT (SCOTLAND) | There are 49 sheriff courts, arranged into six geographical areas ('Sheriffdoms'), each overseen by a sheriff principal. Sheriffs have limited sentencing powers (e.g. up to 3 years' imprisonment and/or an unlimited fine in solemn cases; 6 months' imprisonment and/or £5,000 fine for summary cases). |
| S.I. | (see *Statutory Instrument*). |
| SOLICITOR | Member of the legal profession chiefly concerned with advising clients and preparing their cases and representing them in some courts. May also act as advocates before certain courts or tribunals; not generally in Crown Courts. |
| SPECIFIC INTENT CRIMES | An offence of specific intent is one for which the prosecution must prove intention with respect to one or more of the elements in the *actus reus*. Recklessness will not suffice (see *basic intent crimes*). The significant distinction between offences of specific intent and basic intent is that where a lack of *mens rea* resulting from voluntary intoxication will excuse in the case of an offence of specific intent, it will not excuse for crimes of basic intent. Specific intent crimes include:<br><br>• Murder<br>• GBH with intent (s.18 OAPA 1861)<br>• Theft (s.1 *Theft Act 1968*)<br>• Burglary with intent to steal (s. 9 *Theft Act 1968*). |
| SPECIAL MEASURES | Measures which can be put in place to provide protection and/or anonymity to a witness, young or vulnerable person in court; this usually means that the witness is screened off in court or gives evidence on video. |
| STATEMENT | A written account by a witness of the facts of details of a matter. |
| STATUTORY INSTRUMENT (S.I.) | Rules or Regulations named within an Act of Parliament and made by a Minister of State. S.I.s affect the practical workings of the original Act (e.g. The *Prison Rules 1999* |

|  | under the *Prison Act 1952*). Also called 'delegated legislation' or 'Secondary Legislation'. |
|---|---|
| SUMMARY OFFENCE | A minor criminal offence triable only in a magistrates' court (see also *indictable* and either-way offence). |
| SUMMING-UP | A review of the evidence and directions as to the law by a judge immediately before a jury retires to consider its verdict. |
| SUMMONS | Order to appear or to produce evidence to a court. |
| SUMMONS (WITNESS) | Court order to appear as a witness at a hearing. |
| SUPERVISION ORDER | An order placing a person who has been given a suspended sentence under the supervision of a probation officer. |
| SUPREME COURT | New Appeal Court, replacing the House of Lords' Appellate Committee. |
| SUSPENDED SENTENCE | A custodial sentence which will not take effect unless there is a subsequent offence within a specified period. |

## T

| TAGGING | Electronic tagging or monitoring. |
|---|---|
| THEFT | To dishonestly appropriate property belonging to another with the intention of permanently depriving them of it. |
| TORT | A civil wrong committed against a person for which compensation may be sought through a civil court (e.g. personal injury; neighbourhood nuisance; libel etc.). |
| TRIBUNAL | A group of people consisting of a chairman (sometimes solicitor/barrister) and others who exercise a judicial function to determine matters related to specific interests, such as an Employment Tribunal. |
| TROUBLES, THE | The Troubles in Northern Ireland (NI): a generic term used to describe a period of sporadic communal violence involving |

paramilitary organisations, the Royal Ulster Constabulary (RUC), the British Army and others in Northern Ireland from the late 1960s until the late 1990s ending with the 'Good Friday Agreement' on 10 April 1998. The violence was extreme and often spilled over into the Republic of Ireland and the UK mainland. The various sides would describe the violence either as terrorist, conflict, guerrilla war or civil war (see *Good Friday Agreement*).

## V

| | |
|---|---|
| VERDICT | The finding of guilty or not guilty by a jury or a bench of magistrates. |
| VICTIM | The victim of an offence. |

## W

| | |
|---|---|
| WARRANT OF EXECUTION | Method of enforcing a judgement for a sum of money whereby a bailiff or sheriff (Scotland) is authorised, in lieu of payment, to seize and remove goods belonging to a defendant for sale at public auction. |
| WARRANT OF POSSESSION | Method of enforcing a judgement for possession of a property whereby a bailiff is authorised to evict people and secure against re-entry. |
| WHITE PAPER | Documents produced by the Government setting out details of future policy on a particular subject. A White Paper is the basis for a Bill before Parliament and allows the government an opportunity to gather feedback from the public before it formally presents the policies as a Bill (see *Bill*). |
| WITNESS | A person who gives evidence in court. |
| WOUNDING OR MALICIOUS WOUNDING WITH INTENT | (See *GBH*) Wounding i.e. causing grievous bodily harm *with intent* (*mens rea* – *Belfon* 1976 CA; *Bryson* 1985 CA; *Purcell* 1986 CA). An offence under s.18 OAPA 1861. The maximum penalty is a term of imprisonment for life (life sentence). To amount to a |

'wound' the inner and outer skin must be broken; a bruise is not a wound ('a break in the continuity of the whole of the skin'; a 'rapture of an internal blood vessel' (*JCC (a minor) v Eisenhower* [1984]). Breaking a collarbone is not 'wounding' under s.18, but amounts to GBH s. 20 OAPA 1861.

## Y

YOI — Young Offender Institution, a prison for young offenders.

YOT — Youth Offending Team. Inter-agency dealing with reports on and community sentences for juveniles.

YOUTH COURTS — Magistrates' courts in England and Wales, exercising jurisdiction over offences committed by children and young persons under 18.

YOUTH JUSTICE BOARD — Government agency dealing with young and juvenile offenders.

# APPENDIX 4 USEFUL WEBSITES AND INTERNET SOURCES

Acts of the UK Parliament: www.opsi.gov.uk
Administrative Justice & Tribunals Council (AJTC): www.ajtc.gov.uk
Algemene Inlichtingen en Veiligheidsdienst (AIVD) – General Intelligence
    and Security Agency of the Netherlands: www.aivd.nl
Amnesty International: http://web.amnesty.org
An Garda Síochána: www.garda.ie
Attorney General's Office: www.attorneygeneral.gov.uk
Audit Commission: www.audit-commission.gov.uk
BBC News Online: http://news.bbc.co.uk
BBC Northern Ireland Service online: www.bbc.co.uk/northernireland
BBC Radio: www.bbc.co.uk/radio
Black Police Association: www.nationalbpa.com
Bloody Sunday Inquiry: www.bloody-sunday-inquiry.org
Border and Immigration Agency (Home Office): www.bia.homeoffice.gov.uk
British Crime Survey (BCS): www.homeoffice.gov.uk/rds/index.htm
British Foreign and Commonwealth Office: www.fco.gov.uk
British Transport Police: www.btp.police.uk
Children's Reporter (Scotland): www.childrens-reporter.org
Commission for Racial Equality and Racism: www.cre.gov.uk
Council of Europe: www.coe.int
Council of Europe Legal Instruments: www. eur-lex.europa.eu
Criminal Cases Review Commission (CCRC): www.ccrc.gov.uk
Criminal Defence Service (Legal Services Commission and legal aid):
    www.legalservices.gov.uk/criminal.asp
Criminal Injuries Compensation Authority: www.cica.gov.uk
Criminal Justice System of England and Wales: www.cjsonline.gov.uk
Criminal Records Bureau (Home Office): www.crb.gov.uk
Crown Prosecution Service (CPS): www.cps.gov.uk
Death Penalty: www.deathpenalty.org
Department for Constitutional Affairs (DCA): www.dca.gov.uk
European Commission: http://ec.europa.eu/index_en.htm
European Court of Human Rights (ECHR): www.echr.coe.int/echr
European Court of Justice (ECJ): www.curia.eu.int

European Parliament: www.europarl.europa.eu

EUROPOL – European Law Enforcement Cooperation:
www.europol.europa.eu

Hansard: www.parliament.the-stationery-office.co.uk/pa/cm/cmhansrd.htm

HM Inspectorate of Prisons: http://inspectorates.homeoffice.gov.uk/hmiprisons

Her Majesty's Court Service: www.hmcourts-service.gov.uk

HM Prison Service: www.hmprisonservice.gov.uk

Home Office: www.homeoffice.gov.uk

House of Lords, UK: www.parliament.uk/about_lords/about_lords.cfm

Howard League for Penal Reform: www.howardleague.org.uk

Human Rights Legislation (Crown Office): www.humanrights.org.uk

Identity Fraud (CIFAS): www.identityfraud.org.uk

International Criminal Court (The Hague): www.icc-cpi.int

Independent Monitoring Boards (IMB): www.imb.gov.uk

Independent Police Complaints Commission: www.ipcc.gov.uk

International Crime Victim Survey:
www.unicri.it/wwd/analysis/icvs/index.php

Interpol (International Criminal Police Organisation): www.interpol.int

Irish Times: www.ireland.com

Judicial Studies Board: www.jsboard.co.uk

Jury Service: www.hmcourts-service.gov.uk/infoabout/jury_service/index.htm

Koran, the Holy Qur'an (online English version):
http://quod.lib.umich.edu/k/koran/browse.html

Law Society of England/Wales: www.lawsociety.org.uk/home.law

Law Society of Scotland: www.lawscot.org.uk

Legal Services Commission (CLS) (formerly 'legal aid'):
www.legalservices.gov.uk

Magistrates' Association: www.magistrates-association.org.uk

Metropolitan Police: www.met.police.uk

MI5 – National Security Service of the UK: www.mi5.gov.uk

Ministry of Justice: www.justice.gov.uk

National Archives: www.nationalarchives.gov.uk

National Assembly for Wales (Cynulliad Cenedlaethol Cymru):
www.wales.gov.uk

National Association of Youth Justice: www.nayj.org.uk

National Association of Probation Officers (NAPO): www.napo.org.uk

National Audit Office: www.nao.org.uk

National Policing Improvement Agency (NPIA) 'Neighbourhood Policing
Programme: www.neighbourhoodpolicing.co.uk

National Probation Service: www.homeoffice.gov.uk/justice/probation

National Reassurance Policing Programme (NRPP): www.reassurancepolicing.
co.uk

Northern Ireland Affairs Committee – UK Parliament: www.parliament.uk/
parliamentary_committees/northern_ireland_affairs.cfm

Northern Ireland Assembly: www.niassembly.gov.uk
Northern Ireland Court Service: www.courtsni.gov.uk
Northern Ireland Office: www.nio.gov.uk
Northern Ireland Prison Service: www.niprisonservice.gov.uk
Northern Ireland Statistics and Research Agency (NISRA): www.nisra.gov.uk
Office of the First Minister and Deputy First Minister for Northern Ireland:
    www.ofmdfmni.gov.uk
Office of National Statistics (UK): www.statistics.gov.uk/glance
Organisation for Economic Cooperation and Development (OECD):
    www.oecd.org
Parole Board: www.paroleboard.gov.uk
Penal Reform International: www.penalreform.org
Police Information Technology Organisation (PITO): www.pito.org.uk
Police Service: www.police.uk
Police Service of Northern Ireland: www.psni.police.uk
Police Service of Northern Ireland Annual Report 2005–2006:
    www.psni.police.uk/cc_report_text.doc
Prison and Probation Ombudsman: www.ppo.gov.uk
Prison population statistics: www.homeoffice.gov.uk/rds/prisons1.html
Prison Reform Trust: www.prisonreformtrust.org.uk
Respect Task Force (Home Office): www.respect.gov.uk
Restorative Justice Consortium: www.restorativejustice.org.uk
Royal Ulster Constabulary (R.U.C.), history of:
    www.royalulsterconstabulary.org/history.htm
Scotsman: www.thescotsman.scotsman.com
Scottish Crown Office and Procurator Fiscal Service:
    www.crownoffice.gov.uk
Scottish Court Service: www.scotcourts.gov.uk
Scottish Government: www.scotland.gov.uk
Scottish Law Commission: www.scotlawcom.gov.uk
Scottish Police: www.scottish.police.uk/mainframe.htm
Scottish Police Federation: www.spf.org.uk
Scottish Prison Service: www.sps.gov.uk
Sentencing, Justice and Prisons: www.homeoffice.gov.uk/justice/what-
    happens-at-court/sentencing/
Serious Organised Crime Agency: www.soca.gov.uk
Statute Law Legal Database (Ministry of Justice): www.statutelaw.gov.uk
UK Parliament: www.parliament.uk
United Nations: www.un.org/english
Victim Support: www.victimsupport.org.uk
World Health Organization: www.who.int
Youth Justice Agency Northern Ireland: www.youthjusticeagencyni.gov.uk
Youth Justice Board: www.youth-justice-board.gov.uk/YouthJusticeBoard

# BIBLIOGRAPHY

Al-Fanar (1995) 'Developments in the Struggle against the Murder of Women against the Background of so-called Family Honour', *Women Against Fundamentalism Journal*, (6): 37–41.

Allen, G. (2001) The Private Finance Initiative (PFI). Research Paper 01/117, Economic Policy and Statistics Section, House of Commons, 18 December.

Amnesty International (1998) Country Report on Pakistan: No Progress on Women's Rights, September. AI Index: ASA 33/13/98.

Amnesty International (1999) Country Report on Pakistan: Violence against Women in the Name of Honour, 22 September. AI Index: ASA 33/17/99.

Amnesty International (2007) Iran continues to pass death sentences on child offenders. News Release, 22 June.

Anderson, D. (1999) 'The Aggregate Burden of Crime', *Journal of Law and Economics*, 42(2): 611–641.

Andreas, P. and Nadelmann, E. (2006) *Policing the Globe: Criminalization and Crime Control in International Relations*. New York/Oxford: Oxford University Press.

Antoun, R. T. (1977) *Arab Village: A Social Structural Study of a Trans-Jordanian Peasant Community*. Indiana University Press.

Ashton, C., Brand, D., Brodie, D. and Chalmers, J. (2003) *Fundamentals of Scots Law*. Edinburgh: W. Green.

Ashworth, A. and Redmayne, M. (2005) *The Criminal Process*, 3rd edn. Oxford: OUP.

Audit Commission (1996) *Misspent Youth: Audit Commission Report*. London: The Stationary Office Ltd.

Audit Commission (1998) *Misspent Youth: A Challenge for Youth Justice. Follow-up Report by the Audit Commission*. London: The Stationary Office Ltd.

Barker, A. (2006) *Shadows: Inside Northern Ireland's Special Branch*. London: Mainstream Publishing.

Barnett, H. (2006) *Constitutional and Administrative Law,* 6th edn. London: Routledge Cavendish.

Batchelor, S. (2001) 'The myth of girl gangs', *Criminal Justice Matters,* 43: 26–27.

Beck, U. (1999) *World Risk Society*. London: Polity Press.

Beck, U. (1992) *Risk Society: Towards a New Modernity*, translated by Mark Ritter, (Theory, Culture and Society Series). London: Sage.

Bentham, J. (1789; 1948 edition by Harrison, W.) *Introduction to the Principles of Morals and Legislation*. New York: Free Press.

Berlins, M. and Dyer, C. (2000) *The Law Machine,* 5th rev. edn. London: Penguin.

Bilton, M. (2003) *Wicked Beyond Belief: The Hunt for the Yorkshire Ripper*. London: Harper Collins.

*Blackstone's Statutes on Criminal Law 2006–2007* (ed., P.R. Glazebrook) (2007) 15th edn. London: Blackstones.

Blekxtoon, R. (ed.) (2004) *Handbook on the European Arrest Warrant*. Cambridge: Cambridge University Press.

Bottoms, A., Rex, S. and Robinson, G. (eds) (2004) *Alternatives to Prison: Options for an Insecure Society*. Cullompton: Willan.

Bowlby, J. (1944) 'Forty-four juvenile thieves', *International Journal of Psychology,* 25: 1–75.

Bowlby, J. (1979) *The Making and Breaking of Affectional Bonds*. London/Baltimore: Harmondsworth-Penguin.

Bowling, B. and Phillips, C. (2002) *Racism, Crime and Justice*. London: Longman.

Bradney, A., Cownie, F., Masson, J., Neal, A. and Newell, D. (2005) *How to Study Law,* 5th edn. London: Thomson/Sweet & Maxwell.

Braithwaite, J. (1989) *Crime, Shame and Reintegration*. Cambridge: Cambridge University Press.

Brand, S. and Price, R. (2000) 'The Economic and Social Costs of Crime'. Home Office Research Study 217. London: Home Office.

Brooks, G. (1995) *Nine Parts of Desire: The Hidden World of Islamic Women*. London: Penguin Books.

Brown, S. and Macmillan, J. (1998) *Understanding Youth and Crime: Listening to Youth?* Oxford: OUP.

Browne, N. (1999) *Francis Ford Coppola's The Godfather Trilogy*. Cambridge: Cambridge University Press.

Brownlee, I. D. (1998) *Community Punishment: A Critical Introduction*. London: Longman.

Bryans, S. (2007) *Prison Governors: Managing Prisons in a Time of Change*. Cullompton: Willan.

Burman, M., Bradshaw, P., Hutton, N., McNeill, F. and Munro, M. (2006) 'The End of an Era? – Youth Justice in Scotland', in J. Junger-Tas and S. H. Decker (eds), *International Handbook of Juvenile Justice*, pp. 439–472. Springer.

Busby, N., Clark, B., Mays, R. and Spink, P. (2003) *Scots Law: A Student's Guide*. London: LexisNexis/Butterworths.

Cabinet Office (2006) Intelligence and Security Committee Report into the London Terrorist Attacks on 7 July 2005. London, May. Cm 6785.

Campbell, A. (1981) *Girl Delinquents*. Oxford: Blackwell.

Campbell, A. (1993) *Men, Women and Aggression*. New York: Basic Books.

Carlen, P. (1985) 'Criminal women, myths and misogyny', in P. Carlen (ed.) *Criminal Women: Autobiographical Accounts*. Cambridge: Polity Press.

Carlen, P. (ed.) (2002) *Women and Punishment: The Struggle for Justice*. Cullompton: Willan.

Carr, J. (2004) *Child Abuse, Child Pornography and the Internet*. The National Children's Homes.

Cavadino, M. and Dignan, J. (2001) *The Penal System,* 2nd edn. London: Sage.

Cavadino, M. and Dignan, J. (2006) *Penal Systems: A Comparative Approach*. London: Sage.

Cawthorne, N. (2004) *The Strange Laws of Old England*. London: Portrait.

Centre for Crime and Justice Studies (2006) *Knife Crime: Ineffective Reactions to a Distracting Problem? A Review of Evidence and Policy*. London: Kings College, CCJS.

Cochrane, J., Melville, G. and Marsh, I. (2004) *Criminal Justice: An Introduction to Philosophies, Theories and Practice*. London: Routledge.

Cohen, S. (1972) *Folk Devils and Moral Panics: The Creation of the Mods and Rockers*. London: Macgibbon & Kee.

Council of the European Union (2004) *The Hague Programme: Strengthening Freedom, Security and Justice in the European Union*. December, No. 16054/04.

Coyle, A. (2005) 'Management of Long-term and Life-Sentenced Prisoners Internationally in the context of a Human Rights Strategy', in N. Browne and S. Kandelia (eds), *Managing Effective Alternatives to Capital Punishment*, occasional paper series 3. London: Centre for Capital Punishment Studies.

Crawford, A., Lister, S. and Blackburn, S. (2005) *Plural Policing: The Mixed Economy of Visible Patrols in England and Wales* (Researching Criminal Justice Series). London: Policy Press.

Creighton, S., King, V. and Arnott, H. (2004) *Prisoners and the Law,* 3rd rev. edn. London: Tottel.

Croall, H. (2001) *Understanding White Collar Crime*. Oxford: OUP.

Crown Prosecution Service (2003) *Race for Justice: A Review of the Crown Prosecution Service Decision Making for Possible Racial Bias at Each Stage of the Prosecution Process*. London. CPS.

Crown Prosecution Service (2006) *See the Other Side: Make the Case. Real Life Stories at the Crown Prosecution Service*. London: Aquarium Writers.

Davies, N. (2004) *Dead Men Talking*. London: Mainstream Publishing.

Dicey, A. V. (1885) *Introduction to the Study of the Law of the Constitution*, 10th edn, 1959. London: Macmillan.

Dickens, C. (1851) 'On Duty with Inspector Field', in *Household Words*. London: Bradbury and Evans (1850–1859).

Dickens, C. (1853; 2003 edn by N. Bradbury) *Bleak House*. London: Penguin.

Downes, D. and Rock, P. (2003) *Understanding Deviance*, 4th edn. Oxford: OUP.

Durkheim, E. (1893 in French) *The Division of Labour in Society*. New York: MacMillan (1933 translation by George Simpson).

Dwyer, C. D. (2007) 'Risk, Politics and the "Scientification" of Political Judgement: Prisoner Release and Conflict Transformation in Northern Ireland,' in *British Journal of Criminology*, 47(5): 779–797.

Easton, S. and Piper, C. (2005) *Sentencing and Punishment: The Quest for Justice*. Oxford: Oxford University Press.

Elliott, C. and Quinn, F. (2008) *Criminal Law*, 7th edn. Harlow: Longman/Pearson.

Elliott, C. and Quinn, F. (2008) *English Legal System*, 9th edn. Harlow: Longman/Pearson.

Esmée Fairbairn Foundation (2004) 'Crime, Courts and Confidence: The report of an independent inquiry into alternatives to custody.' Chaired by Lord Coulsfield ('The Coulsfield Inquiry'). London: The Stationary Office Ltd.

Etzioni, A. (1997) *The New Golden Rule: Community and Morality in a Democratic Society*. London: Basic Books.

European Commission (2007) 'British Airways plc v Commission'. Decisions by the Court of Justice and other Courts (2/93): EU Commission Press Release 15/3/2007. Bulletin EU 4-2007.

European Council for the Prevention of Torture and Inhuman or Degrading Treatment (2001) *11th General Report on the CPT's activities*. Strasbourg: Council of Europe.

Fairhurst, J. (2007) *Law of the European Union*, 6th edn. Harlow: Pearson/Longman.

Fattah, E. A. (1978) 'Some Theoretical Developments in Victimology', *Victimology: An International Journal*, 4 (2): 198–213.

Fattah, E. A. (1999) 'From a handful of Dollars to Tea and Sympathy: The Sad History of Victim Assistance,' in Van Dijk, Van Kaam and Wemmers (eds), *Caring for Crime Victims: Selected Proceedings of the 9th International Symposium on Victimology*, pp. 187–206. Monsey, New York: Criminal Justice Press.

Fattah, E. A. and Sacco, V. F. (1989) *Crime and Victimization of the Elderly*. New York and Berlin: Springer Verlag.

Fay, M-T., Morrissey, M. and Smyth, M. (1999) *Northern Ireland's Troubles: The Human Costs* (Contemporary Irish Studies). London: Pluto Press.

Fitzgerald, M., Stockdale, J. and Hale, C. (2003) *Young People and Street Crime*. London: The Youth Justice Board.

Foucault, M. (1977; 1991 new edn. translation by A. Sheridan) *Discipline and Punish: The Birth of the Modern Prison*. London: Penguin.

Garland, D. (1990) *Punishment and Modern Society: A Study in Social Theory*. Oxford: Clarendon.

Gibson, B. (2004) *Criminal Justice Act 2003: A Guide to the New Procedures and Sentencing*. Winchester: Waterside Press.

Gibson, B. (2007a) *The New Ministry of Justice: An Introduction*. Winchester: Waterside Press.

Gibson, B. (2007b) *The New Home Office: An Introduction*. Winchester: Waterside Press.

Gibson, B. and Watkins, M. (2004) *The Criminal Justice Act 2003: a guide to the new procedures and sentencing*. Winchester: Waterside Press.

Giddens, A. (1991a) *The Consequences of Modernity*. London: Polity Press.

Giddens, A. (1991b) *Modernity and Self-identity: Self and Society in the Late Modern Age*. London: Polity Press.

Gillan, A. (2003) 'Race to save new victims of child pornography', *Guardian* Newspaper, November 4.

Glueck, S. (1934) 'Probation and Criminal Justice', *California Law Review*, 22(2): 235–237.

Glueck, S. and Glueck, E.T. (1950) *Unravelling Juvenile Delinquency*. Cambridge, MA: Harvard University Press.

Goldson, B. (ed.) (2000) *The New Youth Justice*. Russell House.

Habermas, J. (1962) *The Structural Transformation of the Public Sphere: An Inquiry into a Category of Bourgeois Society* (Strukturwandel der Öffentlichkeit. Untersuchungen zu einer Kategorie der bürgerlichen Gesellschaft – translated in 1989 by Thomas Burger and Frederick Lawrence; new edn. 1992). London: Polity Press.

Hale, C., Hayward, K., Wahidin, A. and Wincup, E. (eds) (2005) *Criminology*. Oxford: Oxford University Press (OUP).

Hall, S. and Jefferson, T. (eds) (1976) *Resistance Through Rituals: Youth Subcultures in Post-war Britain*. London: Unwin Hyman.

Halsbury, H. S. G. (1973) *Halsburys Laws of England* London: Butterworths.

Hatherall, J. and Hopkins, B. (2006) *Evidence: Key Facts*, 2nd edn. London: Hodder Arnold.

Heidensohn, F. (1968) 'The Deviance of Women: A Critique and an Enquiry', *The British Journal of Sociology*, 19(2): 160–175.

Heidensohn, F. (1985) *Women and Crime*. Basingstoke: Macmillan.

Heidensohn, F. (1994) 'Gender and crime', in M. Maguire, R. Morgan and R. Reiner (eds), *The Oxford Handbook of Criminology*. Oxford: Clarendon Press.

Heidensohn, F. (1996) *Women and Crime*, 2nd edn. London: Macmillan.

Heidensohn, F. (2002) 'Feminist Approaches to Criminology', in M. Maguire, R. Morgan and R. Reiner (eds), *The Oxford Handbook of Criminology,* 3rd edn. pp. 507–523. Oxford: OUP.

Heidensohn, F. (2006) *Gender and Justice: New Concepts and Approaches*. Cullompton: Willan.

Hentig, von H. (1948) *The Criminal and His Victim*. New Haven: Yale University Press.

Herring, J. (2008) *Criminal Law*. 3rd edn. London: Palgrave Macmillan.

Hirschi, T. (1969) *Causes of Delinquency*. California: Sage.

HM Inspectorate of Prisons (2003) Report on an unannounced inspection of HMP Kilmarmock (13–14 August 2003) by HM Chief Inspector of Prisons. London: The Stationary Office Ltd.

HM Inspectorate of Prisons (2005) Report on an unannounced inspection of HMP Rye Hill (11–15 April 2005) by HM Chief Inspector of Prisons. London: The Stationary Office Ltd.

Home Office (1997) 'No More Excuses: A new approach to tackling youth crime in England and Wales'. A government White Paper. London: The Stationary Office Ltd.

Home Office (2000) 'The economic and social costs of crime', by Sam Brand and Richard Price. HORS 217. London: The Stationary Office Ltd.

Home Office (2003a) 'Re-offending of Adults: Results from the 2003 Cohort', Statistical Bulletin 20/06 online: www.homeoffice.gov.uk/rds/pdfs06/hosb 2006.pdf

Home Office (2003b) 'Reducing Homicide: a review of the possibilities', by Fiona Brookman and Mike Maguire. Home Office Online Report 01/03: http://www.homeoffice.gov.uk/rds/pdfs2/rdsolr0103.pdf

Home Office (2004a) 'Juvenile reconviction: results from the 2001 and 2002 cohorts', online report 60/04: www.homeoffice.gov.uk/rds/onlinepubs1.html

Home Office (2004b) 'Reassurance policing: an evaluation of the local management of community safety' by Lawrence Singer. Home Office Research Study 288. November. London: The Stationary Office Ltd.

Home Office (2004c) 'Population in custody, August 2004 England and Wales: monthly tables'. London: Home Office.

Home Office (2004d) 'The future of netcrime now: threats and challenges', by Sheridan Morris. Research Paper 62/04. London: The Stationary Office Ltd.

Home Office (2005a) 'The impact of corrections on re-offending: a review of "what works"'. 3rd edn, edited by Gemma Harper and Chloë Chitty. Research Study 291. RDS, February 2005. London: The Stationary Office Ltd.

Home Office (2005b) 'Domestic Violence: A National Report', March 2005. London: The Stationary Office Ltd.

Home Office (2006a) 'Re-offending of adults: results from the 2003 cohort 20/06,' by Adrian Shepherd and Elizabeth Whiting from the Reconviction Analysis Team, Home Office Research, Development and Statistics Directorate (RDS) NOMS: 20/60. November. London: The Stationary Office Ltd.

Home Office (2006b) 'Prison population projections 2006 – 2013, England and Wales', 11 July 2006, by Nisha de Silva, Paul Cowell, Terence Chow, Paul Worthington. Statistical Online Bulletin.

Home Office (2006c) 'Young People and Crime: Findings from the 2005 Offending, Crime and Justice Survey', by Debbie Wilson, Clare Sharp and Alison Patterson. NOMS: 17/06. London: The Stationary Office Ltd.

Home Office (2007a) 'A rapid evidence assessment of the impact of mentoring on re-offending: a summary,' by Jolliffe and Farrington. Online Report 11/07: www.home office.gov.uk/rds/pdfs07/rdsolr1107.pdf

Home Office (2007b) 'Crime in England and Wales 2006–07'. Statistical Bulletin, edited by Sian Nicholas, Chris Kershaw and Alison Walker, 2nd edn. London: The Stationary Office Ltd.

Home Office (2007c) 'The British Crime Survey: Crime in England and Wales 2005/06'. HOSB 12/06: www.homeoffice.gov.uk/rds/pdfs06/crime0506summ.pdf

Hood, R. (2002) *The Death Penalty: a Worldwide Perspective,* 3rd rev. edn. Oxford: OUP.

Hood, R. and Seemungal, F. (2006) *A Rare and Arbitrary Fate: Conviction for Murder, the Mandatory Death Penalty and the Reality of Homicide in Trinidad and Tobago. A Statistical Study of Recorded Murders and Persons Indicted for Murder in 1998–2002.* Centre for Criminology. University of Oxford.

Hopkins Burke, R. (2004) 'Policing contemporary society revisited', in R. Hopkins Burke (ed.), *Hard Cop, Soft Cop: Dilemmas and Debates in Contemporary Policing.* Cullompton, Devon: Willan Publishing.

Hopkins Burke, R. (2005) *An Introduction to Criminological Theory,* 2nd edn. Cullompton, Devon: Willan Publishing.

Hornsby, R. and Hobbs, D. (2007) 'A Zone of Ambiguity: the political Economy of Cigarette Bootlegging', *British Journal of Criminology,* 47(4): 551–71.

House of Commons (2007) Northern Ireland Affairs Committee: The Northern Ireland Prison Service: Government Response to the Committee's First Report of Session 2007–08. First Special Report of Session 2007–08. 27 February 2008. HC386.

Houchin, R. (2005) 'Social Exclusion and Imprisonment in Scotland', report to the Scottish Executive. Glasgow Caledonian University.

House of Commons (2004) 'The separation of paramilitary prisoners at HMP Maghaberry'. Second Report of Sessions 2003–04. Northern Ireland Affairs Committee. HC 302-1. London: The Stationary Office Ltd.

House of Commons (2003) *The Steele Report on HMP Maghaberry in Northern Ireland.* Submitted to the Secretary of State for Northern Ireland. EV 107. London: The Stationary Office Ltd.

House of Lords – Select Committee on the European Communities (1997) *Europol: Confidentiality Regulations.* London: The Stationary Office Ltd.

Hoyle, C. (ed.) (2002) *New Visions of Crime Victims.* London: Hart.

Huebner, B. M., Varano, S. P. and Bunum, T. S. (2007) 'Gangs, Guns and Drugs: Recidivism Among Serious, Young Offenders, *Criminology Public Policy,* 6(2): 187ff.

Hungerford-Welch, P. (2004) *Criminal Litigation and Sentencing,* 6th edn. London: Cavendish.

Hutton, G. and Johnston, D. (2007) *Blackstone's Police Manuals: Evidence and Procedure,* 2nd edn. Oxford: OUP.

Huxley-Binns, R. and Martin, J. (2005) *Unlocking the English Legal System.* London: Hodder Arnold.

Huxley-Binns, R., Riley, L. and Turner, C. (2005) *Unlocking Legal Learning.* London: Hodder Arnold.

James, A., Bottomley, K., Liebling, A. and Clare, E. (1997) *Privatizing Prisons: Rhetoric and Reality.* London: Sage.

Johnston, L. (2000) *Policing Britain: Risk, Security and Governance.* London: Longman.

Jolliffe, D. and Farrington, D.P. (2007) 'A rapid evidence assessment of the impact of mentoring on re-offending: a summary.' Home Office Online Report 11/07: ww. homeoffice.gov.uk/rds/pdfs07/rdsolr1107.pdf.

Jones, S. (2006) *Criminology,* 3rd edn. Oxford: Oxford University Press.

Kant, I. (1781; reprint 2002) *Kritik der reinen Vernunft* (The Critique of Pure Reason, translated edition by Werner S. Pluhar). Indianapolis: Hackett.

Keane, A. (2006) *The Modern Law of Evidence,* 6th edn. Oxford: Oxford University Press.

Keil, T., Vito, G. F. and Andreescu, V. (1999) 'Perceptions of Neighbourhood Safety and Support for the Reintroduction of Capital Punishment in Romania: Results from a Bucuresti (Bucharest) Survey', *International Journal of Offender Therapy and Comparative Criminology,* 43(4): 514–34.

Kennedy, H. (1992) *Eve was Framed. Women and British Justice.* London: Chatto & Windus.

Kesteren, J. N. van, Mayhew, P. and Nieuwbeerta, P. (2000) *Criminal Victimisation in Seventeen Industrialised Countries: Key-findings from the 2000 International Crime Victims Survey.* The Hague: Ministry of Justice, WODC.

Kilbrandon, Lord (1964) Report of the Committee on Children and Young Persons, Scotland, known as the Kilbrandon Report. Cmnd 2306. London: The Stationary Office Ltd.

Knowles, J. and Thomas, P. (2006) *Effective Legal Research.* London: Thomson/Sweet & Maxwell.

Kury, H. and Smartt, U. (2006) 'Domestic Violence: Recent Developments in German and English Legislation and Law Enforcement', *European Journal of Crime, Criminal Law and Criminal Justice,* 14(4): 382–407(26).

Kury, H., Obergfell-Fuchs, J. and Smartt, U. (2002) 'The evolution of public attitudes to punishment in western and eastern Europe' (Chapter 5), in J. Roberts and M. Hough (eds), *Changing Attitudes to Punishment: Public Opinion, Crime and Justice.* Cullompton: Willan.

Lister, D. (2004) *Mad Dog: The Rise and Fall of Johnny Adair and 'C' Company.* London: Mainstream Publishing.

Lombroso, C. (1895; 2004 – new edn.) *Criminal Man.* New York: Duke University Press.

Lombroso, C. and Ferrero, W. (1895) *The Female Offender.* London: Fisher Unwin.

Lombroso, C. and Ferrero, G. (2004 – new edn. by N. Hahn-Rafter) *Criminal Woman, the Prostitute and the Normal Woman.* New York: Duke University Press.

Loveland, I. (2006) *Constitutional Law, Administrative Law and Human Rights: A Critical Introduction,* 4th edn. Oxford: OUP.

MacQueen, H. (2004) *Studying Scots Law.* London: LexisNexis/Butterworths.

Maguire, M., Morgan, R. and Reiner, R. (eds) (2007) *The Oxford Handbook of Criminology,* 4th edn. Oxford: OUP.

Mansfield, M. (1993) *Presumed Guilty.* London: Heinemann.

Marshall, T. (1999) *Restorative Justice. An Overview.* London: Home Office.

Martin, J. and Turner, C. (2005) *Unlocking Criminal Law.* Abingdon, Oxon: Hodder & Stoughton.

Matravers, A. (2003) *Sex Offenders in the Community: Managing and Reducing Risk.* Cullompton: Willan.

Mauer, M., King, R. S. and Young, M. C. (2004) *The Meaning of 'Life': Long Prison Sentences in Context.* Washington, DC: The Sentencing Project.

McAra, L. (2006) 'Welfare in Crisis?: Key Developments in Scottish Youth Justice', in John Muncie and Barry Goldson (eds), *Comparative Youth Justice.* London: Sage Publications.

McColgan, A. (2000) *Women under the Law: the False Promise of Human Rights.* London: Longman.

McConville, S. (ed.) (2003) *The Use of Punishment.* Cullompton: Willan.

McCullough, K. P. (1996) 'When Women Kill', *Journal of Criminal Justice,* 24(4): 375–376.

McEvoy, K. (2001) *Paramilitary Imprisonment in Northern Ireland: Resistance, Management, and Release.* Oxford: OUP.

McIvor, G. (2004) *Women Who Offend* (Research Highlights in Social Work Series). London: Jessica Kingsley.

McKittrick, D. and McVea, D. (2001) *Making Sense of the Troubles.* London: Penguin.

McLaughlin, E. (2007) *The New Policing.* London: Sage.

McLaughlin, E. and Muncie, J. (eds) (2006) *The Sage Dictionary of Criminology.* 3rd edn. London: Sage.

McLaughlin, E., Fergusson, R., Hughes, G. and Westmarland, L. (eds) (2003) *Restorative Justice: Critical Issues.* The Open University. London: Sage.

McVean, A. and Spindler, P. (2003) *Policing Paedophiles on the Internet.* The John Grieve Centre for Policing and Community Safety. Goole: New Police Bookshop.

Merton, R. (1938) 'Social Structure and Anomie', *American Sociological Review,* 3.

Milke, T. (2003) *Europol und Eurojust* (German). Osnabrück: V & R Unipress GmbH.

Ministry of Justice (2007a) *Population in Custody: Monthly Tables, December 2007, England and Wales,* RDS/NOMS. London: Her Majesty's Stationary Office.

Ministry of Justice (2007b) *Offender Management Careload Statistics 2006.* RDS/NOMS: Her Majesty's Stationary office.

Muncie, J. (2001) 'Prisons, Punishment and Penalty', in Eugene McLaughlin and John Muncie (eds), *Controlling Crime,* 2nd edn. London: Sage.

Muncie, J. (2004) *Youth and Crime,* 2nd edn. London: Sage.

Muncie, J. and McLaughlin, E. (2001) 'Crime, Order and Social Control', in *The Problem of Crime series,* 2nd edn. London: Sage.

Muncie, J. and Wilson, D. (eds) (2004) *Student Handbook of Criminal Justice and Criminology.* London: Cavendish.

Muncie, J., McLaughlin, E. and Hughes, G. (eds) (2002) *Youth Justice: Critical Readings.* London: Sage.

Murphy, P. (2005) *Murphy on Evidence,* 9th edn. Oxford: OUP.

Nagin, D. S. (1998) 'Deterrence and incapacitation', in M. Tonry, (ed.), *The Handbook of Crime and Punishment,* New York: Oxford University Press.

National Audit Office (2007) *Targeting Inequalities: Performance Measurement Practice*. London: NAO.

Newburn, T. (2003) *A Handbook of Policing*. Cullompton: Willan.

Newburn, T. (2007) *Criminology*. Cullompton, Devon: Willan Publishing.

Northern Ireland Office (2005a) 'Northern Ireland Prisoner Population Projection 2005–2009', by K. Amelin and C. O'Loan. Research and Statistical Bulletin 12/2005. Research and Statistical Office, Belfast: Stormont.

Northern Ireland Office (2005b) (2007) 'An Evaluation of the Northern Ireland Youth Conferencing Service', by Catriona Campbell, Roisin Devlin, David O'Mahony, Jonathan Doak, John Jackson, Tanya Corrigan and Kieran McEvoy. NIO Research and Statistical Series: Report No. 12. Belfast: Statistics and Research Branch Criminal Justice Policy Division.

Northern Ireland Prison Service (2003) 'HM Chief Inspector of Prisons, Report of a full announced inspection of HMP Maghaberry, 13–17 May 2002'. Belfast: The Stationary Office Ltd.

O'Byrne, D. (2005) *Human Rights: An Introduction*. Harlow: Pearson/Longman.

Office of National Statistics (2000) 'Psychiatric Morbidity Among Young Offenders in England and Wales.' ONS Online: http://www.statistics.gov.uk/CCI/nugget.asp?ID= 853&Pos=1& ColRank=2& Rank=112

O'Mahony, D. and Deazley, R. (2000) *Juvenile Crime and Justice*. Belfast: Criminal Justice Review Group: Her Majesty's Stationary Office.

O'Mahony, D. and Campbell, C. (2004) 'Mainstreaming Restorative Justice for Young Offenders through Youth Conferencing – the experience of Northern Ireland' (unpublished).

O'Mahony, D., Chapman, T. and Doak, J. (2002) *Restorative Cautioning: A Study of Police Based Restorative Cautioning Pilots in Northern Ireland*. Belfast: Northern Ireland Statistical and Research Agency (NISRA).

Ormerod, D. (2008) *Smith and Hogan: Criminal Law*, 12th edn. Oxford/London: LexisNexis, Butterworths.

Ormerod, D. (2005) *Smith and Hogan: Criminal Law. Cases and Materials*, 9th edn. Oxford/London: LexisNexis, Butterworths.

Pierrepoint, A. (1974, Harrap; 2005) *Executioner Pierrepoint: An Autobiography*. London: Eric Dobby Publishing Ltd.

Prison Reform Trust (2004) *England and Wales – Europe's lifer capital*.

Puzo, M. G. (orig. 1969; new edn. 1991) *The Godfather (Part I)*. London: Arrow Books.

Race Bannon, D. (2003) *Race Against Evil: The Secret Missions of the Interpol Agent Who Tracked the World's Most Sinister Criminals: A Real Life Drama*. London: New Horizon Press.

Radzinowicz, L. and Wolfgang, M. (eds) (1977) *The Criminal under Restraint*, 2nd edn. in Crime and Justice, Vol 3. New York/London: Basic Books Inc. Publ.

Ramsbotham, Sir David (former Chief Inspector of Prisons) (2003) *Prisongate: The Shocking State of Britain's Prisons and the Need for Visionary Change*. London: Simon & Schuster.

Rawlings, P. (1999) *Crime and Power: A History of Criminal Justice 1688–1998*. London: Longman.

Rawlings, P. (2001) *Policing: A Short History*. Cullompton: Willan.

Rawls, J. (1971; 1999 reprinted edn.) *A Theory of Justice*. Oxford: OUP.

Raynor, P. (2002) 'Community Penalties: Probation, Punishment, and "What Works"', in M. Maguire, R. Morgan and R. Reiner (eds), *The Oxford Handbook of Criminology*, 3rd edn, pp. 1168–1196. Oxford: OUP.

Rebellon, C. J. (2002) 'Reconsidering the broken homes–delinquency relationship and exploring its mediating mechanims(s)', *Criminology*, 40(1): 103–136.

Rehman, J. (2003) *International Human Rights Law: A Practical Approach*. Harlow: Pearson/Longman.

Reichel, P. L. (2005) *Comparative Criminal Justice Systems*, 4th edn. Upper Saddle River, NJ: Pearson/Prentice Hall.

Reichel, P. L. (ed.) (2005) *Handbook of Transnational Crime and Justice*. Thousand Oaks/London/New Delhi: Sage.

Reiner, R. (2000) *The Politics of the Police*, 3rd edn. Oxford: OUP.

Roach Anleu, S. L. (2005) *Law and Social Change*, revised edn. London: Sage.

Roberts, J. and Hough, M. (2002) *Changing Attitudes to Punishment: Public Opinion, Crime and Justice*. Cullompton, Devon: Willan.

Robertson, G. (1999) *The Justice Game*. London: Vintage.

Robertson, G. (2006) *Crimes Against Humanity: The Struggle for Global Justice*. London: Penguin.

Rock, P. (1994) *Victimology*. Aldershot: Dartmouth.

Rock, P. (ed.) (2004) *Constructing Victims' Rights: The Home Office, New Labour, and Victims*. Oxford: OUP.

Runciman, W. G. (1996) *Relative Deprivation and Social Justice: A Study of Attitudes to Social Inequality in 20th century England*. London: Routledge & Kegan Paul.

Samuels, A. (2005) 'The Meaning of Recklessness', *Justice of the Peace*, 169, 19 November: 918–919.

Sanders, A. and Young, R. (2007) *Criminal Justice*. 3rd edn. Oxford: OUP.

Santiago, M. (2000) *Europol and Police Cooperation in Europe*. London: Edwin Mellen Press Ltd.

Scottish Executive, The (2002) Audit Committee, 5th Report, Report on Public Accounts. SP Paper 615. Scottish Executive Oral Hearing on 30 April 2002 (Audit Committee 7th Meeting 2002 (Session 1)). Edinburgh: Scottish Parliament Stationary Office Ltd.

Scottish Executive, The (2003) 'Building strong, safe and attractive communities: guidance for submissions. Guidance to local authorities and their community planning partners on preparing submissions for wardens and other community based initiatives to tackle anti-social behaviour'. Edinburgh: Scottish Executive.

Scottish Parliament, The (2003) 'Anti-social behaviour: Community Wardens and related issues,' by Jude Payne. SPICe Briefing, 03/78 of 29 September.

Sebba, L. (1996) *Third Parties, Victims and the Criminal Justice System*. Columbus: Ohio State University Press.

Sherman, L. (1990) 'Police Crackdowns: Initial and Residual Deterrence', in M. Tonry and N. Morris (eds), *Crime and Justice: A Review of Research*, Vol. 12. Chicago: University of Chicago Press.

Shute, S., Hood, R. and Seemungal, F. (2005) *A Fair Hearing? Ethnic Minorities in the Criminal Courts*. Cullompton: Willan Publishing.

Slapper, G. and Kelly, D. (2006) *The English Legal System,* 8th edn. London: Routledge/Cavendish.

Smartt, U. (1999) 'Constitutionalism in the British Overseas Territories', *European Journal of Crime, Criminal Law and Criminal Justice*, 3, June: 300–314.

Smartt, U. (2001a) 'The stalking phenomenon: trends in European and international stalking and harassment legislation', *European Journal of Crime, Criminal Law and Criminal Justice, 9/3:* 209–232.

Smartt, U. (2001b) *Grendon Tales: Stories from a Therapeutic Community*. Winchester: Waterside Press.

Smartt, U. (2006 a) *Criminal Justice*. Course Companion. London: Sage.

Smartt, U. (2006 b) 'Honour Killings', *Justice of the Peace Journal*, 170: 4–7.

Smartt, U. (2006c) *Media Law for Journalists*. London: Sage.

Smartt, U. and Kury, H. (2002) 'Prisoner-on-Prisoner Violence: Victimization of Young offenders in Prison. Some German Findings', *Criminal Justice Journal*, 2(4): 411–437.

Smartt, U. and Kury, H. (2007) 'Domestic Violence: Comparative Analysis of German and UK Research Findings', *Social Science Quarterly*, 88(5): 1263–1280.

Smartt, U., Kury, H., Obergfell-Fuchs, J. and Würger, M. (2002) 'Attitudes to Punishment: How Reliable are International Crime Victim Surveys?', *International Journal of Comparative Criminology*, 2: 133–150.

Smith, P. and Natalier, K. (2004) *Understanding Criminal Justice: Sociological Perspectives*. London: Sage.

Smyth, J. and Ellison, G. (1999) *The Crowned Harp: Policing in Northern Ireland*. London: Pluto Press.

Stafford Smith, C. (2007) *Bad Men: Guantanamo Bay and The Secret Prisons*. London: Weidenfeld & Nicolson.

Steiner, J., Woods, L. and Twigg-Flesner, C. (2007) *Textbook on EC Law,* 9th edn. Oxford: Oxford University Press.

Stephenson, M. (2007) *Young People and Offending: Education, Youth Justice and Social Inclusion*. Cullompton: Willan.

Sturge, L. F. (1950) *Stephen's Digest of the Criminal Law (Indictable Offences)*, 9th edn. London: Sweet & Maxwell.

Sullivan, D. and Tifft, L. (2006) *Handbook of Restorative Justice: A Global Perspective.* London: Routledge.

Surrey Alcohol and Drug Advisory Service (SADAS) (2006) 'Caring For People Affected by Alcohol and Drugs in Surrey'. Annual Report March 2004 – March 2005. Guildford: SADAS.

Taylor, D. (1998) *Crime, Policing and Punishment, 1750–1914.* London: Palgrave Macmillan.

Taylor, P. (1998) *The Provos: IRA and Sinn Fein.* London: Bloomsbury.

Treadwell, J. (2006) *Criminology* (Sage Course Companion). London: Sage.

Uglow, S., Cheney, D., Dickson, L. and Fitzpatrick, J. (1999) *Criminal Justice and the Human Rights Act.* 2nd edn. London: Jordans.

Vanstone, M. (2004) *Supervising Offenders in the Community: A History of Probation Theory and Practice.* Aldershot, Hants: Ashgate.

Van Zyl Smit, D. (2005) 'Life Imprisonment Issues in National and International Law', in N. Browne and S. Kandelia (eds), *Managing effective alternatives to capital punishment*, Centre for Capital Punishment Studies occasional paper series 3. London: CCPS.

von Hirsch, A. (1999) *Criminal Deterrence and Sentence Severity: An Analysis of Recent Research.* Oxford: Hart.

von Hirsch, A. and Ashworth, A. (2005) *Proportionate Sentencing: Exploring the Principles.* Oxford: OUP.

Waddington, P. A. J. (1999) 'Police (canteen) sub-culture. An appreciation', *The British Journal of Criminology*, 39: 287–309.

Wadham, J. and Mountfield, H. (2003) *Blackstone's Guide to the Human Rights Act 1998*, 2nd edn. London: Blackstones.

Walker, C. and Starmer, K. (1999) *Miscarriages of Justice: A Review of Justice in Error.* London: Blackstone Press.

Walker, L. E. (2008) *The Battered Woman Syndrome,* 3rd edn. New York: Springer Co. Inc.

Walklate, S. (2004) *Gender, Crime and Criminal Justice,* 2nd edn. Cullompton, Devon: Willan.

Watson, A. (2004) 'A Reckless Decision?', *Justice of the Peace,* 168 (17 January): 32–33.

Welsh Assembly Government (2006) 'Perceptions of young people in custody' by R. Powell, R. Smith, G. Jones. and A. Reakes. Slough: National Foundation for Educational Research.

Wertham, F. (1949) *Dark Legend: A Study In Murder.* London: V. Gollancz Publ.

Whitfield, D. (2001) *Introduction to the Probation Service.* Winchester: Waterside Press.

Williams, G. L. and Smith, A. T. H. (2006) *Glanville Williams: Learning the Law.* London: Sweet & Maxwell.

Wilson, J. Q. and Kelling, G. L. (1982) 'Broken Windows: The Police and Neighbourhood Safety', *Atlantic Monthly*, 249: 29–38.

Wilson, J. Q, Kelling, G. L. and Coles, C. M. (1998) *Fixing Broken Windows: Restoring Order and Reducing Crime in Our Communities.* New York: Simon & Schuster Inc.

Wolfgang, M. E. (1958) *Patterns in Criminal Homicide.* Philadelphia: University of Pennsylvania Press.

Worrall, A. (2001) 'Girls at risk? Reflections of changing attitudes to young women's offending', *Probation Journal*, 48(2): 86–92.

Worrall, A. (1990) *Offending Women.* London: Routledge.

Worrall, A. and Hoy, C. (eds) (2005) *Punishment in the Community: Making Offenders, Making Choices.* Cullompton: Willan.

Wright, M. (1996) *Justice for Victims and Offenders. A Restorative Response to Crime*, 2nd edn. Winchester: Waterside Press.

Wright, M. (1999) *Restoring Respect for Justice.* Winchester: Waterside Press.

Zander, M. (2000) *The State of Justice* (the Hamlyn Lectures). London: Sweet and Maxwell.

Zedner, L. (2007) *Security.* London: Routledge.

Zedner, L. (1999) 'Victims', in M. Maguire, R. Morgan and R. Reiner Leded, *The Oxford Handbook of Criminology*, 2nd edn, pp. 577–612. Oxford: OUP.

Zimring, F. E. and Hawkins, G. (1995) *Incapacitation: Penal Confinement and Restraint of Crime.* Oxford: Oxford University Press.

# INDEX

Maguire, Mike 155–6
malice aforethought 197–8
malicious wounding 85–7, 198
*Management of Offenders
   (Scotland)
   Act 2005* 124, 130
mandatory orders 27
Mannheim, Marvin 11
manslaughter 77–83, 198
   gross negligence 82–3
   involuntary 81–2
   unlawful act 81–2
Marshall, T. 11
Masson, J. *see* Bradney,
   Anthony *et al*
Master of the Rolls (MR) 24
Mattan, Mahmood
   Hussein 148
Mauer, M. *et al* 150
Mayhew, Pat *see* Kesteren, J.N.
   van *et al*
measuring crime and
   criminality 8–10
media
   and fear of crime 6
Mellor, Gavin 151
*mens rea* 72–4, 195–6, 198–9
*Mental Health Act 1983* 93
mercy killing (euthanasia) 80
Merton, Robert 5
Metropolitan Police 102
Milke, T. 66
Milosevic, Slobodan 145
Ministry of Justice (MOJ)
   100, 199
Mitchell, Luke 162
mitigation 199
*M'Naghten* Rules 93, 95
Mohnhaupt, Brigitte 150
Montesqieu 139
moral wrong and criminal
   wrong 4
Multi Agency Public
   Protection Arrangements
   (MAPPA) 124
Muncie, John 14, 156, 170
Munro, M. *see* Burman, M. *et al*
murder 199
   and manslaughter 77–83
   *mens rea* for 77
Murray v United Kingdom
   [1996] 138

Nadelmann, Ethan 55, 70
Natalier, Kristin 14
National Assembly for
   Wales 19
National Criminal Intelligence
   Service (NCIS) 104
National Offender
   Management Service
   (NOMS) 119, 123, 126,
   165, 199
National Policing Improvement
   Agency (NPIA) 104
Neal, A. *see* Bradney,
   Anthony *et al*

'necessity' 93
neighbourhood and community
   policing teams 157
neighbourhood decay 5, 101
Nelson, Brian 44
Newburn, Tim 14, 118
Newell, D. *see* Bradney,
   Anthony *et al*
Nicholls of Birkenhead,
   Lord 145
Nieuwbeerta, Paul *see* Kesteren,
   J.N. van *et al*
norms 5, 6
Northern Ireland
   court structure 46–51
   institutions 45–6
   Northern Ireland Assembly
      45–6
   St Andrew's Agreement
      (2006) 34, 45
   'The Troubles' 43–5, 203–4
      case study 51–2
   'Good Friday Agreement'
      (1998) 34, 43, 44–5, 194
Northern Ireland Assembly 199
*Northern Ireland (Elections) Act
   1998* 45
*Northern Ireland (Emergency
   Provisions) Act 1973* 50
*Northern Ireland (Sentences) Act
   1998* 131

Obergfell-Fuchs, Joachim
   *see* Kury, H. *et al*;
   Smartt, U. *et al*
objective recklessness 76–7
offences against the person 83–7
*Offences Against the Person Act
   1861* (OAPA) 7, 9, 32,
   72, 83
*Offender Management Act
   2007* 126
Old Bailey (Central Criminal
   Court) 114
O'Mahony, D. 163, 166
Ombudsman 127
Omerod, David 98
on-the-spot fines 103
open justice principle 199
'Orders in Council' 36
Osman, Hussain 65
Owers, Anne 132
*Oxford Handbook of
   Criminology* 118

PACE Codes 7, 101, 102–3
Paisley, Ian 34, 45
parental deficit 103, 155
parenting academies 157
Parenting Order 160
Parker, Lord 72
Parliament (Westminster)
   18–19, 200
*Parliamentary Constituencies
   and Assembly Electoral
   Regions (Wales) Order
   2006* 19

Parliamentary sovereignty 18
Parental Compensation
   Orders 166–7
Parole Board 128, 200
Partnership for a Better
   Scotland 130
Peel, Robert 100
peer group pressure 155
penal codes 17
Penalty Notice of Disorder
   (PND) 103
Peniston, Kamilah 155
Phillips, C. 101
Pimental, Edward 150
Plato 139
pleas 110, 200
Police Authorities 102
Police Community Support
   Officers (PCSO) 101, 104
*Police and Criminal Evidence
   Act 1984* (PACE) 7, 102–3
*Police and Justice Act 2006* 104
*Police (Northern Ireland) Act
   2000* 46
*Police (Scotland) Act 1967* 104
Police Service of
   Northern Ireland
   (PSNI) 105
policing
   England and Wales 100–4
   carrying firearms 102
   community policing 103–4
   key performance indicators
      (KPI) 102
   Northern Ireland 104–5
   Scotland 104
Polmont 165
Ponto, Jürgen 150
poor school attainment 155
Powell *et al* 164
power of arrest 200
*Powers of Criminal Courts
   (Sentencing) Act 2000* 160
precedent 17, 36, 200
President of the Family
   Division 24, 25
President of the Queen's Bench
   Division (QBD) 24
Pretty, Diane 80
*Prevention of Terrorism Act
   2005* 146
Price, R. 10
primary legislation 200
   Northern Ireland 46
'priority crime' 3
prison *see* imprisonment
prison governance 126–7
Prison Reform Trust 151
*Prison Rules 1999* 129
Private Finance Initiatives
   (PFI) 129
private prisons 129
Privy Council 25
Probation Order 42, 122
Probation Service 123, 199
   Scotland 129–30
*Proceeds of Crime Act 2002* 116